THE TIWA ETHNOHISTORY

Raktim Patar

notionpress.com

INDIA · SINGAPORE · MALAYSIA

Notion Press

No. 8, 3rd Cross Street
CIT Colony, Mylapore
Chennai, Tamil Nadu – 600004

First Published by Notion Press 2021
Copyright © Raktim Patar 2021
All Rights Reserved.

ISBN
Hardcase: 978-1-63781-572-4
Paperback: 978-1-63745-517-3

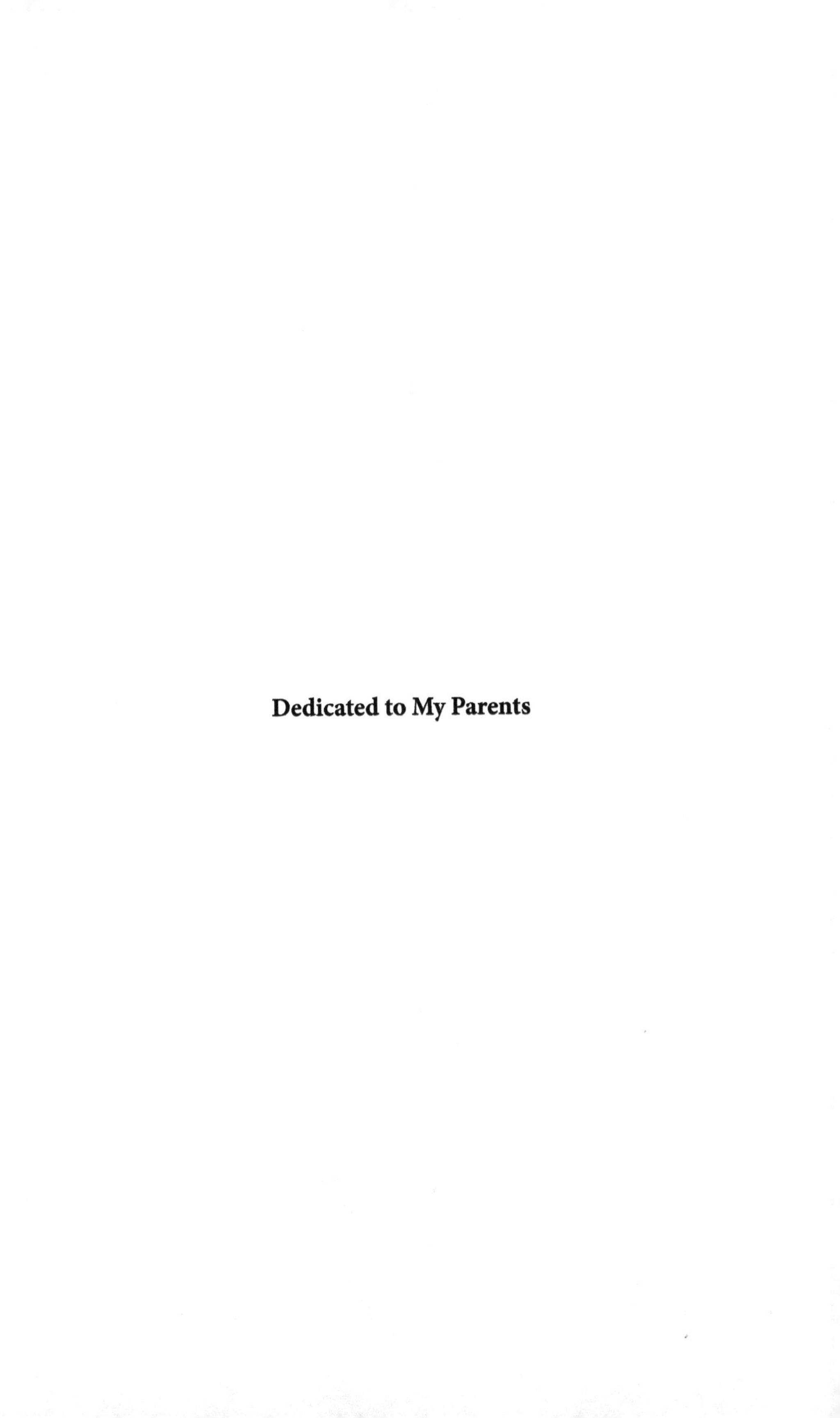

Dedicated to My Parents

Contents

Preface

This book aims at presenting as far as possible a comprehensive understanding of the ethnohistory of the Tiwa people. I have endeavoured to incorporate all the areas that are necessary to cover in an etnohistorical study. It is an attempt to reconstruct the early history of the Tiwa and to depict the traditional and the changes that are taking place in contemporary Tiwa society on the basis of extensive fieldwork supplemented by archival and other sources. The necessity of such a work has long been felt primarily on account of the fact that no full-length ethnohistorical study on this tribe has been attempted earlier.

The earliest reference to the Tiwa tribe is found in the *Buranjis* (Ahom Chronicles), where they were referred to as the '*Datiyaliya*' or the people of the margins. This was followed by references to the Tiwa under the nomenclature of 'Lalung' in colonial writings. The information available in colonial records is very scanty and full of perplexity. They refer to them a semi-Hinduised tribe, who represent a branch of the Kachari or as descendants of the Chutiya of Upper Assam. There is little information on their origin, migration, settlement pattern or social organization, polity formations, and traditional belief system. Similarly published works of the post-Independence period do not provide a clear understanding of this tribe. In their writings most of the authors did not make any distinction between the Tiwa of the hills and those of the plains, often mixing up the features of both groups without taking note of the fact that they display distinct socio-cultural features. Available published works are descriptive accounts of the socio-economic and cultural features of the Tiwa, as they appear in recent times. There is no mention of their early history or the circumstances leading to the bifurcation of the Tiwa into two groups with distinct patterns of social organization and belief system. Furthermore, there is neither enough information on the socio-political institutions of the Tiwa nor an adequate understanding of the continuity and the changes that are taking place among them. It is against such a backdrop, that systematic documentation, description, and construction of the history of the Tiwa are necessary and which the present work seeks to address.

This book consists of seven chapters. The first chapter gives a brief background of the land and the people and brief discussion on the ethnohistorical approach of study. The second chapter discusses the origin, migration and the settlement pattern of the Tiwa. This chapter has analysed various oral traditions supplemented by written sources like the Ahom chronicles and the colonial records to ascertain the origin and migration of the Tiwa into the present habitation to throw light on the settlement pattern. The third chapter deals with the religion and belief system of the hill Tiwa. This chapter describes the traditional Tiwa concepts of reality and destiny which are deeply rooted in the spirit world. In continuance to the previous chapter, the fourth chapter deals with the religious practices of the Tiwa living in the plain districts of Assam. In view of the changes in the religious beliefs and practices of the plain Tiwa, it is necessary to discuss it as a separate chapter. In the fifth chapter the kinship patterns, the principles of marriage, descent and residence, village administration, and development of chieftainship with special reference to Gobha chief has been discussed. The sixth chapter provides an understanding on the traditional economy of the Tiwa. The seventh chapter deals with the issues of continuity and change among the Tiwa. Here brief overviews of the theories of change as well as the factors that have contributed to change among this tribe have been discussed. The concluding chapter includes an overview of the work and highlights the major findings of the study.

I take this opportunity to express my humble gratitude to Prof. Cecile A. Mawlong, the Dean of Social Science, North-Eastern Hill University, Shillong for her valuable suggestions and comments and taking active interest on the book. I owe a great deal of appreciation to Prof. A.K. Thakur, Department of History NEHU, who has been a source of inspiration during the work and consistently encourage me to publish this book. I am indebted to all the esteemed informants some of whom have since passed away without whom I would not have finished this work. I am greatfull to my friends and colleagues especially to Dr. Lallianzuali Chhangte, Mr. Robert Lumphuid, Dr. Dimbeshwar Das, Ms. Shyamolima Saikia, Mr. Ajit Konwar, Mr. Leander Lumphui and Mr. Bipul Bordoloi for taking keen interest on the book and helping in various ways. Last but far from the least, I sincerely acknowledge the sacrifices that my wife Mrs. Pumpa Patar has made by shouldering all the responsibilities while I was consistently away for my field studies.

Department of History   RAKTIM PATAR
Gargaon College, Assam, India
29th December, 2020

Distribution of Tiwa Population

Chapter I

Introduction

The Tiwa is an Indo-Mongoloid tribe and descendent of the Bodo family of the Tibeto-Burman branch of the Sino-Tibetan speech family. Settled in Morigaon, Nagaon, Kamrup, Jorhat, Dhemaji and Karbi Anglong districts of Assam and Ri-Bhoi district of Meghalaya, the Tiwa has long been referred to as "Lalung" or "Laloo"[1] by other neighbouring groups (Khasi-Jaintia, Karbi). The *Buranjis*[2] (Ahom chronicles) used terms like 'Lalung', 'Garo' and 'Dantiyalias' interchangeably to denote the Tiwa people.[3] The people in question, however, refer to themselves as Tiwa. They are divided into two socio-cultural groups, those settled in the plains who speak Assamese and follow a patrilineal descent[4] system bearing Assamese patronyms, and those residing in the hills, speaking a Tibeto-Burman language of the Bodo-Garo group, that follow a matrilineal descent[5] system. Thus, the Tiwa follow a *bilateral descent*[6] system which recognises that descent may be traced from either the father or mother, depending on the decision taken at the time of marriage. In most cases, the husband goes to live with his wife's family (matrilocality), and their children are included in the mother's clan. However, if the woman goes to live with her husband (patrilocality), the children take the name of their father. Thus, the Tiwa follow the ambilocal or biolocal marriage residence rule where a newly married couple is free to choose whether they will live with, or near to, either the parents of the bride or the parents of the groom.[7] B.C. Allen[8] also reiterates the point that a Lalung (Tiwa) woman may enter either her husband's clan or the husband may enter the wife's clan, but the right of property and lineage goes to the clan which was agreed upon at the time of marriage.

The large villages of the Hill Tiwa are located in the Amri development block in the West Karbi Anglong district of Assam and in the Ri-Bhoi district of Meghalaya. These villages are situated on elevations ranging between six to nine hundred meters. They practice both wet and shifting cultivation depending upon the physical features of the land. Shifting cultivation is practiced on the high slopes where irrigation is not possible. For shifting cultivation they would use a plot of land for three consecutive years to grow varieties of crops. In the first year, the above-mentioned crops were cultivated but from the second and third year onwards they would cultivate only paddy. After that, they would leave the patch for eight to ten years to regenerate. However, changes have taken place in the pattern of cultivation and they now cultivate only once in a plot of land sowing broom and bamboo saplings along with other food crops. In the first year, they harvest paddy and vegetables. From the second year onwards they harvest broomsticks which have a growing market outside North-East India. Similarly, trade-in bamboo is lucrative as there is a high demand from the paper mill at Jagiroad. This strategy has largely benefitted not only the Hill Tiwa but also other tribes like the Khasi-Jaintia, Karbi, and Nepali. Wet cultivation is done in the valleys where rainwater from the surrounding hills irrigates the fields. Umsawai, Morten, Ulukhunji, and Bormarjong are the main valleys where wet rice cultivation is done by the Hill Tiwa. However, the method applied for wet cultivation is different from that of the plains. Until recently instead of ploughing the field, water buffalos were used for preparing the ground for rice cultivation.

The Plain Tiwa are mainly settled in Nagaon, Morigaon, Kamrup and in some pockets of Titabor sub-division of Jorhat district of Assam. A few Tiwa villages are also located in the Dhemaji district on the north bank of Brahmaputra and Sadiya sub-division of Tinsukia district of Assam.

While the Hill Tiwa professes their 'traditional' religion, the Plain Tiwa are by, and large, Hindu. The process of Hinduisation of the Plain Tiwa began in the mid-17th century with the subjugation of Tiwa chiefs of Gobha, Nelli and Khola by the Ahoms. Subsequently, the conversion of chiefs of the minor Tiwa principalities collectively known as *Satu-raja* (seven kings) and *Pasu-raja* (five kings) to Neo-Vaishnavism led to the conversion of more Tiwas into the fold of the latter. However, a large section still follows the traditional religion. According to B. C. Allen "… the Tiwa religion is based on the worship of natural forces and of the ordinary animistic type and is chiefly concerned with the propitiation of the evil spirits and with sacrifices to ensure prosperity".[9] However, since the 1950s, there has been a growing number of converts to Christianity especially among the Hill Tiwa.

Despite the differences between the Hill and Plain Tiwa cited above, both groups claim a common ancestry. They both claim a close association with the principality of Gobha,[10] which is mentioned in the *Buranjis*[11] since the early 17th century, as an important center of trade and politics between the Ahom and the Jaintia Kingdom. They further claim that the Gobha *raja* belonged to a Tiwa clan and that his territory covered more or less, the Tiwa-dominated areas both in the hills of West Karbi Anglong and Ri-Bhoi district of Meghalaya and in the plain areas covering Morigaon, Nagaon and Kamrup districts of Assam. The reverence displayed by the Tiwa to the legendary Gobha *raja*[12] depicted as a sacred figure is significant and appears to be a binding factor for the Hill and Plain Tiwa.

The Tiwa under the nomenclature of 'Lalung' has been recorded as a Scheduled Tribe since the first Constitution Order (1950) for the state of Assam. The 2011 Census Report[13] shows 371,000 (approx) 'Lalung' in Assam, while the Tiwa population in the Ri-Bhoi district of Meghalaya is roughly estimated to be around 5000.[14] The total number of Tiwa language speakers as recorded in the 2011 Census is 34,800.[15] The following table shows the Tiwa population recorded in different census reports: The census data mentioned in the table are collected from different sources.[16]

Table: I

Year	Tiwa Population
1872	34859
1881	47650
1891	52423
1901	35513
1911	39219

Year	Tiwa Population
1921	41033
1931	43448
1941	51308
1951	52352
1961	61315
1971	95609
1981	-
1991	143746
2001	170622
2011	371000

Conceptualising Ethnohistory:

Ethnohistory is an interdisciplinary approach to the study of indigenous, colonial and post-colonial culture and history that developed as a coherent field of study in the United States during the 1950s. Ethnohistory developed as an approach to study non- European and non-literate tribal cultures in order to document their past experiences.

Erminie Wheeler-Voegelin[17] defined ethnohistory as the "study of identities, locations, contacts, movements, numbers, and cultural activities of primitive peoples from the earliest written records concerning them, onward in point of time." This definition however was criticized by subsequent scholars as too general. Her explanation, minus the brief consideration of written records, was believed to better serve as a definition of anthropology instead of ethnohistory. One such critic is anthropologist Gene Weltfish[18] who argued that the evidence base for ethnohistory should include more than just written records. He further states that by examining only written records, ethnohistorians limit their studies to the historical present giving disproportionate weight to surviving written documents. According to Weltfish ethnohistory encompasses "the study of ethnic groups in their continuity over time from the present as far back as we can identify them, and that the techniques of anthropology, coupled with the ethnic interpretation of written historical records should furnish the intellectual instruments of the study." Into the pool of evidence that ethnohistorians should draw upon are also "arrangements of things in tombs, archaeological artifacts, names and their linguistic significance, folklore, institutional forms, personal reminiscences, direct observations, and interviews."[19]

Charles Hudson,[20] an anthropologist interested in folklore, agreed with Weltfish's assessment that ethnohistory needed to incorporate more diverse source material into its evidentiary base. Unlike Weltfish, however, Hudson believed that ethnohistory, as practiced in the 1950s and 1960s, relied too heavily on Western Eurocentric interpretations. Indeed, he argued, one could not readily tell the difference between "ethnohistory" and "history." In 1966, he called for the inclusion of folk history into the definition and conception of ethnohistory. Hudson defined folk history as an attempt to "find what people in another society believe 'really happened' as judged by their sense of credibility and relevance." Hudson's claim that ethnohistorians ignored the "ethnos" in their title by relying upon European ideas of time, space, and linear thinking resonated with some anthropologists and a few historians, but did not revolutionize the idea of ethnohistory in the way that Hudson would have wished. Thus, his contention was that the methodology of ethnohistory is essentially "etic".

Anthropologist Robert Euler, defined ethnohistory as, "an advancement of the understanding of culture or cultural process by analysis of human group behavior through time using protocols of a historic nature, preferably analysed for purposes other than those originally intended by the authors, and in categories based upon modern ethnographic field investigation".[21]

According to James Axtell, ethnohistory is essentially "The use of historical and ethnological methods and materials to gain knowledge of the nature and causes of change in a culture defined by ethnological concepts and categories."[22] He further writes "whether we consider ethnohistory a form of cultural history or a sub-discipline of cultural anthropology, we can agree that it represents a common-law marriage of history and ethnology, whose purpose is to produce scholarly offspring who bear the diachronic dimensions of history and the synchronic sensitivity of ethnology."[23]

P.T. Strong,[24] who combined the approaches of history, cultural anthropology, and archaeology, posits that ethnohistory centers on reconstructing the history of non-European people including their experiences of colonisation and resistance. She states that "There are strong connections between ethnohistory and other forms of interdisciplinary inquiry such as historical anthropology, historical archaeology, social history, oral history, subaltern studies, colonial studies and indigenous studies, but ethnohistory is a fairly coherent scholarly formation that remains true to its particularistic and empirical roots."[25]

From the above discussion, it can be concluded that ethnohistory is an inter-disciplinary approach that draws on diverse sources written, spoken and material, to study the history and past experiences of non-European, pre-literate societies. Given the fact that the Tiwa is one of the pre-literate societies of North East India that have not documented their past in written form, this approach we believe is appropriate for the present study and has been used as a methodology to study the Tiwa of North East India.

The earliest reference to the Tiwa tribe is found in the *Buranjis*,[26] where they are referred to as the *'Datiyaliya'* or the people of the margins. This was followed by references to the Tiwa under the nomenclature of 'Lalung' in colonial writings.[27] The information available from British records is very scanty. They refer to the Tiwa as a semi-Hinduised tribe, who represent a branch of the Kachari or as descendants of the Chutiya of Upper Assam.[28] There is little information on their origin, migration, settlement pattern or social organization. Similarly, published works[29] of the post-Independence period do not provide a clear picture of this tribe. In their writings most of the authors do not make any distinction between the Tiwa of the hills and those of the plains, often mixing up the features of both groups without taking note of the fact that they display distinct socio-cultural features.[30] Available published works are descriptive accounts of the socio-economic and cultural features of the Tiwa, as they appear in recent times. There is no mention of their early history or the circumstances leading to the bifurcation of the Tiwa into two groups with distinct patterns of social organization and belief system. Furthermore, there is neither enough information on the socio-political institutions of the Tiwa nor an adequate understanding of the same. It is against such a backdrop, that systematic documentation, description, and construction of the history of the Tiwa has been felt to be necessary and which the present work seeks to address.

Given that the study intends to focus primarily on the early history of the Tiwa-an area largely ignored by earlier works-the study will extend from the pre-colonial period (as far back as the sources allow) to the creation of the state of Meghalaya from the erstwhile undivided state of Assam in 1972. This was an important turning point when the Karbi Anglong (Mikir Hills) and Dima Hasao (North Cachar Hills) having been given the option to either remain with the state of Assam or join the autonomous state of Meghalaya, chose the former. These political changes had far-reaching consequences which did not leave the Tiwa unscathed, bringing in its wake the politics of identity into the region which are however beyond the scope of the present study.

the *Deodhai Asam Buranji*,[31] under the chapter *Datiyalia Buranji* a manuscript collected from Mohorsing Deka of Nagaon district. In this chronicle, the Tiwa is referred to as the *Datiyaliya* or the people of the margins. It speaks about Ahom relations with the small Tiwa principalities of Gobha, Nelli, Khola, Topakuchia, Dandua, and Baropujia. It recounts Assamese soldiers' encounter with the Tiwa whom they called *Datiyalia*. It gives an interesting account of Ahom soldiers sent to survey a Tiwa village by the Rohial Baruah, head of the Roha *Chokey* after he saw smoke rising from the top of the adjacent hills. The account narrates the interactions of the Ahom soldiers with the Tiwa who initially fled out of fear. During the encounter, the Ahom soldiers insisted the Tiwa people to renounce their matrilineal descent system in favour of a 'better' system of inheritance and promised, if they came down to the plains, they will be placed under the control of the Ahom king. The *Buranji* also highlights the settlement of twelve 'Lalung' and 'Mikir' (Tiwa and Karbi) families in the plains bordering the Jaintia Hills in the 17th century.

Another Ahom chronicle the *Jayantia Buranji*[32] which deals with the diplomatic relations between the Ahom and the Jaintia gives an account of the Ahom assault on the Tiwa villages of Marjong and Amri. Interestingly in this chronicle, the people of these villages were described as Garo. Probably the Ahoms were unaware of their ethnic identity and hence used the common word 'Garo' denoting the hill dwellers. It further narrates the role of the Tiwa principality of Gobha, Khola, and Nelli in the diplomatic exchanges between the Ahom and the Jaintia kingdom from the early 17th century to the late 18th century.

During the colonial period, no separate study or ethnographic account of the Tiwa was carried out. Nevertheless, brief information about this tribe can be obtained from some of the official reports. John M'Cosh[33] was the first colonial officer to record about the Tiwa. He stated that 'Lalung' tribe did not have a fixed habitation or a population large enough for them to have a government of their own. Hence these people attached themselves with other rulers. A.J.M. Mills[34] stated that the 'Lalungs' were inhabitants of the Jaintia Hills and their religion, customs, social habits and prejudices resembles those of the 'Khasias'. According to him, the dialect that they spoke was different from the dialects spoken in other parts of Jaintia Hills.[35] R. B. Pemberton[36] also gives an account of the Gobha principality ruled by Tiwa chiefs. He recorded that there was a feud between the *raja* of 'Khyram' and 'Jayantia' to control the Gobha principality which had proved to be seriously injurious to the prosperity of the Gobha. E. T. Dalton,[37] provided a very brief account of the 'Lalung' who he believed were descendants of the 'Chutiya' of upper Assam. However, he also added that it was unlikely that all Lalungs were 'Chutiya' descendants. According to W. W. Hunter,[38] the origins of the Lalung were obscure but he thought that they are the aborigines of Cachar as their customs, habits, occupations, and religion resemble those of the 'Cachari'. He estimated the total population of this tribe at 32,818 in 'Nowgong' district. According to L. A. Waddell,[39] the Lalungs were a semi-Hinduised tribe of the plains and a branch of the Kachari that had mixed Garo and Mikir blood. He also noted that some of them referred to themselves as Tiwa. B. C. Allen's[40] brief description of the Lalung refers to the legends of this tribe which suggests that they were originally the inhabitants of the Khasi and Jaintia Hills, before the majority of them descended to the plains of 'Nowgong', apparently, because they disliked the Khasi descent system. He further mentions that the Lalung are divided into a number of clans and except for the 'Masorang' (Mosorong) clan, all others are exogamous. However, our field study has highlighted the falsity of this statement as all Tiwa clans including the Mosorong clan, are exogamous. He states that the rule of the inheritance among this tribe is peculiar. He found that a Lalung woman may either enter her husband's clan or the husband may enter the wife's clan, but the right of property and lineage goes to the clan which was adopted at the time of marriage. B. C. Allen in another work[41] refers to the practice of human sacrifice prevalent among the Lalung. He described the Tiwa as a member of the Bodo family and their language as a link between the Bodo of the plains and Dimasa or Hill Kachari. He gave a brief description of their demographic pattern and traditional beliefs in the 'Nowgong' district of Assam. G.A. Grierson[42] spoke about the Lalung speaking population in the south-west corner of the 'Nowgong' district and the adjoining areas of Kamrup and Khasi and Jaintia Hills. He enumerated 40160 Lalung speakers. He also mentions that no Ahom and Koch historian recorded anything about this tribe. According to him, some Lalung in 'Nowgong' claim that their ancestors migrated from the 'Jayantia' territory. In the tour diary of A.E. Heath,[43] the Sub-Divisional Officer of Jowai, who visited a few Tiwa villages and recorded some of the Tiwa customs. He is said that the Lalungs of 'Unswai' (Amsai) and 'Maranggaow' (Marjong) did not know their history or where they came from. According to him, they were in these hills from time immemorial. He gave a brief description of the Tiwa traditional village administration composed of the following functionaries: one *Doloi*, one *Langdoh*,[44] one *Pator*, one *Hatari*, one *Sangot*, one *Maji*, two *Dhulias* and two *Barakhs* or *Chutiyas* who were appointed by the '*Dolloi*' (*Doloi*) of 'Nurtiang' (Nartiang). However, he further added that they settled all disputes at the level of their village and seldom troubled the '*Nurtiang Dolloi*' to settle any issue. Apparently, the Tiwa informed him that they seldom go to 'Nurtiang' or the southern hats. Instead, they go to 'Nowgong' for trade. He further gave a brief description of certain customs related to the village Bachelors' dormitory '*Chummadi*'(*Shamadi*), marriage, divorce, inheritance, dress, and burials. He also gave a comparative vocabulary of English, Tiwa, and Mikir (Karbi).

While the above mentioned colonial accounts about the Tiwa are important, they are quite clearly limited as compared to accounts/ ethnographic works available on other tribes of northeast India.[45] The information on their origin, culture, religious beliefs, socio-political institutions, etc., is inadequate to provide a coherent account of the Tiwa.

In the post-Independence period, a few anthropological studies were undertaken on the Tiwa, specifically the Plain Tiwa under the sponsorship of the Tribal Research Institute of Assam and the Anthropological Survey of India. Among Indian ethnographers, N. K. Shyamchoudhury and M. M. Das[46] provided an account of the society of the Plain Tiwa. In their work, they made an attempt to describe the marriage system, religious beliefs and give a brief account of their economy. The *All Assam Tiwa Yuva-Chatra Sanmilan* (All Assam Tiwa Student-Youth Association) also brought out a book[47] comprises of several articles dealing with the marriage system, and rituals associated with cremation as practiced by the Plain Tiwa. G. C. Sharma Thakur[48] recorded some stories that are prevalent among the Plain Tiwa regarding their origin. He also described their material culture, social institutions, religious beliefs and festivals. In his *Tiwa Samaj*[49] and *Tiwa Janajati aru Bhashar Itihas*,[50] Maneshwar Dewri briefly discusses the society and culture of the Plain Tiwa and provides an analysis of the Tiwa language based on phonetics and grammar and the influence of Sanskrit on the Tiwa language. L. Gogoi's *Tiwa Sanskritir Ruprekha*,[51] Shailendra Kumar Agnihotri's *The Lalungs*[52] and Rupa Deka Pator's *Tiwa Samaj aru Sanskritir Acherenga*[53] although useful, do not provide any new information or insights into the culture and society of the Plain Tiwa.

A significant departure from the above-mentioned works is B.K. Gohain's *The Hill Lalungs*,[54] that focuses on the Hill Tiwa. It is the only ethnographical account that deals with the Hill Tiwa. The work describes the domestic, social and religious life of the Tiwa living in the hills of West Karbi Anglong district of Assam. The author provides a brief analysis of the factors that have influenced them significantly such as the market economy, wage system, *jhum* cultivation and use of modern technology etc. ushering in change among the Hill Tiwa. He later brought out a revised edition of his work under the title *Continuity and Change in the Hills of Assam: Karbi Anglong District of Assam*,[55] where he further elaborated on the same topics mentioned above. His work was largely concentrated on documenting the contemporary socio-cultural practices as observed during the latter part of 1980s.

As with the other works discussed earlier, Gohain's work is brief and does not adequately address the issues of origin, migration, settlement patterns, and socio-political institutions etc. of both the Hill and Plain Tiwa. Despite their shortcomings, the above literatures were invaluable for the present work.

Notes and References:

[1] The Khasi-Jaintia refers to the Tiwa as 'Lalung'. Interestingly the Tiwa maintain that the Khasi-Jaintia refer to them as 'Laloo' which is also the name of a founding clan in the Jaintia Hills district of Meghalaya. It may also be mentioned that the Hill Tiwa have an oral tradition which claims that the Tiwa assisted the Jaintia king in erecting megaliths at Nartiang and were subsequently absorbed as a clan within Jaintia society. An analysis of this oral tradition has been taken up in chapter III under the theme Religion and Belief System: The Hill Tiwa.

[2] S. K. Bhuyan (ed.), *Deodhai Asam Buranj*(4[th]edn.), DHAS, Guwahati, 2001 and S.K. Bhuyan(ed.), *Jayantia Buranji* (3[rd]edn.), DHAS, Guwahati, 2012.

[3] The *Deodhai Asam Buranji* contained a chapter, entitled *Dantiyalia Buranji* which talks about the people of the margins/borders adjacent to the Ahom territory.

[4] Patrilineal descent is traced only through the male and the children of both sexes belong to the kin group of their father.

[5] The majority of Tiwa living in the hills of West Karbi Anglong district of Assam and the Ri-Bhoi district of Meghalaya follow the matrilineal descent pattern. According to oral tradition maintained by the Hill Tiwa, there were twelve sisters who were the progenitors of twelve original clans of the Tiwa, suggesting that the Tiwa were originally a matrilineal society. However there has been a drastic change in the descent system of the Hill Tiwa since the early part of the 1980s primarily because of the impact of their patrilineal counterparts in the plains. Moreover improved means of transport and communication and establishment of markets in the areas dominated by the Hill Tiwa are also responsible for the changes in their descent system.

[6] The term 'bilateral descent' has been defined by Thomas R. Williams in his book *Cultural Anthropology*, Prentice Hall, New Jersey, 1990, p. 267, wherein he writes, "…if descent is recognized culturally as taking place more or less equally in both the male and female line it is called bilateral descent".

[7] Thomas R. Williams, *op. cit.*, p. 265.

[8] B.C. Allen, *Assam District Gazatteers, Vol X: The Khasi Jayantia Hills, The Garo and the Lushai Hills*, Allahabad, 1906, p.62.

[9] B.C. Allen, *op. cit.*, p. 62

[10] Presently Gobha is a revenue village under Morigaon district of Assam and is located in the foothills bordering the Karbi Anglong district of Assam and the Ri-Bhoi district of Meghalaya.

[11] S. K. Bhuyan (ed.), *Deodhai Asam Buranji, Jayntia Buranji, Kamrup Buranji,op.cit.*

[12] The Tiwa believe that the first Gobha *raja* was born in a mountain called Thinimaklang or Timowflong situated between the present borders of the West Karbi Anglong district of Assam and the East Khasi Hills district of Meghalaya. He is closely associated with the *Junbil/Jonbil* fair organized every year in the month

of January near Jagiroad, where the Tiwa, Khasi-Jaintia and Karbi people exchange their commodities with the plains people on the first day of the fair.

13 Registrar General & Census Commissioner of India, General Census, 2001 online accessed www.censusindia.govt.in on 17/09/2015.

14 According to some leaders of the *Tiwa Mathonlai Tokhra* or the Tiwa Sahitya Sabha, a literary body of the Tiwa based in Jagiroad, Assam, the Tiwa population in Ri-Bhoi district of Meghalaya is estimated to be around five to six thousand. They state that the number of Tiwa population has been dwindling because many of them have identified themselves as Khasi instead of Tiwa in the census reports primarily to gain socio-political benefits from the government of Meghalaya where the Tiwa are not recognised under Scheduled Tribe category. It is an interesting development that has been going on for the last several decades which needs to be studied in detail.

15 Registrar General & Census Commissioner of India, *op. cit.*

16 Census data of 1872, 1881, 1891 and 1901 has been collected from, B.C. Allen, *Census of Assam, 1901*(Reprint), Manas Publishing, New Delhi, 1984, p. 157. The data of 1911, 1921 and 1931 has been collected from J.H. Hutton, *Census of India, 1931*, *op. cit.*, p. 549. The data of 1941, 1951 and 1961 has been collected from, E.H. Pakyntein, *Census of India 1961*, Vol. III, Assam, Part-V-A, Scheduled Tribes and Scheduled Castes, Govt. of India, Delhi, 1964, p. 3. The census data of 1871 is collected from G. C. Sharma Thakur, *The Lalungs(Tiwa)*,Tribal Research Institute, Assam, Guwahati, 1985, p. 15. The census of 1981 in Assam is blank on account of the Assam agitation. The data of 1991 and 2001 has been collected from the Registrar General & Census Commissioner of India website www.censusindia.govt.in accessed on 17/09/2015.

17 Erminie W. Voegelin, "An Ethnohistorian's Viewpoint, "*Ethnohistory* 1, 1954, p. 168.

18 Gene Weltfish, "The Question of Ethnic Identity, an Ethnohistorical Approach," *Ethnohistory* 6, 1959, p. 335

19 *Ibid.*

20 Charles Hudson, "Folk History and Ethnohistory", *Ethnohistory* 13, 1966, p. 54.

21 Robert C. Euler, "Ethnohistory in the United States," *Ethnohistory* 19,1972, p.201

22 James Axtell, "Ethnohistory: An Historian's Viewpoint," *Ethnohistory* 26, 1979, p. 2.

23 *Ibid.*

24 P.T. Strong, "Ethnohistory," In James D. Wright (ed.), *International Encyclopedia of the Social and Behavioral Sciences*(2nd edn.), Vol, 8, New York, 2015, pp. 192-197.

25 *Ibid.*

26 S.K. Bhuyan(ed.), *op.cit.*

27 *See* A.J.M. Mills, *Report on the Khasi and Jaintia Hills 1853*, NEHU, Shillong, 1985, p.5; R.B. Pemberton, *The Eastern Frontiers of India* (Reprint), Delhi, 1979, p. 22. E. T. Dalton, *Descriptive Ethnology of Bengal*, Calcutta, 1872, p. 78; L. A. Waddell, *The*

Tribes of Brahmaputra Valley: A Contribution of Their Physical Types and Affinities (reprint), New Delhi, 2000, p. 54.

[28] *Ibid.*

[29] See, N. K. Shyamchoudhury & M. M. Das, *The Lalung Society: A Theme for Analytical Ethnography*, Calcutta, 1973; All Assam Tiwa Yuva-Chatra Sanmilan (ed.) *Tiwa Sampradyar Parichay*, Asom Sahitya Sabha, Jorhat, 1975; G.C. Sharma Thakur, *op. cit.,*; Maneshwar Dewri, *Tiwa Samaj*, Asom Sahitya Sabha, Jorhat, 1983; L. Gogoi, *Tiwa Sanskritir Ruprekha*, Harihar Mandir, Nagaon, 1986.

[30] Both the Hill and Plain Tiwa display differences in their systems of marriage, rituals associated with birth and death and descent. Festivals celebrated by the Hill Tiwa, such as *Sogra, Wanchuwa, Khelchawa, Langkhon* are not performed by the Plain Tiwa. Moreover, the Hill Tiwa are primarily dependent on *Jhum* cultivation whereas the Plain Tiwa are dependent on wet rice cultivation. Similarly the settlement pattern of both the groups also differs from each other.

[31] S.K. Bhuyan (ed.), *op. cit.*, 2001.

[32] S.K. Bhuyan(ed.), *op. cit.*, 2012.

[33] John M'Cosh, *Topography of Assam*, Calcutta, 1837, p. 166.

[34] A.J.M. Mills, *op. cit.*, p. 5.

[35] Perhaps Mills was not aware of the fact that the Tiwa speaks a language that belongs to Tibeto- Burman branch of the Sino-Tibetan language family and Khasi language is a branch of Mon-Khmer language family and both the language differ from each other.

[36] R. B. Pemberton, *op. cit.*, p. 22.

[37] E. T. Dalton, *op. cit.*, p. 78.

[38] W. W. Hunter, *A Statistical Account of Assam, Vol. I*, London, 1879, p.184.

[39] L. A. Waddell, *op. cit.*, p. 54.

[40] B. C. Allen *op.cit.*, p. 62.

[41] B.C. Allen, *Assam District Gazetteers, Nowgong,*Part:VI, City Press, Calcutta, 1905,p. 72

[42] G.A. Grierson, *Linguistic Survey of India*, vol.2, Calcutta, 1903

[43] Tour diary of the Sub-divisional officer, Jowai Mr. A.E. Heath, for the month of November and December 1882, submitted to the secretary to the Chief Commissioner of Assam on 17th February 1883, Assam State Archives collected on 17/10/2015.

[44] Among the Khasi the *Lyngdoh* is the village priest. Among the Tiwa the village priest is called the *Loro*.

[45] British administrators and missionaries wrote several accounts on various tribes in North East India. Some well-known monographs include *The Khasis* by P.R.T. Gurdon, *The Garo* by A. Playfair, *The Naked Naga* by J.P. Mills and J. Hutton's and Furer Haimendorf, *The Kacharis* by S. Endle, *The Lotha Nagas* by J. P. Mills,

The Mikirs by Charles Lyalls are some of the important works that were produced during the colonial period.

[46] N. K. Shyamchoudhury & M. M. Das, *op. cit.*

[47] All Assam Tiwa Yuva-Chatra Sanmilan (ed.), *op. cit.*

[48] G. C. Sharma Thakur, *op. cit.*

[49] Maneshwar Dewri, *op. cit.*

[50] *idem.,Tiwa Janajati aru Bhashar Itihas*, Tribal Research Institute, Guwahati, 1988.

[51] L. Gogoi, *op. cit.*

[52] Shailendra Kumar Agnihotri, *The Lalungs*, S. Kumar &Associates, Delhi, 1996.

[53] Rupa Deka Pator, *Tiwa Samaj aru Sanskritir Acherenga*, Tribal Research Institute, Guwahati, 2007.

[54] B. K. Gohain, *The Hill Lalungs*, ABILAC, Guwahati, 1992.

[55] *Idem, Continuity and Change in the Hills of Assam: Karbi Anglong Distrct, Assam,* Omsons Publication, New Delhi, 2006.

Chapter II

Origin, Migration and Settlement Patterns

It is always difficult and sometime controversial to study the origin and migration of ethenic groups especially due to lack of verifiable sources. Nevertheless, the application of ethnohistorical approach which encompasses all oral, written and archaeological sources has proved to be important in this regard. The origin and migration of the Tiwa and settlement at different places from the earliest period to the present day can be traced from oral traditions, enduring customs, Ahom chronicles, and colonial writings. We have primarily focused on the collection and interpretation of oral traditions and eduring customs to attain a logical understanding of the Tiwa origin and migration history.

For long the paradigm of reconstructing histories based on written sources virtually denied oral tradition its rightful place in historical methodology. However, historians like Jan Vansina[1], David Hanige[2], H.M. Wright[3] and others have shown that oral tradition is a dependable source and that it is history in its own right. They have also argued that the custodians of traditions are both informants and historians at the same time. Oral tradition is a means by which people transmit cultural knowledge. Culture is transmitted from generation to generation through stories, myths and reenactment of rituals and ceremonies. A common form of oral tradition is storytelling, an art form passed down from one generation to another through word of mouth. One of the main purposes of these stories is to reflect upon 'traditional' values of the past in order to make sense of the moral changes of the present. A significant part of oral tradition comprises of origin myths. Classical cultural evolutionists such as J. Frazer[4] and E.B. Tylor[5] contended that such components of 'primitive Ideas' should be identified with mythological thought. Franz Boas[6] and B. Malinowski,[7] however argue that pre-literate cultures need not be classified in such a demeaning way. Malinowski suggested that myth, like religion, fulfills a universal human need for unraveling the unexplained phenomena. Boas unlike Malinowski maintained that myths have an explanatory function. In his view myths are taken seriously because they deal with the most fundamental aspect of 'native' life, such as their beliefs on the nature and origin of their world. Claude Levi-Strauss[8] considered myth as historically specific, since it is almost always set in some timeframe 'long ago' and ahistorical because the narrative is 'timeless'. He brushed aside the individuality of the texts of myths in favour of looking at patterns, systems and structures contained therein. Levi-Strauss emphasized the idea that structures are universal, hence they are timeless. This model fits with what the traditional societies believed: that the events described in their myths took place at the dawn of creation. They viewed the world as a unified creation whose characteristic patterns did not vary through time.

In this regard, C. L. Imchen[9] writes, "for some people myth may be 'false believe' or irrational. But it is important to realize that myth is a distinct form of thought for which scientific standard of 'truth' and 'falsehood' have no meaning". Myth makes no distinction between a subjective world's personal experience and the objective world that is deciphered through empiricism. He furthers states that, myth are unique in the sense that they stimulate human thought patterns and emotions that allow them to make sense of particular dimensions of their world which cannot be here usually explained away.[10] Considering the immense value of myths in the context of northeast India, M. Momin,[11] contended that,

> This region is a treasure-strove of myths pertaining to the people's customs, beliefs and values, which have been handed down from generation to generation by word of mouth and the stories tell us about the origins of people and their claim to particular areas, about the emergence of socio-political institutions and about the regulation of human actions *vis-à-vis* those institutions, among other things.

Ethnologically, the Tiwa are related to the Bodo-Garo linguistic group under the Tibeto-Burman linguistic family who are living in different parts of Brahmaputra valley, Karbi Anglong districts of Assam and parts of the hills of Meghalaya.

Origin myths prevalent among the Tiwa can be divided into two types: one which is related to the term 'Lalung' and the other with the 'Tiwa'. The stories related to the word Lalung is basically more popular among the plain Tiwa. However the Hill Tiwa do not like to be called Lalung as they believed that the name Lalung was coined by outsiders.

Origin of Tiwa:

The Ahom chronicles and colonial documents recorded the Tiwa people as 'Lalung'. Even today many of the neighbouring tribes such as the Karbi, Khasi-Jaintia and people from the plains call them Lalung/ Langlu or Laloo. Until recently the term 'Lalung' has been used in all government records. However, the Tiwa especially the Hill Tiwa addresses themselves as 'Tiwa'. Some Hill Tiwa are of the view that they are known to others as 'Lalung' but they never identify themselves as 'Lalung'. According to them, they are the Tiwa people, their language is Tiwa and their culture is Tiwa culture. They have never used the word 'Lalung' to describe their ethnicity or culture.

B.K. Gohain[12] writes "The word Tiwa has its origin in the words *ti-phar-wali* meaning a clan living near water". He referred to a story which describes 'Sodonga raja'.[13] According to the story, once a girl of the Maloi-wali clan was excommunicated by her parents and villagers because she conceived a child out of wedlock. Subsequently, she gave birth to a baby boy near the bank of the Kiling River in West Karbi Anglong district of Assam. However, after few days the baby happened to have disappeared in the river. Eventually he was found alive by some villagers in a pond near Umtengam. Before long he was considered to be the child of the entire village and brought up with great love and affection. With the progress of time, the child grew up into a fearless hero participating in the affairs of the village council and becoming keenly interested in the welfare of his people. Subsequently, he was chosen as the leader of the village and later the chief of the tribe because of his courage and intelligence. As the chief was found in water/river, the people whom he represented became known as *Ti-phar-wali* or Tiwa.

However, the above story about how the Tiwa derived its name from their king 'Sodonga Raja' does not sound convincing as the evolution of political institution or Kingship in any tribal society takes place at a much higher stage. Surajit Sinha[14] writes that,

> The state emerged primarily out of the endogenous ethnic based evolutionary process. It has a significant correlation between the degree of surplus generated through appropriate technological innovations and the level of functional differentiation, stratification and centralization of a polity.

Therefore it is obvious that polity formation is an evolutionary process and there is no evidence to suggest that a tribe derives its name from its chief or ruler.

Nevertheless, there is ample scope to believe that the term 'Tiwa' was derived from *Ti -Phar- Wali*. *Ti* means water, *Phar*, meaning bank and *Wali*[15] denotes matriclan. It means people living on the banks of a water body. According to Tiwa scholars, in the course of time the word "*Phar*" disappeared and the people came to be known as Tiwali or Tiwa. According to E. A. Gait[16] the river Brahmaputra was known as *Ti-lao* in the early days of the Ahom rule. He further states that another name for this river was Lohit or Lohitya (red) a Sanskritised term for the original name of *Ti-lao*. The *Kalika Purana*, mentioned that the river Lohitya/Lohit is so-called because Parasuram a legendary figure in the Ramayana washed off his bloody stain in it. Gait concluded that the frequent occurrence of the prefix *ti* or *di*, the Bodo word for water, in the names of the tributaries of Brahmaputra River like Dibru, Dikhu, Dihing, Dihong, Disang, Dimla, testify that in the past the Bodo dominated these areas for a long duration. S.K. Chatterji[17] also has similar views regarding the relationship of the river Brahmaputra and its Bodo origin. He stated that "the Brahmaputra also came to be better known in the Hindu world outside Assam as *Lauhitya*, which would appear to be an 'Aryanisation', in Sanskrit, of the Indo- Mongoloid, Bodo name. He concluded that the areas of the Luhit River presently occupied by several tribes of Arunachal

Pradesh, appear to have been inhabited by Bodo speakers because the main channels of the Luhit, Dibang and Dihang have a common Bodo element for water or river, *Ti* or *Di*. S.K. Phukan who has done extensive work on the onomastics[18] of Assam contended that the name Luhit has come from two words Lao+Ti and Dihong comes from Di+Hong.[19] He further concluded that the present name of the rivers of upper Assam such as Dilao, Dimak, Dima, Dikhow, Dichang, Dilih often mentioned in a number of Ahom chronicles as Tilao, Timak, Timao, Tikhow, Tichang and Tilih respectively which according to him starts with '*Ti*' a Tiwa word for water or river.[20] During our fieldwork we have found that the neighbouring Naga groups such as the Ao and Konyak still call the river Dikhow as Tikhow and Dilih as Tilih and Dichang as Tichang.[21] Further derivations linking the Tiwa and water/Brahmaputra have been highlighted by several Tiwa scholars. They are of the view that the Luhit was known as *Leu-ti* or Long River and the river Dibang was originally known as *Ti-bonge* among the Tiwa. In Tiwa language, *ti* means river/water and *bonge* means water flowing forcefully/abundantly. Thus *Ti-bonge/Dibang* means, a river with abundant water flowing forcefully. Further, they are of the view that the river Dihang came from the Tiwa word *Ti-hong* which means, the river came out of a hole or *hong*. Thus, it is quite certain that the term 'Tiwa' has a strong connection with the river Luhit or *Leu-Ti* which originates in the Himalayan Mountains and that the Tiwa lived on its banks in the area roughly covering the Tibet region and subsequently in eastern Assam. It is to be noted that several Tiwa oral traditions suggest about their close connection with the Himalayan region and eastern Assam where they inhabited for a considerable period of time before migrating towards the lower Brahmaputra valley in the remote past.

Origin of the Term Lalung:

There have been many theories and conjectures by various authors based on oral traditions to describe the meaning of the word 'Lalung'. However, after careful investigation, it has become clear that there is no word called 'Lalung' in Tiwa language. The people especially the Hill Tiwa never use the word 'Lalung' among themselves to describe their ethnicity. The word does not have any meaning in their language nor is there any root Tiwa word from which this word could have originated or be derived from and as such, it is a foreign word for them. Nevertheless, the Tiwa have been recorded as Lalung in the Ahom Buranjis, British reports as well as various government records of the post-independent period. Until the 1990s the caste certificates issued by the government refer to the Tiwa as 'Lalung'. Mills report of 1853 recorded the Tiwa as 'Lalung' whom he identified as one of the original inhabitants of Khasi-Jaintia Hills.[22] A.E. Heath[23] who paid a visit to Tiwa villages of Amsai, Marjong and Amkha in 1881, found people introduced themselves as Lalung but not as Tiwa. It suggests that both the terms 'Tiwa' and 'Lalung' were used by this tribe to identify themselves.

Regarding the name, meaning and origin and derivation of the term "Lalung", there were various views and opinions which are discussed below:

A popular legend prevalent among the Plain Tiwa believes that Siva created a god by the name "Lungla Mahadeo", *Lung* means saliva arising out of Shiva's mouth and *la* means the formation of a living being out of that saliva. The union of lord *Lungla* and 'Joyanti Devi' produced three daughters. Subsequently, these three daughters produced three persons who were the ancestors of the Karbi, the Khasi and the Tiwa respectively.[24] An interesting aspect of this story is that it advocates the brotherly relation between the three tribes and their close social and cultural ties since a very remote past.

A similar story with little variation also described, once upon a time Mahadeo and his consort Parvati were enjoying the scenic beauty of Mansarovar Lake in the Makha Koja(red mountain). The soothing beauty of the lake and its surroundings were so enchanting that Siva soon fell asleep on the banks of the lake. When awoke, he saw five drops of his saliva had fallen on the ground and created five men out of the five drops of saliva. On the other hand, his consort Parvati created five women who were married to those five men. As such their offspring came to be known as 'Lalung'.[25]

Another popular legend behind the term 'Lalung' is that, once the Tiwa were ruled by a demon king called Bali, who was a faithful devotee of Vishnu. So he wanted all his subjects should worship Vishnu as their principal deity. However, a section of people refused to accept the dictate and continued to adhere to their traditional way of worship. As a result, the king ordered to expel those who opposed his will from the kingdom after imprinting a red (*lal*)[26] mark on the forehead. Later, those bearers of red marks on the forehead came to be known as the Lalung.[27]

The stories related to the origin of the word 'Lalung' is closely associated with the Hindu deity Siva, Parvati and Vishnu. There is no denying the fact that Tiwa especially the Plain Tiwa has adopted and incorporated the Hindu traditions in their society since the last several centuries. Perhaps these stories may have developed when the Tiwa chief of Gobha migrated to Gobha near Jagiroad from Amsai in the West Karbi Anglong and become influential.

Another myth popular among the plain Tiwa recorded by Maneshwar Dewri[28] during 1980s, states that after staying for several centuries in the 'Jayatha'(Jaintia) Hills an internal conflict emerged among the Tiwa people on the issue of selection of their chief through the matrilineal descent system.[29] One group led by one Hura preferred the matrilineal descent system and another group led by Thongra opted for patrilineal descent. Later, as a result of this feud, Thongra (some other says Hura) was killed by the supporters of Hura. Hence, in order to escape from being punished for the crime, Hura and his followers decided to flee from the hills. But the supporters of Thongra requested them not to leave and stay at a place called Tiwa Junthung[30]. However, they refused to remain in the hills and came down towards the Brahmaputra Valley. Meanwhile, while coming down towards the plains they happened to cross a river. While battling to go across the river some of them were drowned and many were rescued by the Mikir (Karbi) people. Thus the Karbis started addressing the Tiwa people as *'langlu-monit'* or people rescued from the water. In Karbi dialect, *lang* means water/river *lu* means rescued and *monit* means people. In due course, the *langlu* became *lalung* in the plains of Assam.

B.K. Gohain recorded that the Hill Tiwa believed that the word 'Lalung' has been derived from the compound word *'lang-lu'* in Karbi which means light blue water. From the above story, it is clear that the word 'Lalung' has a close connection with the Karbi word *'lang'* meaning water. The Tiwa are still addressed by the Karbi as *'Langlu'* in Karbi

Anglong. Thus in our opinion, the word '*langlu-monit*' could be a direct translation of the term 'Tiwa' which means people settled along the river. It appears '*ti*' which means water/river in Tiwa and '*lang*' which means water/ river in Karbi is interrelated. It suggests that the Karbi had translated the term '*Tiwa*' in their own language as '*langlu*' which has a similar connotation with the term Tiwa. It is to be noted that the Karbi have a tradition of identifying some Tiwa clans as an equivalent of some of their own clan (*kur*)[31]. During our fieldwork,we have found that the Karbi has equivalent clans for several Tiwa clans. The following are the different Tiwa clans identified by the Karbi as equivalent to their own clans:

Table II

Tiwa clan	Equivalent Karbi Clan
Mithi, Madar	Engti/Ingty
Malang	Ronghang
Amshi, Amsong	Teron, Millick
Puma	Timung
Maslai	Hanse
Kholar	Bey
Sagra	Kro

Interestingly, the Karbi considers marriage between the equivalent clans of Karbi and the Tiwa unacceptable. Though the Tiwa and Karbi are two different tribes but while deciding any marriage proposal, the Karbi forbids the marriage with the Tiwa clan equivalent to theirs. In this connection, Philippe Ramirez[32] made an extensive study and found that the Karbi, Tiwa and Khasi have equivalences between surnames. He contended that equivalences could have contributed to a large extent to inter-ethnic matrimonial relationships. Whatever may be the reasons for identifying the Tiwa clans with that of equivalent Karbi clan, the above discussion shows that it could be possible that the Tiwa were addressed as '*Langlu*' by the Karbi because they found it to be equivalent to the word 'Tiwa' meaning the people settled along the rivers/waters.

Some of the Tiwa scholars believe that the Lalung word has come from a Tiwa word 'Libing' or 'Libung' which means person/individual. It is interesting to note that while describing themselves the Tiwa people identify themselves as Tiwa libing/libung meaning a Tiwa person. It may have possible that with the progress of time the non-Tiwa people started addressing them as Libung or Lalung instead of Tiwa Libung.

From the above discussion, it has emerged that there is no consensus opinion on the origin of the word Lalung. It is to be noted that several tribes in North East India were known by names conferred by outsiders rather than the actual name of the tribe. For example, Nishis were known as *Dafla,* a term given by the people of the plains, the Achik Mande were known to the outsiders as Garo a term conferred on them by the plains people meaning 'hill dwellers'. Francis Hamilton recorded that 'Garo' is a Bengali word to describe different groups of people having a name peculiar to it.[33] In the case of the Karbi, they were known as Mikir to outsiders but they never identified themselves by that name. Mizo were known by the outsiders as Kuki which is a Bengali word meaning "wild Man" to designate all hill people who cultivated their land by *jhuming.*[34] Similarly the Naga or naked is a generic term coin by the people of the plains to denote several ethnic groups such as Ao, Lotha, Sema, Konyak, Chakasang etc. inhabiting the hills of present Nagaland. From the above instances it has come to the light that several ethnic groups in North-East India have two names; one that is conferred by outsiders and the other the original one by which a tribe identifies themselves. The name given by others is always regarded as derogatory by the individuals of the particular tribe as it is not their actual identity.

Dafla, Naga, Mikir, Garo and Lalung are some of the examples of *exonyms* or *xenonyms* similarly Nishi, Ao, Lotha, Sema, Konyak, Chakasang, Achik Mande, Tiwa are *endonyms* or *autonyms. Exonym* or *xenonym* is a name used by foreigners or outsiders to refer to a people or ethnic group that the group itself does not use. On the other hand *endonym* or *autonym* is a name by which a people or ethnic group refers to itself; self- designation.

Migration Stories:

The history of migration of the Tiwa can be studied from their oral traditions and religious practices. During our field study, we have come across a folk song that was sung in the olden days during the *jhum* cultivation which speaks about different places where the Tiwa lived. The song goes like this:

> *Makhakojaw chorega*
> *Borthongkara na phijuga,*
> *Tumramakha son phiga*
> *Sera Siri na phijuga.*[35]

Free translation:

> *We started from Makha Koja (the red mountain) arrived at Bor Thongkara (great plains) then went to Tumara Hill (near Khetri to the south of NH 37) and arrived at Sera Siri (a hill above the Umswai valley).*

This folk song narrates the migration story of the Tiwa people. It states that they started their journey from the Makha Koja or the red mountain. According to the Hill Tiwa, Makha Koja is the Himalayan Mountain from where they came to the present habitat. From the song, we can infer that the Tiwa once lived in the Himalayan mountain range possibly in the Tibetan plateau on the bank of river Luhit or *Leu-Ti*. The possibility that Makha Koja was the place of origin of Tiwa people can further be ascertained from a ritual associated with the *Phidri-Chongkhong* ceremony that takes place at the beginning of the agricultural cycle. During this ceremony, it is observed that the Tiwa are forbidden to show their backs towards the 'east' on the day of the ceremony as it is considered to be sacred in their religious beliefs. On examination, the *Hadari*[36] of Amsai village stated that according to Tiwa tradition they have come from the eastern direction where Makha Koja is located therefore they are forbidden to show their backs towards that direction in honour of their ancestors.

In this connection S. Endle[37] writes that the Mongoloid features and appearance of the people suggest Tibet and China, the two trans-Himalayan countries to be the original home of the 'Bodo' race. The fact that the Tiwa are ethnically Mongoloids, and linguistically belong to the Sino-Tibetan or more precisely Bodo-Garo speech family needs no further reference. S.K. Chatterji, locates the original home of the Sino-Tibetan speakers to the northwest of China, the headwaters of Hwang-ho and 'Yangtzekiang' rivers and observed that the Mongoloid tribes of the Tibeto-Chinese speech family appeared to have been pushing south and west from their original homeland from pre-historic times.[38] The imperial Gazetteer of India[39] states that the upper courses of the Yangtzekiang and the Hwang-ho rivers in North West China were the original home of the Tibeto-Burman races. Based on the above views corroborated by the Tiwa oral traditions as stated above, it may be inferred that the original home of the Tiwa lies in the Tibet region of the Himalayas.

Different scholars have suggested different routes of migration of the Bodo-Garo speech family. R. Rahul,[40] in his work *Himalayan Borderlands*, refers to three prominent routes connecting Tibet with Assam and Bengal through Bhutan. These routes are the Manas river valley, the Kariapara Duars and the Paro valley. He writes that formerly there was a flourishing trade between India and Tibet with the Bhutanese as carrying agents. From Bengal and Assam, the Bhutanese used to collect dyes, *endi* or *eri* cloth and cocoons, areca nuts, tea, tobacco etc., and exchanged them with the Tibetans for wool, salt, musk etc. R.M. Nath,[41] writes that there was an ancient route from China along the course of the Lohit river or *Lao-tu* (wide water) to the north-eastern corner of Assam. He concluded that by this route the 'Zuh-This' people (Austric) came to the Assam Valley. He mentions that there was a trade route from Yunan in south China through the Shan states, Hukawng Valley, the Brahmaputra River, and Kamarupa to Pataliputra (Patna) and Sravasti. There was another route from Lhasa which led into Assam along the lower Brahmaputra which took four months to reach Chounahat on the Border of Assam. According to S.K. Chatterji,[42] a meager stream of the trade from China used to filter into Assam through the Kirata country comprising Tibet, Sikkim, Bhutan, Manipur and adjacent areas. He quotes Changkiang, the Chinese General and explorer of Central Asia in the 2nd century B.C. as having referred to such trade routes connecting North-East India and Western China. P.C. Choudhury,[43] provided four possible routes of migration of various races into Assam. First through the mountain passes of Tibet, Nepal and Bhutan; second, through the valley of the Ganges and the Brahmaputra from India; third, by sea or the Bay of Bengal, passing through Bengal or Burma and fourthly the Assam-Burma routes, one over the Patkai passes in the North East, leading from the 'Lidu'- Margherita road to China through the Hukawng Valley in Burma (Myanmar) and another through Manipur and Cachar in the South-East or South Assam. He is of the view that the route through the mountain passes between Tibet and Assam were extensively used for trade.

Now the question is which route was followed by the Tiwa while entering the Brahmaputra valley. In this regard, there seems to be a consensus of opinion among scholars that the likely route appears to be along the north and north eastern direction. G.A. Grierson,[44] mentioned that the upper courses of the Yangtze and the Hwang-ho in North-West China were the original home of the Tibeto-Burman races and they entered Assam through the courses of the river Brahmaputra, Chindwin, Irrawaddy, Salween, Mekong, Menam and mountain passes of Assam and Burma through the North-East and South-East direction. The Imperial Gazetteers of India states that the north-eastern route was followed by the Lalungs (Tiwa), Mikirs (Karbi) and Boros.[45] S. Endle[46] refers to two great immigrations at different times, one entering from the North-East Bengal and Western Assam through the valleys of Teesta, Dharla and Sankosh etc. and the other making its way through the Subansiri, Dibong and Dihong valleys into eastern Assam.

P.C. Choudhury[47] suggests that the Tibeto-Burman tribes entered Assam from the North- East direction. A similar view was expressed by B.M. Das[48] regarding the original home of the Tibeto-Burman speakers of Northeast India. According to him, they migrated to the hills and plains of Assam in successive waves from the upper courses of the Yangtzekiang and Hwang-ho via Tibet. B.K. Barua[49] opined that the Lalung (Tiwa) migrated to the Brahmaputra valley along with the other Tibeto-Burman tribes such as the Dimasa, Garo, Rabha, Maran, Chutiya, Tipra and the

Koch from their original home in Western China near Yangtzekiang and the Hwang-ho River. He further stated that after they "migrated towards the courses of the Brahmaputra, one of the Tibeto-Burmese speaking groups ascended the Kapili Valley and the neighboring streams into the hills of Khasi and Jaintia Hills".[50] In our opinion the group which ascended the Kapili Valley was the Tiwa. According to B. K. Gohain,[51] the Tiwa had their original homeland in North-Eastern China and later settled in Tibet from where they migrated to the Brahmaputra valley several millennia before the birth of Christ.

To locate early Tiwa settlements in Assam and its adjoining areas, there are suggestive evidences that provide us with ample scope to establish the fact that they had lived and thrived in the Brahmaputra valley before entering the hills of the present West Karbi Anglong and Jaintia Hills.

According to one legend recorded by Maneshwar Dewri[52] in the 1970s among the Tiwa of Dhemaji district described that the original abode of the Tiwa was at the Tibetan plateau. Their ancestors entered the Brahmaputra valley through the North-Eastern direction and settled at Sadiya and Dhemaji. Subsequently, under the leadership of two brothers, they established a principality called Khola. Envied by their prosperity they were frequently attacked by the neighbouring Dafla (Nishi) and Abor (Adi) people. Hence they had to migrate along the course of Brahmaputra River and established themselves at Hillali corresponding to present Halem in Darrang district. Subsequently, they were again attacked by the neighbouring tribes which forced them to seek a new beginning in the Jaintia Hills. The story suggests a probable route of Tiwa migration from Tibet along the Brahmaputra valley through the North-Eastern direction.

A story still current among the Hill Tiwa states that Saripahai (the Tiwa deity) provided the hoe (*pakhu*) and spade (*khangra*) to their ancestors that included twelve males and females to cultivate at Lagrathuli, Makha Koja, Bortongkhara, Tumra Makha and at Sera Siri. They undertook cultivation at those places consistently without any rest till they arrived at Sera Siri where they were given a big fat pig by their god for a feast. The story is suggestive of the migration route of the Tiwa. The appearance of a pig while in Sera Siri in the story suggests on the founding of a permanent settlement in that area after a long period of struggle. It also symbolizes prosperity that was achieved at Sera Siri by the Tiwa people.[53]

The Plain Tiwa:

According to the census of 2001[54] the total tribal population of Assam was 3,308,570 which constitute 12.4% of the total population. The Tiwa population is 1,70, 622, which constitutes 5.2% of the total scheduled tribe population of the state. Major concentrations of the Tiwa people are found in Nagaon and Morigaon districts of Assam, which constitute 92.79% of the total Tiwa population.[55] This section deals with the aspect of migration of the Tiwa in the plains of Brahmaputra valley, more precisely into the Kolong and Kapili valley.

The data generated during our fieldwork at Amsoi (Sohori), Marjong Gaon, Silchang, Manikpur, Morigaon and Baropujia suggested that the ancestors of these villages came from Jaintia Hills.[56] According to some prominent Plain Tiwa; their ancestors migrated to the Brahmaputra valley long ago from the east and moved into the Jaintia Hills. Subsequently, they again came down to the valley in search of a better livelihood. They contended that the Tiwa are one of the several Tibeto-Burman groups that came down from Tibet through the upper course of the Brahmaputra. Initially, they settled at various places along the valley of the Brahamaputra and its tributaries before reaching Sera Siri in West Karbi Anglong and Jaintia Hills. In course of time, some of their ancestors again moved down to the Kolong and Kapili valleys in search of agricultural land. Moheswar Pator an inhabitant of Marjong Gaon in Amsoi stated that their ancestors came down and settled at the present area several centuries ago from their root village at Bormarjong in the West Karbi Anglong. A resident of Silchang village informed that the founder of their village came from the root village called Amnibaro, located around thirty kilometer in the hills of West Karbi Anglong. Their ancestor Khalasing Puma founded the Khola kingdom in 1429 C.E. and made Silchang its capital. Suren Konwar[57] told us that Amsoi in the Nagaon district was established by a few families who came from Amsai, a Tiwa root village in the West Karbi Anglong. Hence, the name of the newly established village was called Amsai. Later it was mispronounced as 'Amsoi'.

Thus the above oral accounts suggest that most of the Tiwa villages in the plains were established by the people who migrated from the neighbouring Hills. In our opinion, the Plain Tiwa must have migrated to the Lolong-Kapili valley from two prominent routes. One group came down through the Nelli-Ulukhunji route and spread across the present Morigaon and Kamrup district. Another group migrated through the Amsoi-Sahari route and settled at different places in the present Nagaon district. It is to be noted that, these two routes are the main arteries connecting the Tiwa inhabited areas of Umswai valley in West Karbi Anglong. During the 1960s before the construction of the PWD roads connecting Nelli with Umswai and Amsoi with Ulukhunji, the people of the hills used to come to the weekly market at Nelli and Phuloguri by scaling down the stiff hilly slopes barefooted. Our informant[58] stated that they used to start their journey to the market one day ahead of the market day as it takes ten hours to cover the distance from their village. Therefore, it can be concluded that these two routes facilitated the flow of Tiwa migration and settlement in the Brahmaputra valley.

All the above discussed oral testimonies suggest that the Plain Tiwa migrated from the West Karbi Anglong and Jaintia Hills in several batches. It may have been possible that while coming down from Tibet and eastern Assam, some of the Tiwa groups were left behind in the Brahmaputra valley while others settled in the hills. However, we do not have definite evidence to testify to this hypothesis as the scholars that we had interviewed acknowledged that their ancestors came to the plains of Assam from the West Karbi Anglong and Jaintia Hills several centuries ago.

In the previous chapter it was mentioned about the the *Datiyalia Buranji*[59] (Chronicle of the frontier people or people of the Margins) compiled under the title *Deodhai Asam Buranji* where an encounter of Ahom and some Tiwa villagers was made. The chronicle describes that during the reign of Jaydhwaj Singha (1648-63) the Rohial Baruah, the head of Roha military post on being curious of the smokes in the neighbouring hills, he sends his troops to ascertain whether there was any human habitation. When the soldiers arrived at a village (apparently a Tiwa village) after a journey of twenty days they found that most of the inhabitants had fled to different quarters. Eventually, the Ahom soldiers found a few old and disabled persons who could not flee and developed a cordial relationship with them. During their stay at the village, they told the villagers that '*Swargodeo Iswar* (the Ahom king) is the son of god Indra who came to the Earth and becomes the master of men and god above human beings'[60] The soldiers further explained that as an honour to *Swargodeo* who rules the country, the king's son becomes the king, the minister's son becomes the minister, the saint's son become saint, and the village officer's son becomes village officer. And if you can afford it, there is no fault in wearing golden ornaments. In reply the *datiyalias*(frontier people)said that in their country the king's son cannot become the king, only the daughter's son can become the king. The king's son has to work as servant. The *datiyalias* further explained that they can only put gold ornaments when it is given by the king, one cannot wear it unless the king approves. Those who wear without his permission, their hands and ears are severed. The Ahom chronicle further recorded that after hearing this custom the Bora (officer-in-charge of the troop) ridiculed it and invited the *datiyalias* to their country and promised to install the king's son as the king after consultation with the *Swargodeo*. Subsequently, after much deliberation, some of *datiyals* decided to migrate towards the Ahom country. Finally, twelve Lalung (Tiwa) and twelve Mikir (Karbi) families were settled at Burhagaon and Tihulia Bill respectively with due permission from the Ahom king. This has been the first recorded event associated with the migration of Tiwa from the hills to the plains. However, there are several oral traditions that described that the Hill Tiwa were in constant touch with the people of the plains and settled at different places in the Kolong-Kapili valley several centuries before the Ahoms came in contact with Tiwa people.

G.A. Grierson[61] recorded that the Lalung of 'Nowgong' believed that they came from 'Jayantia' Hills. B.C. Allen recorded a legend which stated that originally the Lalung (Tiwa) were the inhabitants of the Khasi and Jaintia Hills, before a majority of them descended to the plains of 'Nowgong', apparently, because they disliked the Khasi descent system and practice of human sacrifice.[62]

Another narrative recorded by Sharma Thakur stated that the Tiwa left the Jaintia Hills as the Jaintia king forcefully recruited them for compulsory military service to assist the Ahom army to fight against the Mohammadans.[63] The authenticity of this legend can be ascertained from the fact that the Ahom King Rudra Singha planned a fresh attack on the Mughals during the last days of his reign just before his death in 1714 for which he organised a powerful army and requested the Jaintia king Jay Narayan to join the war effort by contributing 10,000 men.[64] It is possible that a section of Tiwa might have left the hills and settled at different places in the present Nagaon and Morigaon districts while they came down to join the ensuing war preparations.

Settlement Pattern:

Settlement patterns are the complex products of social and political relations. It helps in the understanding of a particular society and culture. According to K. C. Chang[65] settlement pattern is the study of physical locale or a cluster of locales where the members of the community lived, ensured their subsistence and pursued their social functions in a delineable time period.

According to G.R. Willey[66],

> The settlement pattern is the way in which man disposed himself over the landscape on which he lived. It refers to the dwellings, to their arrangement and to the nature and disposition of other buildings pertaining to community life. These settlements reflects the natural environment, the level of technology on which the builders operated and various institutions of social interaction and control which the culture maintained. Because settlement patterns are to a large extent, directly shaped by widely held cultural needs, they offer a strategic starting point for the functional interpretation of archeological cultures.

The definition shows that the study of settlement patterns not only provides examples of human adaptation to the environment but also provides insights into a broad spectrum of human behaviour that were influenced by both cultural and ecological factors. An analysis of the settlement pattern provides information on environmental strategies and on social organization. The ecological approach considers the settlement pattern as a product of the interaction of environment and technology.[67]

The Hill Tiwa live in the West Karbi Anglong district of Assam, particularly in the Amri, Chinthong, Rongkhang, Howraghat and Lumbajong area and in the Ri-Bhoi district of Meghalaya. The plain Tiwa mainly inhabit the Morigaon district, Nagaon Sadar revenue circle, Kaliabor revenue circle, Raha revenue circle, Lanka revenue circle, Kampur revenue circle of Nagaon district and Tribal Belt of Sunapur revenue circle of Kamrup district, some parts of Dhemaji district and in Titabor sub- division of Jorhat district in Assam. The topography and natural environment have a noticeable influence on the life and culture of this ethnic group. Hence, there are socio- cultural variations among the Tiwa living in the hills and those living in the plains. These variations are visible in the dress and agricultural patterns, food habits etc.

The study of the Tiwa settlement pattern is divided into two sections, one for the hills and the other for the Plain Tiwa. Among the Hill Tiwa, wet rice cultivation is mainly practiced on the narrow valleys of Umswai, Marjong, Ulukhunji and Morten. *Jhum* or shifting cultivation is done on the hilly slopes in and around the Tiwa inhabited areas to grow paddy and other vegetables. The oral traditions and songs describe the method of cultivation that existed among the Tiwa before the introduction of modern machines. Their implements of *jhum* cultivation consist mainly of a hoe (*pakhu*) and spade (*khangra*). According to one legend their god gave them hoe and spade to cultivate at Langrathuli, Makha Koja, Bortongkhora, Dumra Makha and Sera Siri. The story implies that the Tiwa were expert *jhum* or shifting cultivators. It also suggests that the Tiwa were already familiar with the use of the hoe and spade for agriculture when they migrated to different places before arriving at Sera Siri hill near the Umswai Valley. Apart from agriculture, the Tiwa economy also depends on animal husbandries such as poultry, piggery and sericulture. Animal husbandry is practiced only for domestic consummation and religious purposes. Pigs, chicken and goats are important animals that every Hill Tiwa household rears. However, rearing a cow is forbidden by their religion. During our fieldwork, we have not noticed any cow or ox reared by the Hill Tiwa. It could be possible that the non-use of a ox for agriculture is the primary cause of their avoidance for cattle rearing. They do not use the plough or oxen to drive the iron ploughshare to till their paddy fields. Instead, they use hoe and water buffalo to tread the soil for cultivation. The absence plough implies that the Hill Tiwa were not familiar with the iron ploughshare in the remote past. Rearing of *eri* larva for *eri* silk is a household activity of Tiwa. The silk procured from the silkworms are used for weaving different types of cloth for both men and women. The Tiwa had a rich tradition of dyeing cloth by using different herbs as natural colour.

The Plain Tiwa villages are surrounded by paddy fields and houses are usually built along the village path. Each house has a small compound with bamboo fencing where coconut and areca nut trees and other fruits and vegetables are grown. In the recent years, the commercial use of areca nut popularly called *tamul* and pan leaf has become a good source of income among the people. Unlike their hill counterpart, the cattle rearing are an integral part of the Plain Tiwa economy as cow and ox are a necessity for all agricultural activity. They mainly depend upon wet rice cultivation and animal husbandry.

Ethnographic evidence reveals that the Hill Tiwa villages are set up near the source of water in the foothills, valleys and in ridges. In absence of a big river in the Tiwa inhabited region in the hills of West Karbi Anglong the settlement pattern of the villages is determined by numerous small streams.

To understand the settlement pattern of the Tiwa, surveys were conducted at Tharakhunji, Bormarjong, Khawrakrai, Hadaw, Singlangkhunji, Khromkhunji, Silaguri and Amsai village in the Amri development block of West Karbi Anglong district of Assam. The survey showed that the Tiwa have settled in different kinds of landscape. Most of these villages are located on hilly slopes and along the narrow valleys of the small hilly streams.

Houses in Tiwa villages are not compact and follow a scattered plan wherein houses are located at some distance from each other. The number of houses in a village generally varies from 20-150 households. Every household has a well-maintained kitchen garden protected by seven to eight feet tall bamboo fencing called *pera*. These bamboo fences protect the family from the intrusion of wild animals and work as a fortified wall. The compound has only one entrance located in front of the house. The entrance is regulated by a bamboo gate called *langra*. It is three to four feet wide made of hanging bamboo tubes attached to a bamboo stick placed at the top supported by two bamboo poles on two ends. While entering the gate one has to draw the bamboo tubes aside and the loud sound thus created while opening the gate works as a doorbell.

The major determinant in house forms is the use of locally available materials. Hence houses are equally constructed using bamboo, wood and grass for thatched roofs.

In the study of the Tiwa settlement pattern, three important structures are prominent:

- Individual house
- Animal shelter
- Bachelor's dormitory.

A Tiwa house is called *nabaro*. The houses are made taking into consideration the sub-tropical monsoon climate of the region. Houses in their villages are simple rectangular structures with slanting roof with an open platform attached to the main house called *comphor*. Houses are constructed on the raised mud platform. In order to keep the floor dry, the mud platform is erected three to four feet above the ground. Bamboo splits are used as walls and the roof is made with thatch.

A Tiwa house is dominated by a slanting roof reaching up to three feet above the ground: it has short walls and lacks windows therefore the interior is dark and smoky. The interior is wide open and divided into different parts, allotted for sleeping, cooking, wine-making, offering etc. For the Tiwa, a house is not only protection against the sun, wind, rain or cold but each and every part of the house has its own meaning and its own distinct functions. The layout and the decoration of the house reflect the beliefs of the people.

Raw Materials:

A typical traditional Tiwa house is made of locally available bamboo, wood and cane. Traditional houses are usually built with the roof made of thatch. For them, a large amount of wood, bamboo and thatch are required for the construction of the house and therefore, the accumulation of building materials is done slowly over a period of a year. The wood collected while felling down trees from the agricultural fields are collected and stored in the backyard of the house or at the new building site. Recently, changes have been observed in the use of house building materials. Some Tiwa families are opting for modern brick houses or partial use of modern materials in the construction of a house. The posts and pillars are made of brick and cement instead of wood. However, in most cases the modern houses are designed on the traditional home plan respecting the traditional architecture. Though wealthy people prefer to have modern concrete houses, a traditional house is also built near the modern house. The traditional house is still used as a place of worshiping the clan gods and for cooking or sitting in the evening around the fireplace with all the family members or as a venue for any other ceremony major or minor sponsored by the house.

There are various considerations to be taken into account before building a house. Rituals are an important aspect in house construction. Before selecting a piece of land, a small ritual is performed to check whether the chosen land is appropriate or not for the construction of a house. The ritual is called `sumanina' in which a chicken egg is thrown on the place by the *Jela*[68] of the family. It is believed that if the egg does not break even after hitting the ground, then the place is considered to be not suitable for house construction.

Great care is taken while selecting the main post of the house which they call *thuna* as it is considered to be the abode of their clan deity and all rituals associated with the family and clan are performed under the sacred pillar. All family rituals and worship of the clan deity are performed under it.

The construction of a house is a group activity in which the whole community is involved. It is a venture in which the whole village participates, at least a male member from each house helps during the construction of the house. During the construction, it is the duty of the owner of the new house to feed the helpers. The participants are served with food, meat and rice beer called *chu magra*. Relatives of the owner of the new house also contribute by feeding the participants.

A Tiwa traditional house, *nobaro* consists of four different units. Open space in front of the house is called the *comphor*. These open platforms are primarily used for drying grain under the sun and also to bask in the sun during the wintry cold. It is an open space used for various purposes such as reception of guest and a place where traditional weaving equipment (*tat*) is fixed for weaving purposes. It is also used for relaxation by the family members of the house and their neghibours. During the daytime, the male members of the house spend their time making bamboo baskets, mats etc. at the *camphor*. The room immediately after the *comphor* is called the *nomaji*. It is the largest room in the Tiwa traditional house and is used for multipurpose activities. It is used as a fireplace-cum-bedroom-cum living room. It also serves as a cooking place in special circumstances. As the region where the Hill Tiwa inhabits gets extremely cold during the winter, the family members usually sleep around the fireplace (*hor-sal*) in order to keep themselves warm. The *thuna*, the sacred post is located on the right side of the entrance of the *nomaji* under which the family offers sacrifices to their clan deity. The area near the base of the *thuna* is considered to be the most sacred spot of the house. In the olden days, no table, chair or anything that are bought from the market were allowed to be taken inside the *nomaji* which is still being maintained by most of the Hill Tiwa families. The Important family members and guests sleep in the *nomaji* in the assigned places around the fireplace. During the olden days, people used to keep the embers burning the whole night as there was a dearth of sufficient clothing. Even today most of the Tiwa households keep the embers burning for the whole night to ward off mosquitoes and other insects. The right side of the fireplace is called the *nomajisa* which is reserved for the grandparents of the family for sleeping. The left side is called the *nomajiguri* where the unmarried girl child and young boys sleep in the night. It is to be noted that according to tradition, the Tiwa boys older than ten years should spend the nights at the village bachelor's dormitory, the *Shamadi*. It is mandatory for the Tiwa family to send their sons to join the *Shamadi* institution after they attain the age of ten. Hence there is no assigned sleeping place for a grown-up boy in a Tiwa traditional house. In case of sickness, the boys can be accommodated in the *nomaji* until he gets physically fit to spend the nights at the *Shamadi*. The *nomaji* is also a place where the guests are entertained with food and rice beer. They sleep on the space near the bamboo partition wall between the *nomaji* and the *nukthi*. According to tradition, under no circumstances is a bed allowed inside the *nobaro*. Hence all the family members including guests have to sleep on bamboo mats placed on the mud floor of the house. In 1882, the Sub-divisional officer of Jowai recorded that the Lalung (Tiwa) sleep on the ground and they have no *machans* of any sort and he found that they were not concerned about the fever and rheumatism that may afflict them due to the dampness of the floor.[69] Nowadays, besides the *nobaro* they also construct a separate house called *noshura* especially for guests where modern equipment like TV, sewing machine, beds etc. are kept.

The Hill Tiwa does not construct a separate granary for the family. They keep their paddy in packs called *maipur* made of straw and sun grasses on stacks inside the *nomaji*. The packs are made in such a way that no air or water can penetrate to protect the paddy inside from moisture and to keep dry and fresh. One paddy pack contains approximately 30 to 35 k.g. of paddy.

The Fireplace or the *hor-sal* located in the *nomaji* is the most important place in a Tiwa traditional house. It is approximately in the middle of the house and various activities revolve around the hearth. But it is equally a private place where outsiders are not directly brought into unless the guest is well-known to family members, otherwise entering the fireplace by an acquaintance during non-ceremonial occasions or without invitation is considered as prying. Over the fireplace (*hor-sal*), there is two- tiered structures suspended one over the other. These tiered structures are made of bamboo and wood and suspended over the hearth where various items of food, chillies, meat and fish to smoke are kept, grains are dried during the rainy season and firewood are also kept for drying. The topmost rack is used for keeping baskets etc. Keeping the bamboo baskets over smoke for a long time increases the strength and durability of the baskets. Maize and vegetables are also hung in rafters above the hearth. The smokiness helps in preservation. Apart from these racks, a few other hanging shelves are also seen on the bamboo walls of the house to keep things away from rats.

The second part of *nobaro* is called *nukthi*. It is an important place for the women member of the family. Generally, the grown-up girls and older women of the family sleep in this room. Since the Tiwa is a matrilineal society, hence when a daughter of the family gets married, she and her husband live in the *nukthi* and the older women of the family are shifted to *nomaji*. There is no separate kitchen room in the *nobaro*. The kitchen is called the *randuni sal*. It is situated inside the *nukthi*. It is also used for storing paddy packets called *maipur* and other agricultural products. The rear part of the *nobaro* is also known as *comphor*. An important section of this part of the house is the *tingki-sal* where grinding and husking of paddy grains are carried out.

The size of Tiwa house varies based on the economic condition and also on the number of family members. Here too the economic status of the people is marked by the size of the house. Usually, in the daytime, the inhabitants spend little time in their structures except the old members of the house who are too weak to go around. During the daytime, usually men do not stay in the house but women when they are not in the agricultural field, spend their time at home- cooking food, weaving, drying grains or pounding rice in the mortar.

Every Tiwa house has separate shelters for pigs, goats and chickens. They build a large rectangular pigpen (*wakodar*) with separate compartments for each pig, within the boundary wall of the house. A chicken coop (*tukodar*) is made within the outer walls of the house. They also have a barn (*prunkodar*) for the goats. Some Hill Tiwa families keep herds of buffalos primarily for agricultural purposes and producing milk and curd to be sold in the weekly markets in the plains. Buffalos are also used for treading soil in wet rice cultivation.

The Bachelor's dormitory or the *Shamadi* is an important part of any Tiwa traditional village. The *Shamadi* is a politico-judicial-religious institution of the Tiwa. Every Tiwa village should have a *Shamadi* which is located at the centre of the village. All the village rituals and ceremonial gatherings are conducted here and social and cultural affairs of the village are also discussed at the *Shamadi*. It is the centre of social and cultural interactions. On certain occasions, cultural programmes are also organised in the *Shamadi*. It is considered to be a sacred place as it is not only a meeting place for the village elders but also the place for conducting community rituals. However, there is a taboo associated with women entering the *Shamadi*. A detailed discussion on the *Shamadi* system among the Tiwa is given in Chapter V.

Apart from the individual houses and animal shelters, activity-specific huts are also used by Tiwa farmers especially the crop watching hut which is constructed in the field. This type of shelter is constructed both on the ground and on treetops. The ground shelter is called *maru* and used in the daytime to take rest and have food while in the *jhum* field. The treehouse is called *thunggi*. It is used to keep a close watch on the *jhum* field against wild animals like the elephant and wild boars.

The settlement pattern of the Tiwa reveals that there has been little change in the house types, building materials and techniques compared to the past. As evident, much of the material used to construct a Tiwa house is made of locally available organic materials.

Figure 1. A Tiwa *Shamadi* Tharakhunji village (*Credit, Raktim Patar*)

Figure 2. A Tiwa Traditional House, *Nobaro* (*Credit, Raktim Patar*)

Figure 3. *Thuna*, the Sacred Post inside *Nomaji* (*Credit, Raktim Patar*)

Figure 4. A Tiwa Kitchen, *randuni sal* (*Credit, Tilok Takuria*)

Figure 5. A View of Bamboo Fence (*pera*) of Two Households Separated by village path *(Credit, Raktim Patar)*

Figure 6. A Tiwa Woman going to the *maiha*, *Jhum* Field *(Credit,Raktim Patar)*

Figure 7. A Chicken Coop, *tukodar* *(Credit, Raktim Patar)*

Figure 8. A Pigsty, *wakodar* *(Credit, Raktim Patar)*

Notes and References:

[1] Jan Vansina, *Oral Traditions as History*, James Currey, London, 1985.

[2] David P. Henige, *The Chronology of Oral Traditions: Quest for a Chimera*, Clarendon Press, Oxford, 1975.

[3] H.M. Wright, *Oral Tradition: A Study in Historical Methodology*, Routledge, London, 1965.

[4] James Frazer, *The Golden Bough: A study of Magic and Religion* (reprint), Macmillan, London, 1980.

[5] E.B. Tylor, *Primitive Culture*, John Murray, London, 1871.

[6] Franz Boas, "Mythology and Folklore" in Franz Boas (ed.), *General Anthropology*, Washington, 1948.

[7] Bronislaw Malinowski, *Magic, Science and Religion*, Collected Essays, Boston, 1948.

[8] Claude Levi-Strauss, *Structural Anthropology* I, Basic Books, New York, 1963.

[9] *See* C. Lima Imchen's paper, "Naga Myths of Origin and Historical Reconstruction" in M. Momin & C. A. Mawlong(ed.), *Society and Economy in North-East India*(Vol. I), Regency Publication, New Delhi, 2004, pp. 118-164

[10] *Ibid.*

[11] *See* Mignonette Momin's paper on "Contextualising Origin Myths of North East India", Proceeding Volume of *North East India History Association,* 22nd Session, Tezpur, 2002, pp. 30-47

[12] B.K. Gohain, *The Hill Lalungs*, ABILAC, Guwahati, 1992, p. 2.

[13] Interestingly in the Jaintia oral tradition Sutunga (Sutnga) was regarded as an important kingdom. For details see B. Pakem's paper "State Formation in Pre-Colonial Jaintia", in Surajit Sinha (ed.), *Tribal Polities and State Systems in Pre-Colonial Eastern and North Eastern India,* K.P. Bagchi & Company, Calcutta, 1987,

[14] Surajit Sinha, *op. cit.,* pp. xiii-xiv.

[15] The Tiwa follow the matrilineal descent system and traces the origin of their clans from twelve sisters. A discussion in this regard is given in subsequent chapters.

[16] Edward Gait, *A History of Assam*(reprint), Lawyers Books Stall, Guwahati, 1997, p. 6

[17] S.K. Chatterji, *Kirata Jana Krti*(4th Reprint), the Asiatic Society, Kolkata, 2014, p. 88.

[18] *Onomastics* is the scientific description or interpretation of names. According to the, *The New Encyclopedia Britannica,* Vol. 24, 1989, the science that studies names in all their aspects is called *Onomastics*

[19] S.K. Phukan, *Onomastics Assam*, Vol. I, Students Store, Guwahati, 2004, pp. 28-29

[20] *Ibid.,* p. 29

[21] *Ibid.,* pp. 140-141

22   A.J.M. Mills, *Report on the Khasi and Jaintia Hills 1853*, NEHU, Shillong, 1985, p. 5.

23   A.E. Heath, *Tour diary of the Sub-divisional officer, Jowai.*, for the month of November and December 1882, submitted to the secretary to the Chief Commissioner of Assam on 17th February 1883, Assam State Archives collected on 17/10/2015.

24   G.C. Sharma Thakur, *The Lalungs (Tiwas)*, Tribal Research Institute, Guwahati, 1985, p.9.

25   Maseshwar Dewri, *Tiwa Janajati aru Bhasar Itihas*, Tribal Research Institute, Guwahati, 1988, p. 5.

26   '*Lal*' is a Sanskrit word, meaning red.

27   G.C. Sharma Thakur, *op. cit.*, p. 9.

28   Maneshwar Dewri, *Tiwa Janajatiaru Bhasar Itihas*, Tribal Research Institute, Guwahati, 1988, p. 6-7.

29   The majority of the Hill Tiwa still practice matrilineal descent system in spite of inroads made by the patrilineal system in their society.

30   A Tiwa village under the Amri development block of KarbiAnglong district of Assam.

31   The Tiwa however do not have any such tradition and do not recognises the linkages.

32   Philippe Ramirez, *People of the Margins: Across Ethnic Boundaries in North-East India*, Spectrum Publications, Guwahati, 2014, pp. 64-75.

33   Francis Hamilton, *An Account of Assam*, DHAS, Guwahati, 1963, p. 93.

34   Dr. Sangkima, *Mizo: Society and Social Change*, Spectrum Publications, Guwahati, 1992, p. 6.

35   This is a fraction of the folk song which speaks of twelve young couples who took up cultivation at different places and the hardships that they had to undergo. The song further narrates how they were given a fat pig for celebration when they arrived at Sera Siri hill which is located above the Umswai valley in the Amri Development block of the West Karbi Anglong district.

36   Phulson Kholar is the present *Hadari*, the personal assistant of the village priest (Loro) of Amsai.

37   Sidney Endle, *The Kacharis* (Indian Reprint), Akansha Publishing, New Delhi, 2010, p. 3

38   S.K. Chatterji, *Kirata-Jana Kriti*(fourth reprint), The Asiatic Society, Kolkata, 2014, p.26-27

39   *Imperial Gazetteers of India*, Vol. XIX, 1908, p. 224.

40   Ram Rahul, *The Himalayan Borderlands*, Vikas Publication, New Delhi, 1970, p. 10.

41   R.M. Nath, *Background of Assamese Culture* (2[nd]edn.), Dutta Baruah& Co, Guwahati, 1978, p. 14.

42   S.K. Chatterji, *op. cit.*, p.37

[43] P.C. Choudhury, *The History of Civilization of the People of Assam to the Twelve Century A.D.* (3rd edn.), Spectrum Publications, Guwahati, 1987, pp.74-76.

[44] G.A. Grierson, *Linguistic Survey of India,* Vol. III, Part 11(Reprint), New Delhi, 1967, pp.1-17.

[45] *Imperial Gazetteers of India,op. cit.*

[46] S. Endle, *op. cit.* p. 4.

[47] P.C. Choudhury, *op. cit.*

[48] B.M. Das, *The people of Assam*, Gyan Pub. House, New Delhi, 2003.

[49] B. K. Barua, *A Cultural History of Assam* (2nd edn.), Lawyers Book Stall, Guwahati, 1969, pp. 6-7.

[50] *Ibid.* p.7.

[51] B.K. Gohain, *op. cit.* p.55.

[52] Maneshwar Dewri, *op. cit.* pp. 7-8.

[53] The Tiwa society considers pig as an indispensable part of their community offering and religious life. It is a symbol of strength and prosperity. In all religious ceremonies whether funerary or birth, offering of a pig as a sacrifice to ancestral spirits/ village gods is essential. Even the penalties for most of the serious social offences are collected in the form of a pig. According to www.symboloic-meanings.com (accessed on October 21, 2017) symbolic meaning of pigs varies according to region and culture. In ancient Egyptian culture the pig was considered a great mother and was a symbol of fertility and abundance. The pig was also a symbol of virility, strength and fertility in ancient Chinese cultures. In Hindu symbolism, the pig is linked to Vajravarahi, the female consort of Vishnu.

[54] Census of India 2001, Assam: "Data Highlights: The scheduled Tribes," Office of the Registrar General, New Delhi India, http://www.censusindia.gov.in/Tables_Published/SCST/dh_ ST_ Assam.pdf (accessed October 20, 2017).

[55] *Ibid.*

[56] Prior to 1972 parts of West Karbi Anglong were under the administrative jurisdiction of Jaintia Hills District. The land documents found at Amsai and Bormarjong village shows that these were issued by the revenue officer of Jowai revenue circle in the Jaintia Hills district of Assam.

[57] He was the former chief of the Sahari principality and a social worker.

[58] Hunaki Amsi, age 80 years a resident of Tharakhunji village stated that, she used to visit the weekly market at Nelli until recently covering a distance of 25 kilometers on foot. She further stated that they would go down to the market carrying different kinds of vegetables and roots on Sunday and spend a night at temporary sheds constructed by Bengali traders. On Monday they would exchange their products with dry fish, cloths, utensils, kerosene oil etc. and come back to their village by evening.

[59] S.K. Bhuyan (ed.), *op. cit.,* 2001, pp. 96-98.

[60] *Ibid.*

61   G.A. Grierson, *op.cit.*

62   B.C. Allen, *Assam District Gazatteers, Vol X: The Khasi Jayantia Hills, The Garo and the Lushai Hills*, Allahabad, 1906, p.62.

63   G.C. Sharma Thakur, *op. cit.*, p. 6.

64   E. Gait, *op. cit.*, pp. 180-81.

65   K.C. Chang, "A Typology of Settlement and Community Pattern in Some Circum-polar Societies," *Arctic Anthropology* 34, 1962, pp. 286-94.

66   Gordon R. Willey, " Prehistoric Settlement Patterns in the Virú Valley, Peru", *Bureau of American Ethnology*, Bulletin 155, Washington, D.C., 1953.

67   *Ibid.*

68   The eldest maternal uncle of the family is called the *Jela*. His presence is essential in all the socio- religious activities of every clan. He acts as the priest of the clan and initiates all offerings and blessings for the family.

69   Tour diary of A.E. Heath, *op. cit.*, p.28.

CHAPTER III

Religion and Belief System: The Hill Tiwa

The religious beliefs and practices are a significant aspect of the ethnohistory of Tiwa as the study of human beings can never be complete unless it includes an inquiry into their religious beliefs and practices. Malinowski[1] contended that there are no people however primitive without religion and magic.

According to Morgan, religion is just too irrational to be understood by scientific means. He writes, "The growths of religious ideas are environed with such intrinsic difficulties that it may never receive a perfectly satisfactory exposition. Religion deals so largely with the imaginative and emotional nature, and consequently with such uncertain elements of knowledge, that all primitive religions are grotesque and to some extent unintelligible."[2]

James Frazer's *The Golden Bough*[3] is considered to be a remarkable work in the study of religion. His most significant contribution is his emphasis on the difference between religion and magic. According to him, magic is pseudoscience and religion is a higher achievement. He further states that magic evolved into religion.

Among all the evolutionary scholars, Lubbock was the one who gave an evolutionary scheme to religion in his book *The Origin of Civilization and the Primitive Condition of Man*[4]. According to Lubbock the most primitive 'savages' lack anything which could be called religion rather he terms the beliefs as 'superstitions' which gradually pass into nobler conceptions that can be called religion.[5] Lubbock calls the first stage of religion 'Atheism'. His scheme is as follows:[6]

Atheism: understanding by the term is not a denial of the existence of a Deity, but an absence of any definite idea on the subject. Fetishism: the stage in which man supposes he can force the deity to comply with his desires. Nature worship or Totemism: in which natural objects, trees, lakes, stones, animals, etc. are worshipped. Shamanism: in which the superior deities are far more powerful than man, and of a different nature. Thus place of abode also is far away, and accessible only to Shamans. Idolatry or Anthropomorphism: in which the gods take still more completely the nature of human being, however more powerful. They are still amenable to persuasion; they are a part of nature, and not creator. They are represented by images or idols. In the next stage the Deity is regarded as the author, not merely a part, of nature. He becomes for the first time a really supernatural being.

Malinowski concluded that,

The faith and cult spring from the crisis of human existences, the great events of life, birth, adolescence, marriage, death…it is about these events that largely focuses the tension of instructive need, strong emotional experiences, lead in some way or other to cult and belief. The art and religion alike sprang from unsatisfied desire.[7]

The religion of the Tiwa may be termed as mixture of fetishism, nature worship or totemism and shamanism. Their religion is the expression of experiences like history, folklore, myth and way of life. Their religion has little direct approach to the high god. It was chiefly connected with the worship of lesser deities and spirits both good and evil and hordes of clan gods and various manifestations of nature. It is also associated with festivals, rites of passage, birth, marriage, death, agricultural activities, sickness, natural phenomena, magic and sorcery, sin and taboo. Tiwa religion is not a code of organized theological doctrine or messianic teaching. It fulfils all the conditions that are necessary to satisfy the human mind. Durkheim placed all religions however primitive in equal rank as it fulfills given conditions of human existences though in different ways. He writes,

> Fundamentally there are no religions that are false. All are true after their own fashion. Some can be said to be superior to others, in the sense that they bring higher mental faculties in to play, that they are richer in ideas and feelings, that they contain proportionately more concepts than sensations and images and that they are more elaborately systematized.. All are equally religious, just as all living beings are equally living beings, from the humblest plastid to man.[8]

B.K. Gohain[9] observed that Tiwa religion is an integral part of the overall pattern of social conduct in all spheres, secular, sacerdotal and spiritual. P.C. Choudhury[10] contended that the traditional religious belief of the Tiwa falls within the purview of Animism. The census report of India 1901[11] described the Tiwa religion as Animism. Animism is the belief that inanimate objects and natural phenomena have souls.[12] Frazer in his '*The Golden Bough*'[13] argues that, animism is not the only nor even the dominating belief in primitive culture. He contended that,

> Early man seeks above all to control the course of nature for practical ends, and he does it directly, by rite and spell, compelling wind and weather, animals and crops to obey his will. Only much late, finding the limitations of his magical might, he does in fear or hope, in supplication or defiance, appeal to higher beings; that is demons, ancestor-spirits or gods.

Traditional Tiwa concepts of reality and destiny are deeply rooted in the spirit world. The activities and the actions of spirit beings govern all social and spiritual phenomena. The spirit world can be divided into two broad categories: non-human spirits (*mindai*) and spirits of the dead (*phidri*). Non-human spirits are placed in a hierarchical order following their importance and the role they play in the religious beliefs of the Tiwa. First in the hierarchy, is the creator, then the deities, spirit embodied objects, ancestors' spirits and other spirits that are non-human, and comprising of both benevolent/harmless and malevolent spirits. Men stand between this array of spiritual hosts in the spirit world and the world of nature.

The Creator:

The Tiwa believe in a deity which is considered to be the creator of the universe, human being, and animals. However, his place in the Tiwa religion is not of much importance in the sense that except in *Wasirawa14* ceremony, no other sacrifices are made for him though invocation of his name is essential in every religious ceremony. It is the lesser gods and spirits both good and evil that are of more immediate importance. According to Tiwa traditional belief, the supreme deity is Sharipahai. He controls all four directions of the earth. It is Sharipahai who created the earth and all other natural objects and animals. The Tiwa call the Earth as the *Sharipahai ne mathi*, meaning Sharipahai's land. It is believed that he looks after the welfare of the people on Earth and has control over human beings. In every prayer (*mindai songa*) the invocation of Sharipahai is essential. Generally, no sacrifices are made in his name during the religious ceremonies. The following song of the *Khelchawa* ritual explains the role of Sharipahai among the Tiwa people:

Aege sharipahai mathi golo sarjedom Aege
sharipahai shong golo sarjedom Mathi sarje
sharipahai piruk taruk sarjega

Shong sarje sharipahai lit sagor khori tilung sorjega Piruk sarje
sharipahai hathi kora sarjega

Taruk sarje sharipahai nor munus sarjega Noor munus
sarje sharipahai khu golo siosga Maha munus sarje
sharipahai la golo si osga Khwgolo si ose sharipahai raja
golo kai osga Raja kai lo paro tha loro kai osga

Loro kai lo sharipahai paro tha nem lor osga Loro kai lo
sharipahai paro tha rokhom lor osga Pe nema shang
sarjeosga

*Pe rokhoma shamadi go sarje osga Pe
shanga lo Shangdoloi kai osga*

*Pe shamadi na lo Shangmaji kai osga Pe
Shangdoloi na khlop golo tonga Pe
Shangmaji na mir golo tonga...*

Free Translation:

In the olden days, Sharipahai created land and the forest. After the creation of the land, Sharipahai created enormous trees, lakes and streams. After that, he created elephants, horses and also human beings. He gave language to humans, then he installed the king and twelve Loro(the village priest). Then he gave twelve rituals to humans. To continue the rituals he created Shamadi (the bachelor's dormitory) and to run the Shamadi he created Shangdoloi and Shangmaji (the leader of the dormitory).

In the song, the role of Sharipahai as the supreme authority of the earth and the Tiwa people is highlighted. He is described as the creator of the Tiwa people, their kings and priests, rules and rituals. He is considered to be above all deities. The importance of Sharipahai as a high god can also be confirmed from a religious song sung during the *Phidri-Chongkhong* ceremony performed annually in April/May. This ceremony is associated with the beginning of the annual agricultural cycle and can be considered as a part of the fertility cult.

*Oh Tiwa panthairaw, oh Tiwa khorlaraw Chare
nem hebe, chare nudi hebe*

*Sharipahai sharikora nem hebe Mathi
sarjena naw; Mathi thaithong Shong
thaithong*

Sharipahai Sharikora mathi sarjena naw.

Free Translation:

Hey Tiwa young men, hey Tiwa young women; whose ritual these are? Whose rites these are? These are the rituals and rites of Sharipahai Sharikora. Let the earth survive, let the earth live long and let the village survive. O Sharipahai Sharikora.

From the above song, it is clear that Sharipahai is the supreme god of the Tiwa as he is considered to be the creator of the earth and their village. The Tiwa believes that he is the protector of the world and gives them all comfort in life.

Village Deities:

The Tiwa do not have any shrine or temple. Iconolatry is absent in their religion. According to them, every spirit and deity has a specific area where they live and control humans and animals. Every Tiwa village has common deities that look after the well being of men and domestic animals. They called these deities as *mindai*. The principal deity of the village is called *mathi-ney-giri* or the master of the area/village.

List of Root Village Deities:

Table: III

Root Village	Village Deities
Amsai	Sharipahai, Moramuji, Palakhongor, Mahadeo, Hulawma, Bodolmaji, Hatja and Yangli
Marjong	Thaliya Thokoriya, Palakhongor, Bodolmaji, Maslang, Sabri Makha, Somphreng.
Amni	Bura Ramsha, Jakor Bura, Bokola Bura
Rongkhoi	Nurshing, Makha, Kamta Poroi, Khona Baula, Silikhongor, Nengorbala, Purimoshor,
Lumphui	Mohon Phador, Bodol Maji, Luki Poroi
Amjong	Khatboroi, Nashuni-Baguni, Athar Baula
Makro	Yangli and Kabla
Ligra	Yangli, Bodolmaji
Amri	Bodolmaji, Silikhongor
Amkha	Palakhongor, Thalia Thokoria
Sagra	Bodolmaji
Mayong	Bodolmaji

Every Tiwa village reserves a patch of forest land for their principal deity where sacrifices are offered at the beginning of the annual agricultural cycle.

Palakhongor is one of the lesser deities which have a profound influence on the Tiwa people of Amsai, Bormarjong and Amkha villages. He lives in a large rock on a hilltop in Umswai area of West Karbi Anglong district of Assam. He is the *mathi-ney-giri* or the protector of the Amsai village. Sharipahai and Moramuji are considered to be his parents. Barmon Khongor and Thiris Thongai are his sons and Rungshu Khunguri and Laisari Khunguri are his daughters. The family life of the deity Palakhongor indicates that the Tiwa lesser gods were identical to human beings. Tiwa oral tradition says that, before the advent of Sodonga Raja (the first Tiwa chief) to Amsai from Thinimaklang/Timowflong in the Jaintia hills, they did not have clothes to wear. After settling at Amsai near Palakhongor hillock they obtained clothes. Thus they started considering the hill as their *mindai* or god. The Hill Tiwa still believe that the Palakhongor hillock has the power to provide anything if it is asked with great affection. The Tiwa believes that all the rituals and dances of Amsai village were given by Palakhongor. They called it *Palakhongore phana mana nem-nudi* or the rituals received from Palakhongor. The following are the thirteen rituals and festivals that are believed to have been given by Palakhongor: *Sogra Baro, Rok kara, Bor-chongkhong, Phidri- Chongkhong, Khram Panthai Lamewa, Yangli, Pisu Rawa, Motih Lawa, Pakhukara, Mahadew Phujiwa, Langkhon Phuja, Thurlu Phuja and Sogra-sa.* Palakhongor occupies a major position among the deities of the Tiwa in the Amsai, Bormarjong amd Amkha villages and their offshoots. In the pre-British period, there was a tradition of offering human sacrifice annually at Chongkhong Sal at the bottom of the Palakhongor hill. The place is bounded by a sacred grove where three British officials were sacrificed in 1832. According to the legend on the occasion of *Phidri-Chongkhong,* a human was sacrificed annually by the priest of the Amsai village. This incident was documented by the R.B.Pemberton[15] in his *Report on the Eastern Frontier of British India.* These sacrifices are believed to have brought prosperity and security to the village against evil spirits. However, this ritual has now been replaced with the sacrifice of a black he-goat.

Besides the principal deity of village, there are other spirits that look after the people and protect them from evil spirits. They believe that these spirits live in natural objects such as large rocks, water bodies, deep forests and caves. The natural objects that are big or potentially hazardous are believed to have a life that is not usually perceptible to the human eye.

A profound belief in different deities and spirits among the Tiwa suggest their fear of spirits and invisible powers which are manifested in various omens and signs. They believe that spirits and deities have the power to inflict harm if they are not given proper respect in the form of sacrifices and offerings. As a result of the power attributed to these deities, it is necessary to maintain friendly relations with them. The intimate relationship between the people and their deities is manifested in their seasonal rites and festivals which mark every stage of the agricultural circle.

Ancestral Spirits:

Ancestor worship was a universal form of religious expression, which emphasized the influence of deceased relatives on the living. E.B. Taylor remarked:

> The *Manes* (ancestor) worship is one of the great branches of the religion of mankind. Its principles are not difficult to understand, for they plainly keep up the social relations of the living world. The dead ancestors, now passed into a deity, simply goes on protecting his own family and receiving suit and service from them as of old; the dead chief still watches over his own tribe, still holds his authority by helping friends and harming enemies, still rewards the right and sharply punishes the wrong.[16]

Among the Tiwa, ancestor-worship is a form of religious expression. They believe in the immortality of the human soul. From cradle to grave, the life of a Tiwa individual is centered upon his great ancestors and all virtues and failures of life are attributed to the intervention of their spirits. Tiwa religious life begins with the invocation of their ancestors or the *phidri*. They play the most important role in day-to-day life of a Tiwa individual as well as society. Incantations to ancestral spirits are part and parcel of every Tiwa family. On every occasion be it the beginning of agriculture, welcoming of newborn or while having new rice after the harvest, an invocation of their ancestors is essential. At the community or village level, they perform *Phidri- Chongkhong* ritual to offer respect to their ancestors before the agricultural cycle takes off. They strongly believe that their ancestors have greatly contributed to their survival and taught them cultivation. Their ancestral spirits look after the well-being of the village. Therefore the surviving members of the tribe have to confer due honour to their ancestors and offer sacrifices to receive blessings on the eve of the agricultural cycle. They further believe that there will be a bumper crop if ancestors are satisfied with the appropriate sacrifices. At the individual family level, dead ancestors are offered sacrifices on important occasions. They believe that dead ancestors visit their former abode during special occasions such as the *Nuwan* ceremony which is performed while having the first meal of the newly harvested rice. They also perform different kinds of divinations at the time of sickness and in accidental deaths to pacify ancestors as they strongly believe that untoward happenings can be inflicted upon surviving members if ancestors are not pleased with the sacrifices. Sacrifices are also offered to dead ancestors to protect living members from evil spirits and to obtain material prosperity. The Tiwa consider their house as an important place of worship and great care is taken to keep the sanctity of the house. No footwear and other goods like TV, sofa, etc. bought from the market are allowed to be taken inside the house. Whenever new things like utensils or essential goods are brought to the house they first need to take permission from the clan deity. It is perhaps because of this factor that the Tiwa *Nobaro* or traditional house is considered to be not only a dwelling house but also a place of worship and sacrifice. During our fieldwork, we have observed that all household religious ceremonies associated with birth and death as well as divinations is performed at the *Nobaro* under the *Thuna* or sacred pillar.

The Village Priest:

In every religion, the priest occupies a significant position. Among the Hill Tiwa, the priest is called the *Loro*. No religious ceremony is complete without the permission and initiative of the *Loro*. He acts as the main interpreter of Tiwa religion. B.K. Gohain[17] recorded that "the position of *Loro* in Tiwa society is such that he exercises temporal powers in matters of religion and social law but does not exercise absolute administrative powers in the matter of settling village disputes".

There are certain rules regarding the selection and installation of *Loro*. In the selection of *Loro* the clan plays an important role. Succession to the post of *Loro* is not through nomination based on qualification like age, marital status, etc. but it is the *Khul* or clan which plays a vital role in the selection process. It is only the *kobiya*[18] of a particular clan having a predominant position in the village who can become a *Loro*. The term *kobiya* means the resident son-in-law that is one who comes to stay with his wife after marriage. In Amsai and Lumphui villages the post of the *Loro* is reserved for the *kobiya* of the Kholar clan. A person who goes to live with his wife of the *Kholar* clan becomes eligible to be the *Loro* of these villages. Similarly in Bormarjong the *kobiya* of the Amsong clan is eligible to become the *Loro*. This shows the dominance of certain clans for the priesthood of the village. It was probably the clan that had originally dominated the village that got the privilege to offer their son-in-law as the *Loro*. For example, the Amsong clan in Bormarjong and the Kholar clan in Amsai and Lumphui have the privilege to provide their son in law as the *Loro*. It is the clan of his wife which determines whether a person is fit for the post.

Apart from being the *kobiya* of a particular clan, a person needs to acquire some essential qualities like knowledge on sacrificial rules or *mendei phujiwaney neim nudi*. After the identification of the incumbent for the post of *Loro*, a divination ceremony (*mindai songa*) is performed to determine the final installation ceremony. If the divination is found to be positive, then all the other members of the village elder's council (*Pisai*) and villagers, as well as people from its branch village (*Phams*) gather at the residence of the future *Loro*. In presence of the gathering, he has to take an oath (*sopot*) to uphold the integrity, purity and divinity of their village. He is expected to lead a humble life and should not commit any sin or indulge in forbidden things. A *Loro* lives a normal life like any other Tiwa individual but he enjoys the most respectable social position in the society. The installation ceremony of a *Loro* is attended by his family members especially the maternal uncle (*mamai*) and aunt (*asi*) Once installed the *Loro* continues to enjoy his position until death. He may, however choose to discontinue from the post.[19] But he cannot be removed by any means.

Religious Ceremonies:

Religious ceremonies of the Tiwa are closely linked to the different stages of agricultural activities. These ceremonies are performed according to the annual agricultural cycle. Different stages of cultivation are marked with a ceremony where offerings and sacrifices are made to the presiding deity of the village/area (*mathi-ne-giri*). It begins with the clearing of the forest, tilling of the soil, sowing of seeds, and finally the harvesting of paddy and other crops. However, rituals associated with the performance of the ceremony may vary from one village to another. Among the Hill Tiwa, some festivals such as the *Yangli, Khelchawa, Kabla* and *Wanchuwa* are celebrated after a gap of four to five years depending upon the financial condition of the village. However, due to several factors, presently these festivals are deferred to more than ten to twelve years. Our informant Pirlu Amsi,(village headman of Tharakhunji) stated that due to financial difficulties religious ceremonies like *Kheclchawa* and *Wanchuwa* are not conducted at the appropriate time. However despite these challenges the Hill Tiwa have been observing the periodic religious ceremonies where the main attractions are the songs and dances. Outlines of the festivals are given in the following pages:

Sogra Festival:

The *Sogra* ceremony marks the beginning of the cultivation season. This festival is celebrated in April. It may be termed as the spring festival observed by Amkha, Amsai, Amri, Marjong and Lumphui village. These are the four root villages that maintain the tradition of celebrating the *Sogra* festival. Generally, it begins on Wednesday and continues till Monday. On these days the youth are actively involved in various activities associated with the festival. Regarding the origin of the *Sogra* festival, there are two different versions of a legend that are current among the Tiwa. According to one version[20] associated with Amsai village, this festival was introduced by an orphan boy named Majibor Sagra. According to the story, one day while Majibor was roaming around in the hills, he found some unusual white flowers which resembled that of snow. When the village elders came to know about the flowers, they thought, it was a gift from the god and decided to celebrate the finding with religious fervour. As the boy belonged to Sagra clan hence this festival was named after his clan, Sagra or Sogra.

Another version of the story associated with the Marjong group[21] tells that one day when Sharipahai, the supreme god was sitting in a meeting with Thalia, Thogriya and Palakhongor, a bunch of flowers fell from the sky. The flowers were very beautiful hence Thalia took them with him and gave it to the young boys of his village. The flowers fascinated the children who started dancing in joy. Seeing their joyfulness the gods decided to commemorate the occasion by having a celebration. It may be noted that the Sogra festival is said to have been first held at Amsai.

During this festival, the village priest or *Loro*, performs a ritual called *mindai likhewa*. In this ritual, the *Loro* recites the names of various deities and events that had happened in the past which may continue for several hours. The recitation ceremony takes place in the middle of the night at the residence of the *Loro* in presence of the *Pisai* (village elders) the *panthai khel* (youth group).

Bor-Chongkhong:

This ceremony is held annually in the villages of Amsai, Marjong and Amkha groups. It is celebrated two weeks after the conclusion of the *Sogra* festival on a Sunday in the latter part of April. In this ceremony, one pig is sacrificed in the name of Palakhongor and twelve fowls are sacrificed in the name of the *nima*,[22] or deities who protects the borders of Palakhongor. In this ceremony the *Pisai* or village elders seek permission from their principal village deity to begin the cultivation season. It is believed that without performing the *Bor-Chongkhong* ceremony, nobody should till the soil or clear jungle for cultivation as it may bring a bad harvest. According to the Hill Tiwa, if anyone begins cultivation before the *Bor-Chongkhong* ceremony is performed, there will be bad omens for the village in the form of attacks by a tiger on human and domestic animals and the occurance of epidemic.

Phidri-Chongkhong:

This ceremony is performed three weeks after the conclusion of the *Bor- Chongkhong* ceremony at the end of April or at the beginning of May. This ritual takes place only on a Thursday. In this ceremony, the *Pisai* (the council of village elders) takes permission from the principal deity of the village and the spirits of ancestors of the village (*Phidri*))to dig canals to bring water from the streams to their paddy fields and to commence the sowing of seeds and saplings in their *jhum* fields. In Amsai village on this occasion, three pigs are sacrificed in the name of the principal deity, Palakhongor and the spirits of the ancestors (*Phidris)* of the village. During this ceremony two pieces of flat stone are erected; one vertically and another horizontally at the *Chongkhong Sal* to mark the annual ceremony. They also plant a flame tree or *mandarphang* near the erected stones. It is believed that if the flame tree survives then, the person who planted it dies. However, if the tree does not survive, then it signifies that the principal deity, as well as the ancestors of the village, is happy with the sacrifice and the entire village will have bumper crops for that year. The erection of stones on the occasion of *Phidri-Chongkhong* is an important aspect of the Tiwa society. The menhir or upright stone is called *orlong thuna* (*orlong-*stone, *thuna*-sacred pillar) and the flat stones or dolmens are known as *phidri tongkhra* (*phidri*-Ancestor, *tongkhra*-flat seating place). Selection and installation of these stones are done by two village officials namely the *Phador* and the *Sangot*. They must fix the megaliths at an appropriate place. These stones are erected from the east to west direction. The Tiwa of Amsai believes that Palakhongor, the principal village deity comes to eat the sacrifice and takes rest at the stones placed there. The size of the menhirs found in the Chongkhong Sal of Amsai village varies from one foot to two feet and dolmens are ten to twenty centimeters wide. During our fieldwork at Amsai, we have counted 2047 numbers of menhirs and dolmens including stones raised in 2017. The tradition of erecting megaliths during this ceremony is of great significance since the megalithic site coincides with the place where human sacrifice was performed in the past thereby suggesting its link with the cult of fertility. This point is further reinforced by the fact that the *Phidri-Chongkhong* ceremony which is celebrated at the same location is associated with agriculture. The entire site is suggestive of a fertility complex.

Mahadeo Phuja:

Mahadeo or Siva is a popular Hindu god which is also worshipped by the Hill Tiwa during June and July. It takes place on a Sunday. Some Hill Tiwa believe that Siva is identical with Sharibahai, the creator and protector of the human and animals. However, the Tiwa has no concept of Siva *Linga* and shrine for the worship of the deity. In the *Mahadeo Phuja*, the *Loro* sacrifices a black he-goat in the name of the deity. After the sacrifice, the *Loro* and the *Pisai* seek permission from Mahadeo to offer rice beer in their paddy fields for a better harvest. It is believed that Mahadeo has the power to provide a good harvest and to bring prosperity to the village.

Pakhukara Ceremony:

Pakhukara marks the ending of the cultivation season. In this ceremony, the *Pisai* (village elders), seeks permission from the presiding deity of the village (*mathi-ne-giri*) to withdraw their hoe (*pakhu*) and handbills (*khangra*) from the paddy fields. It is a thanksgiving ceremony after a successful agricultural session. During the ceremony, the *Loro* and other members of *Pisai* invoke the *mathi-ne-giri* to protect their seeds and saplings from birds, animals and insects. In this ceremony, the Tiwa of Amsai sacrifices two fowls, one for the principal deity Palakhongor and another for his mother Moramuji.

Thurlu Phujiwa:

Thurlu is a small flute type musical instrument made of bamboo pipes with three holes. The Tiwa believe that they should not play the *thurlu* or for that matter any other musical instrument without taking permission from their village principal deity, the *mathi-ne-giri*. It is believed that, if someone plays the *thurlu* without performing the *Phuja*, there will be danger to humans from the wild animals especially leopards (*sokati*) which would come to the village by following the sound of the musical instrument. Hence it is completely forbidden to play any musical instrument especially the *thurlu* before the *thurlu Phujiwa* is performed. As the Tiwa villages are surrounded by thick jungle and hills, casualties and injuries by wild animals like tigers and leopards were a common problem in the past. Hunter[23] recorded that the British administration had to spend a part of their collected revenue to keep down the tigers and leopards in 'Nowgong' district. He stated that during the period 1864-69, the total number of deaths due to these animals was 254. The taboo associated with this religious ceremony suggests about the danger that the Tiwa ancestors had to face from the ferocious wild animals lurking to strike at an opportune moment. This ceremony was to seek protection from these wild animals from the principal deity. The *thurlu* ceremony is celebrated in early September soon after the *pakhukara* ceremony. At this time of the year, all the villagers are free from their daily work associated with cultivation. Now they get ready to spend time in the village bachelor's dormitory (*Shamadi)* by playing various musical instruments and singing of folk songs.

Langkhon Phuja:

Langkhon is a twenty to twenty-five feet long bamboo pole decorated with different patterns. It is an annual festival celebrated by the Rongkhoi, Amni, Amsai and Marjong groups (root villages) in late September. It is commonly believed that wild vegetables and fermented bamboo shoots (*damlong)* should not lay dry under the Sun before the *Langkhon* ceremony is performed. During this ceremony the village priest (*Loro*) and the council of elders (*Pisai*) invoke the presiding deity of the village (*mathi-ne-giri*) for the well-being of the people and the standing crops. The main ceremony is held at the *Loro's* residence where sacrifices are offered to the presiding deity of the village. After the sacrifice, the village youth dressed in ceremonial attire perform dances in front of the *Loro* and *Toloi/Doloi*[24] house and thereafter go to the village bachelor's dormitory (*Shamadi*). After spending several hours dancing in the courtyard of the *Shamadi*, the *Langkhons* (decorated bamboo poles) are erected in front of the *Shamadi* and left for the night. The next day these *Lankhons* are deposited at the designated place called the Langkhon Sal located outside the settlement area of the village.

The Tiwa have different versions of the story on the origin of the *Langkhon Phuja*. The legend associated with the Amni village, tells that, once Buraramsa, the presiding deity of Amni village inflicted punishment to the villagers as he was angry for not getting sacrifices. Due to this, the villagers had to suffer from disease and a shortage of food. Subsequently, they had to go down to Silchang in the plains in search of food but failed to procure it. Eventually, the deity took pity on them and appeared in a dream of a person called Sogrolublanoi. The deity told him that if the villager offers sacrifice to him and perform the Langkhon Phuja then all the problems will disappear and they will be able to live happily. Soon with the celebration of the Langkhon Phuja, once again the village started to prosper. Thus they call this ceremony the *Buraramsa ney nem-nudi* or the ritual received from deity Buraramsa.

Wasirawa Ceremony:

The *Wasirawa* ceremony marks the beginning of the collection of bamboo and other forest products for the repair and construction of new dwellings houses. The Tiwa do not procure wild bamboo and thatch from the forest without performing this ceremony. This ceremony is performed on a Saturday during October - November. It is performed at the Chongkhong Sal and sacrifices are made in the name of Sharipahai who is the creator and savior of all the living and non-living things.

Apart from the annual religious ceremonies the Tiwa also observe some festivals which take place once in five or six years. These festivals are celebrated large scale and bear a lot of socio-religious significance. The stories associated with these festivals throw some light on the evolution of the Tiwa culture.

Yangli Phuja:

Yangli is considered to be the deity of wealth and prosperity. It is one of the important religious festivals of the Amsai, Marjong, Rongkhoi and Magro groups (root villages). The Tiwa of these villages believes that the invocation of *Yangli* yields bumper crops and protect them from evil spirits.

The origin of the *Yangli* festival can be traced through the oral traditions associated with the ceremony. According to a legend,[25] After the creation of the Earth, god Sharipahai and Mahadeo created trees, animals, and insects and finally human beings. They instructed all creatures to eat fruits and flowers for survival. However, except humans, all other creatures prospered. So, they asked humans to eat the wild potatoes. But it did not help humans. Seeing their pathetic condition they started searching for food everywhere on the Earth. Subsequently, they came to know about the paddy called *Barobuni*, which was lying on the sea bed. They requested *Barobuni* to become food for humans. On persistent requests, she decided to come to the surface and offered to become food for humans. However, soon after she surfaced, humans, insects, animals and ghosts started eating her. On account of these atrocities, *Barobuni's* mother came down to Earth and took her away to heaven. Once again the humans started suffering from a lack of food. Considering the dismal condition of the humans, Sharipahai and Mahadeo again searched for food to be given to humans. This time they found *Satbuni*, another variety of paddy at the bottom of the sea. The gods requested seven *Khamar* or blacksmiths to build a boat to bring *Satbuni* to the surface. Among the *Khamar* only Khariya Dhatura could build a boat. With this boat, the gods went to *Satbuni* to bring her to the Earth. They took varieties of gold and silver ornaments to allure her. But she refused to come with them. Eventually, the gods requested *Mausuwa Thanduwa*, the king of the rats to convince *Satbuni* and bring her to the Earth. However, once again she refused to come. Now, the gods brought chickens, ducks and pigeons to attract her. By looking at those birds *Satbuni* agreed to come to the earth. When vegetables such as brinjal, chilli, cucumber, pumpkin, ginger, turmeric came to know about the decision of Satbuni to come to the Earth, they also rushed to board the boat. Soon the boat full of vegetables and paddy arrived at the shore. Looking at these the animals and insects once again attacked them. But this time the humans overcame them and welcomed *Satbuni* and the vegetables into their village with a grand celebration. After that rice and vegetables become the staple food for humans.

A closer look at the story reveals the importance of paddy in the life of the Tiwa. The appearance of boat and sea in the story indicates their historical connection with the Brahmaputra Valley. Further, the story also suggests on their struggle for survival in the remote past. Thus we can assume that the seeds of the paddy *Baruboni* and *Satbuni* must have come from the plains.

On the day of the *Yangli Phuja* members of the *Pisai* (village elder's council) and the members of the *panthai khel* (youth group) gather at the *Loro's* house. The festivals formally begin with the offering of seven sachets of betel nut and leaf for *Satbuni*, twelve sachets for the *Barojela*[26] and eighteen sachets for various other deities (*mindai*).

In the evening the ceremony continues with the dance performance, *yangli misawa*. The young boys (*panthai)* perform dances to the tune of the drum *(kharm)* and the flute *(pangsi)*. On the following day, the *Loro* and *Pisai* take the deity to a designated place called *Yangli Sal* located just outside the village. Here the *Loro* installs the deity on a raised mud platform built specifically for the ceremony. Subsequently, he would sacrifice three white he-goats for three deities *Kamtha Boroi, Moko Boroi* and *Bodolmaji*, three black he-goats for *Mahadeo, Satbuni*, and *Nursing*, and one goat for *Songpali*. They also sacrifice one female pig for mother earth (*Bosmoda*) and two male pigs for *Mosuwa-tandawa* (evil spirit) and other evil spirits. In the evening the *Yangli* is taken to a pond and put in a small boat to symbolize her journey to the earth. They sing the story of how she was brought to the earth by *Sharipahai* and *Mahadeo* and how she provided food for the humans on earth.

Wanchuwa Festival:

Wanchuwa is an important religious festival of the Amkha and Marjong villages. It is celebrated once in five or six years. Generally, this festival takes place between June and August. The ceremony usually starts on a Tuesday and ends on a Thursday. The main function takes place on a Wednesday at the residence of *Shangdoloi*, the head of the *Shamadi*, the village bachelor's dormitory where the 'Sham' (wooden mortars) are located. These mortars are partly buried underground and arranged in a circular pattern. While dancing to the rhythm of the *khram, pangsi* and *thurang* (musical instruments) members of the *Shamadi* pound the wet rice with a *'lomphor'* (wooden pestle) till it turns into powder. After the dance, the rice flour is mixed with water and sprinkled on the people present at the ceremony. The remaining flour is distributed among the villagers to prepare *wanrusa,* a type of steamed rice cake. The next morning they bring the *wanrusa* to the *Shangdoloi's* house and offer it in the name of Sodonga Raja and Maldew Raja. By the late evening of Thursday, the *Wanchuwa* festival comes to an end. The Tiwa of the Amkha and Marjong group considers the *Wanguri* or the flour pounded on the day of the *Wanchuwa* festival to be sacred rice. According to a legend[27] associated with the *Wanchuwa* ceremony, There was a couple by the name of Rampha and Ramma. They were very poor and could not afford to have nutritious food. They gradually lost their health and became lean and thin. One day they approached *Sodonga Raja* and *Maldew Raja* to share their problems whereupon the duo advised the poor couple to eat the roots of the Sun grass but it did not eradicate their hunger. So once again they approached the duo for better food. This time the duo asked them to eat the wild potatoes. However, the wild potato was also insufficient to satisfy their hunger. Consequently, they were advised to eat two varieties of rice called *Satbuni* and *Barobuni* which eventually made the couple satisfied. Hence, the Sodonga Raja and Maldew Raja advised the humans to cultivate *Satbuni* and *Barobuni* for food. Subsequently, twelve young men and women started cultivation of rice at different places. They cultivated at Makha Koja, Makha Kojom, Mathal Baro, Mathal Pisa, Borkholong, Tekhon Dao, Khoraphada, Borlemphra, Borsira, Sera Seri etc. They worked for twelve years day and night without any rest. However, even after so much effort put into cultivation, they could not produce sufficient food for themselves. Hence they decided to take the help of other humans to address the issue. This time together with other humans they were able to produce sufficient food for all. This brought immense pleasure to the twelve young couples and they advised their fellow people that they should continue the process of cultivation. Subsequently, the humans could produce sufficient food grain which brought prosperity to them. One day the humans discussed celebrating their success of producing a good harvest. Finally, they decided to start the *Wanchuwa* ceremony to thank the twelve male and female ancestors who taught them how to cultivate and produce food. It appears from the story that *wanchuwa* is a thanksgiving ceremony to their twelve ancestors. It is a celebration of the success of the Tiwa people to produce surplus food.

Kabla Phuja:

Kabla Phuja is an important religious festival observed by the Magro group (root village). This ceremony which takes place once in five years is dedicated to the god *Kabla*. It is celebrated at the house of the village priest (*Loro*) of Phad Magro village in the Ri-bhoi district of Meghalaya. Sacrifices are offered to their village principal deity *Kabla* on the occasion of the ceremony. Our field study suggests two major differences between the *Kabla Phuja* and other Tiwa religious festivals. First, in this ceremony, the sacrifices are made in the western direction whereas other Tiwa religious ceremonies are performed facing towards the east. Secondly, it is the only Tiwa religious ceremony where girls also take part in dancing along with the boys.[28] The Tiwa of the Magro group considers *Kabla* as the giver of food and prosperity. Hence, every branch of the Magro village contributes both materially and physically and celebrates this ceremony with pomp and gaiety.

During our field study, we have found an interesting legend[29] which described the origin of the *Kabla Phuja*. According to the story, once there was a poor widow in a village called Phad Magro. One day the god Kabla disguised as human came to her house seeking food and shelter and told her that he is god. She gave shelter to Kabla but could not offer any food as she could not afford it. By looking at her sadness Kabla told the widow that if she sacrifices an animal in his name, then in return he can bring prosperity to her. When the widow agreed to perform the sacrifice, her house was immediately filled with paddy and other valuable materials. On the night of the *phuja*, a group of boys and girls came down from the sky with *Tumding, Togor* and *Muhuri* (musical instruments) and performed dance and played musical instruments at the courtyard of the widow's house. At the daybreak, they would disappear and would resume once the night falls. The dance performed during the Kabla Phuja is called the Moinarikanthi. Meanwhile, a person belonging to the Maslai clan, who was lost in a deep jungle while hunting wild potato, came to the house of the widow and asked for shelter. Initially, she refused to entertain him but after repeated requests, she allowed him to stay in her house. That night he also saw the dance and music which mesmerized him so much so that he prayed *Kabla* to allow the same rituals for his village as well and promised to offer sacrifice. Eventually, after getting permission from *Kabla,* he discussed with his fellow villagers and they decided to offer sacrifice to *Kabla* and celebrate the *Moinarikanthi* festival.

Human Sacrifice:

The process of human sacrifice is called *pokhya tana.* In the Tiwa language, *pokhya* means a victim (human) and *Tana* means sacrifice. We have already mentioned earlier that the practice of human sacrifice was prevalent among the Tiwa before the consolidation of the British administration in Assam. The census report of 1901 stated that the Tiwa used to sacrifice eight human beings annually before their god.[30] R.B. Pemberton[31] mentioned that out of the four British officials abducted by the Gobha raja's men, three were sacrificed at the shrine of Kali. During our fieldwork, we have found a legend associated with the sacrifice of three British officials at Chongkhong Sal of Amsai. There is a place called '*khugri polo gumawa thai*' meaning the place where the white dog escaped, apparently the place where one of the four British officials escaped from the custody of Gobha Raja's men.

According to our informant[32] of Amsai, earlier the *Loro* and the *Pisai* used to sacrifice a human being at the Chongkhong Sal every year on the occasion of the *Phidri-Chongkhong* ceremony. It is believed that the deity who selects the victim for sacrifice and sends it to the village. When the time for sacrifice approaches, the victim (*pokhya*) would arrive at the village and ask for food and shelter at the *Loro's* house. This is believed to be a sign to identify the chosen victim. The *Loro* then proceeds to feed him sumptuously in a specially designed plate made of brass called *pokhya mai chanane khangsi* till the day of sacrifice arrives. It is also believed that the *pokhya* would eat on the special plate and stay within the periphery of the village till the day of sacrifice. Apparently, the 'chosen one' would not attempt to escape even if the person was made aware of his fate. The process of feeding the victim till the day of sacrifice was called *pokhya rakhena*. On the day of sacrifice, the *pokhya* would be dressed in a fashion similar to that of the *Loro* and the *Pisai*. Adorned with a white floral garland, he would be taken to the place of sacrifice or Chongkhong Sal and after the rituals are performed he would be sacrificed with the sacrificial sword called *pokhya tanane khara*. After the sacrifice, the body of the *pokhya* would be thrown into the jungle to be devoured by wild animals. He further stated that the practice of human sacrifice was abandoned due to an incident where the *pokhya* who happened to be a Melang,[33] killed the *Loro* by snatching the sacrificial sword (*khara*) and escaped to Palakhongor hill. This was a bad omen; therefore they gave up the practice.

Another story we have collected from the *Dewri*[34] of *Deosal*[35] located near Jagiroad suggests that earlier humans were sacrificed at that place in the name of *Bodolmaji,* the Gobha Raja's principal deity. However, on one occasion when the head priest of the Gobha Raja could not procure any humans for the sacrifice, the Raja instructed his officials to sacrifice any human found to be looking towards the east the following morning. Consequently the following morning the officials found one of the Raja's sons looking towards the east. Hence they sacrificed him at the altar of *Deosal.* Later in the evening when the Gobha Raja learned of the incident, he was shocked and extremely saddened. He blamed his principal deity *Bodolmaji* for this incident and promised not to perform any more human sacrifices or to visit the *Deosal.*

According to our informant who is the assistant priest of Amsai, during Jaintia rule, the *pokhya tanane khara* or the sword for human sacrifices was procured from 'Norteng' (Nartiang) in Jaintia hills. It is to be noted that earlier Nartiang was an important centre of the Jaintia state. The *Jayantia Buranji* refers to this place several times in connection with the Ahoms' political relations from the reign of Pratap Singha to Rudra Singha with the Jaintia Kings.[36] P.R.T. Gurdon[37] recorded that the tradition of human sacrifice was prevalent in the Jaintia kingdom. He had mentioned that it was generally believed that the 'Syntengs' took to the practice of human sacrifice only after the conversion of the Jaintia royal family and the principal noble families to Hinduism. However, he also stated that he had reason to believe that this practice was prevalent among them long before they were converted.[38] The Tiwa may have adopted the practice of human sacrifice under the influence of the Jaintia authority. The procurement of the sword, the *Khara* by the Tiwa from Nartiang further confirms its links with the Jaintia state. According to Suren Konwar, the Raja of Sahari,[39] human beings were sacrificed in their ancestral place of worship at *Kalikha Thaan* which is now replaced by the sacrifice of a Turtle. While describing the origin of the human sacrifice he mentioned that their ancestors obtained this tradition from the Jaintia Kingdom. This view is based on a tradition that states that the selection of a victim for human sacrifice among the Tiwa is done by placing a Jaintia coin on a busy road after rituals performed by the royal priest. They would then wait for the coin to be picked up by a male individual who became the victim (*pokhya*) for sacrifice. Apparently, the coin was supplied by the Jaintia King when the Tiwa were under the political control of the Jaintia state and it was used during important religious ceremonies. It was believed that the individual who picked the coin

The above description shared by the present *Raja* of Sahari about their ancestors' relations with the Jaintia kingdom suggests that the Tiwa had borrowed the practice of human sacrifice from the neighbouring Jaintia people in the past.

Birth ceremonies:

Birth ceremonies among the Hill Tiwa are very simple. Soon after the birth of a baby, the umbilical cord is cut with a sharp piece of bamboo. A similar practice is recorded by Gurdon among the Khasis. He writes, "When a baby is born umbilical cord is cut by a sharp splinter of bamboo: no knife can be used on this occasion."[40] After the baby's birth, a fowl is sacrificed in the name of the clan spirits of the family for a healthy life.

Mortuary Rituals:

According to Malinowski, Death is the gateway to the other world in more than the literal sense."[41] Among the Tiwa, death due to old age and prolonged illness are considered to be natural. The persons meeting their natural death are generally cremated. Every clan in a Tiwa village has a specific place to cremate their clansmen within the cremation ground (*mangkhor sal*) of the village. It is located in the periphery of a village covered by wild vegetation and bamboo groves. While cremating, the corpse is placed on the funeral pyre in a north-south orientation. However the deceased are buried in cases of unnatural death such as motor accidents, epidemics or suicide. After burial the grave is fenced with bamboo staves planted around it forming a conical shape called as *mangkhor chura*. If a man dies in his wife's house while living as a resident son-in-law or *kobiya*, information of his death is immediately passed to his family members through a messenger. The family member also informs the village headman and the *Shamadi* or bachelor's dormitory by offering a bottle of rice beer (*chu-magra*). Last rites among the Tiwa are attended by all the fellow clan members of the deceased as well as by other clan members of the village. According to tradition cremation is always done during the daytime. Soon after the death of a person, his feet are kept tied with a white thread. It is believed that it prevents the evil spirits from dwelling inside the corpse. The corpse is laid on a bed covered in new clothes. Before the corpse is taken to the cremation ground, the family members have to inform the village headman regarding any pending debt of the deceased. If such things remained unsettled by the person, while alive, then the family members have to pay a nominal penalty or fine to the village headman. After this formality, the corpse is taken to the cremation ground on a bamboo-bier made of seven long bamboo pieces. In case the deceased was a *kobiya* within the same village, then the corpse is taken to his ancestral house for a moment before proceeding towards the cremation ground (*mangkhor*). It symbolizes the return of the deceased to his birthplace. After the funeral party leaves the house of the deceased, the spot where the corpse was laid before taking to the cremation ground need to fill with ash and cover under the bamboo basket. Later, after the return of the funeral party, the spot is observed if any signs are left on the layers of the ash. Depending on the footprint it is forecast whether the deceased will be reborn as human or animal. If the marks are identified as human feet or palm it is believed that the deceased will be reborn as a human being. However, if no mark is found on the ground then it is believed that the deceased will not be reborn. While proceeding to the cremation ground, the people accompanying the corpse sing about the good deeds the deceased person has accomplished in his/her lifetime. Meanwhile, a woman ties a white thread from one big tree to another which falls along the way to the cremation ground. According to the Hill Tiwa the white thread symbolizes a bridge across the channels and streams which the soul of the deceased has to cross during its onward journey. Before the corpse is placed on the funeral pyre made of bamboo and stacks of wood, the deceased is offered rice, liquor and other edibles made for the purpose. Subsequently, the corpse is placed on the pyre with the head towards the northern direction and covered under firewood. Before lighting the fire, one of the sons of the deceased goes seven times around the platform and lights the funeral pyre. In case there is no son close kin of the deceased performs the task. If the pyre sets on fire easily it is believed to be a good omen. But if it takes some time to burn then it is presumed that the deceased wants to eat something which he used to have during his lifetime. Hence food and liquor are offered in the name of the deceased. During the cremation, if the right leg rises, it is perceived as a bad omen for the family of the deceased. In case the left leg rises, it is considered to be a bad omen for the entire clan. If the eyes burst out while burning, it is believed that the deceased was jealous of other's prosperity in its lifetime. After the corpse gets completely burnt, the ashes are washed by spraying cold water. Subsequently, these ashes are arranged in a human shape aligning in the north-south direction. Over the shape, a small hut of bamboo and sun grasses is constructed. On the following day, the family members along with their clan members go to the cremation ground to see whether the food offered during the cremation was eaten or not. If they find that the food had been eaten by animals or birds it is considered to be a good omen and symbolizes satisfaction on the part of the departed soul.

Except the Malang, no other Tiwa clan practices preservation of the bones of the deceased. The Malang clan use stone cairns called *kungri* to preserve the bones. According to an oral tradition,[42] the *phidri* or the ancestor of the Malang clan brought this tradition from 'Norteng' (Nartiang) in Jaintia hills. The story further tells that the Malangs were originally called *Nungthung wali* who came from a place called Nungthung in the Jaintia hills. This story suggests that the Malang were influenced by the Jaintia tradition.

After the return of the funeral party, water dipped in metals like silver, copper, gold and basil leaves sprinkled on them. Moreover, they need to cross a burning stick before entering the house of the deceased. It is to ward off the bad spirits that might follow the funeral party while returning from the cremation ground. The family members offer food and liquor to the funeral party after they return from the cremation ground. The Hill Tiwa does not practice fasting to mourn the deceased. There is no food restriction for the family members of the deceased. The family members continue to have their usual meal. A ceremony in honour of the deceased called *khari chawa*, is observed after the completion of one year. In this ceremony, all the departed souls within that particular year are remembered by offering food and rice beer. This ceremony is attended by all the villagers and clan members of the deceased. During this ceremony, the villagers help the family in collecting bamboo, firewood and banana leaf etc. required for the ceremony.

The Afterlife and Reincarnation:

The Tiwa strongly believe that after the death of a person, they become the *phidri* or the spirit and live in the world of spirits. According to them after death, the soul becomes a member of the spirit world and rejoins with all the dead ancestors. However only good souls are welcomed among the spirits and wicked souls are not allowed to enter and have to take shelter in jungle, hills and mountains. To ascertain whether the deceased have found solace or not in the spirit world, the family members visit a fortune teller, (*phamari*).[43] The discussion with the spirit through the *phamari* is called *mindai songa*. While visiting the *phamari,* the family members offer food and other edibles to the deceased. After the performance of some rituals, the *phamari* invites the spirit of the deceased and answers questions put by the family members. Generally, the family member asks the spirit about the cause of death and any unfulfilled desires. The spirit is also asked whether he has received any trouble in his afterlife. As per the interaction with the spirit through the *phamari* the family member performs sacrifices for the solace of the deceased. The sacrifices are performed at the residence of the deceased with the help of other clansmen.

The Tiwa believe in the reincarnation of the soul. The reincarnated soul is called *jalai* and the individuals belonging to the same soul but born in different families address each other as *shauce*. A few days after the birth of a child a small divination ceremony is performed to ascertain the reincarnated soul. This divination can be performed by any member of the family including the mother. When a newborn baby does not suckle the mother's milk and repeatedly cries out, it is believed that the baby is asking its mother to find the *jalai* or reincarnated person. The process to ascertain the reincarnated soul is called *jalai pashena*. When the baby cries, the mother or any female relative of the family would tie a piece of thread on the wrist of the baby while pronouncing the names of close family members who have died recently. It is believed that the baby stops crying after hearing the names of the reincarnated individual. If the mother fails to identify the reincarnated soul then the parent would go to the Shaman (*Oja*) for a divination ceremony. The *oja* conducts a small divination ceremony with two split bamboo sticks. He would continue to toss the sticks on the ground while pronouncing names of recently demised close family members until it finds a definite sign. If the name and sign coincide then it becomes clear that the baby is the reincarnation of a particular person. After the identification of the baby with the reincarnated person, the parents conduct a small ceremony to welcome the reincarnated soul by sacrificing a fowl. After this ceremony, the baby gets two identities: the name given by the members of the family and the name of the reincarnated individual.

If the reincarnated person died of some accident or was killed by animals or snake bite, then an elaborate ritual called *khordeng* has to be performed for the safety of the baby in the present life. In this ceremony all the clan members are invited and the *Jela* (clan elder) sacrifices a pig and a fowl in the name of ancestral spirits and seeks protection from evil spirits. It is believed that if *khordeng* is not performed, then the same incident that killed the person in his previous life may be repeated.

Among the Tiwa, it is believed that the spirits of the deceased are reincarnated among its close relatives such as daughters, sons, sisters and brothers etc. If a father dies, it is expected that he will reincarnate in his daughters' and sons' families. However, his soul may take several rebirths in his close family member's house. Similarly, a mother is expected to reincarnate as a daughter in her sons' or daughters' house. One soul can be reborn into several family members' houses within the clan or *maharsha*[44] which can continue up to four generations.

In fact among the Tiwa, all individuals both male and female are the reincarnated soul of their previous life. Everyone has a dual identity; the present name and the name of their previous life. In the course of fieldwork, we found the Hill Tiwa individuals have two names. For example Imlang Lumphui is the reincarnation (*jalai*) of his mother's maternal uncle Nikon Lumphui who was married into the Maslai clan as a *kobiya*. Hence he is also known by the name of his previous life as Nikon. His elder brother Leander Lumphui is the reincarnation (*jalai*) of his maternal grandfather Soipha Maslai. Therefore Leander is also known as Soipha among the family members.

The *jalai* system is also observed among Tiwa Christian converts. According to an informant, most of the Tiwa Christians still believe in the reincarnation of the soul. However, the Catholic Tiwa does not go to the Shaman for divination to identify the reincarnated soul. Instead, mother identifies the reincarnated soul by tying a cotton thread to the baby's wrist. Unlike their counterparts, the Catholic Tiwa do not make any sacrifice or offerings to the reincarnated soul after its identification. They invite friends and family members to bless the baby and perform prayer services for the well-being of the baby in the present life.

Totemism:

According to James Frazer totemism is "an intimate relation which is supposed to exist between a group of kindred people on the one side and a species of natural or artificial objects on the other side, which objects are called the totems of the human group."[45] Sigmund Freud stated that,

> Totem is, as a rule, an animal (whether edible and harmless or dangerous and feared) and more rarely a plant or a natural

phenomenon (such as rain or water), which stands in a peculiar relation to the whole clan. It is an intimate relation that is supposes to exist between a group of kindred people on one side and a species of natural or artificial objects on the other side, which objects are called the totem of the human group. In the first place, the totem is the common ancestor of the clan; at the same time it is their guardian spirit and helper, which sends them oracles and, if dangerous to others, recognizes and spares its own children. Conversely, the clansmen are under a sacred obligation (subject to automatic sanctions) not to kill or destroy their totem and to avoid eating its meat (or deriving benefit from it in other ways). The totemic character is inherent, not in some individual animal or entity, but in all the individuals of a given class. From time to time festivals are celebrated at which the clansmen represent or imitate the motions and attributes of their totem in ceremonial dances. [46]

Malinowski contended that,

The totemism has two sides: it is a mode of social grouping and a religious system of beliefs and practices: as religion it expresses primitive man's interest in his surroundings, the desire to claim an affinity and to control the most important objects above all, animal or vegetable species more rarely useful inanimate objects, very seldom man made things.[47]

Some of the Tiwa clans consider certain animals as their totem and refrain from hunting or eating the meat of that animal. The first Tiwa chief of Gobha was believed to have been born out of *mali* fish. His clan came to be known as Maloiwali. They are forbidden to eat the *mali* fish as it is considered to be their totem. Among the Hukai clan, it is believed that their first ancestor was a tiger. The story of the Hukai clan, says that when they were living in 'Khairam',[48] A woman Padmavati by name conceived supernaturally from the moon. Hence she was driven out of the village but soon received shelter at Amsai village. Subsequently, she gave birth to a tiger which was released in the jungle. Later she also gave birth to a boy. This boy who was the half-brother of a tiger was said to be the ancestor of the Hukai clan. Therefore the members of the Hukai clan never kill any tiger nor do they take part in any hunting expedition. Syamchaudhury and Das[49] recorded that killing of a tiger by a member of the Hukai clan would be an act of patricide. They further state that if the Hukai clan comes to know about the death of a tiger, they would collect the corpse and arrange for its cremation similar to that of other clan members. They would mournfully carry the corpse as if it were a dead man to the cremation ground on a stretcher made of bamboo, covered in white cloth. Those who helped in the cremation would take bath before they entered their house. On that day, the people of the Hukai clan refrain from doing agricultural and other physical work. Women do not weave and no one touches the granary to denote mourning of their totem.

The Mithi clan also has a similar belief that the ancestor of their clan was nurtured by a tiger. The legend describes that once a couple who were married in the same clan was excommunicated and therefore had to live in a jungle. One day the husband disappeared while going to fetch water from a nearby stream. Sensing danger, the wife hurriedly went out in search of her husband while leaving her newborn baby at her house. When the baby screamed, a tigress came and fed the baby with her milk. From that day onwards the boy was reared by the tigress. After attaining adulthood, he left the jungle and lived among humans, and became the ancestor of the Mithi clan. Hence the members of this clan do not kill any tiger and consider it as their ancestor spirit.

Taboo:

Taboo is a rule or conduct that is proscribed by society as improper or unacceptable, forbidden or prohibited. According to Mary Douglas,[50]

> A taboo is a ban or prohibition; the word comes from the Polynesian language where it means a religious restriction, to break which would entail som automatic punishment. She further writes, "In essence it generally implies a rule which has no meaning or one which cannot be explained. To the outsider it is irrational; to the believer its rightness needs no explaining.

According to Freud,[51]

> The meaning of 'taboo', as we see it, diverges in two contrary directions. To us it means, on the one hand, 'sacred', 'consecrated', and on the other 'uncanny', 'dangerous', 'forbidden', 'unclean'. Taboo restrictions are distinct from religious or moral prohibitions. They are not based upon any divine ordinance, but may be said to impose themselves on their own account.

Among the Tiwa, there are several activities that are termed as *namyawa* or taboo. Some of the taboos are clearing of the jungle for *jhum* cultivation or plaughing before the *Phidri-Chongkhong* ceremony is considered to be a taboo. Similarly playing *Thurlu* (flute) and other musical instruments before the *Thurlu Phuja* ceremony is forbidden. The entry of women inside the bachelor's dormitory, the *Shamadi* is taboo. Similarly, presence of women at the ceremonies like *Phidri-Chongkhong, Langkhon* and *Thurlu* is taboo. Untimely celebration of festivals and singing of religious songs and recitation of hymn/religious prayers (*mindai lekha*) is also considered to be taboos. Shyamchaudhury and Das[52] observed certain taboos during the four days of celebration of the *Sogra* festival in Tiwa villages. According to them, during these four days villagers were forbidden to husk and pound paddy, ride a bicycle or any other vehicle and to engage in fishing, weaving, hoeing, cutting of bamboo or firewood and touching of the granary.

The killing of certain animals by some clans is considered as Taboo. The Hukai and Mithi clan cannot kill a tiger as it is considered to be a clan ancestor or *phidri*. Whenever they see a tiger they are forbidden to pronounce its name. Instead, they use a different synonym to indicate a tiger as it is taboo to pronounce the name of the clan deity. The killing of any animals specifically reared for religious ceremonies is a taboo. They believe that the act of killing such an animal will bring misfortune and sickness on the person responsible for the act. Similarly, rearing of cows is also a taboo among the Hill Tiwa. A.E. Heath[53] recorded that cattle rearing was forbidden among the Lalung (Tiwa) by their religion. According to him they never kept cows, as violation of this tradition would bring bad omens in their society. The Hill Tiwa still continue to adhere to this tradition.

It is difficult to explain why every society has certain taboos associated with human acts. Mary Douglas[54] contended that "some of the taboos are said to avoid punishment or vengeance from gods, ghosts and other spirits. Some of them are supposed to produce automatically their dreaded effects. Crop failures, sickness, hunting accidents, famine, drought, epidemics, they may all result from breach of taboos." According to our informant[55] violation of taboo is not considered a crime but it is a moral obligation that every member of society is expected to abide by. The Tiwa believed that they are surrounded by their deities and spirits and hence if someone violates a taboo, though unobserved by humans, it is not hidden from spirits. Hence they have to answer on their deathbed. It may even come and haunt them in their next life in the form of various sicknesses on the body of the *Jalai* or the reincarnated soul.

The traditional religion of the Tiwa has since been influenced by Hinduism. It can be discerned from certain elements connected to their religious beliefs and practices. The worship of Mahadeo, use of basil leaves, copper, gold and silver as a part of the purification ceremony is a Hindu custom incorporated into the traditional Tiwa religion. B.K. Gohain,[56] commented that the influence of Hinduism among the Tiwa must have been transmitted through the Jaintia because of their long association with them. It is to be noted that the Jaintia are one of the immediate neighbours of the Hill Tiwa. Moreover Tiwa oral traditions suggest that there had been a close connection with the Jaintia in the past. However, there is ample scope to infer that the Tiwa essentially came in contact with the Vedic Hindu tradition at a very ancient time. These traditions gradually become a part and parcel of the Tiwa traditional believe system.

Figure 1. *Wanchuwa* Ceremony *(Credit, Topesh Malang)*

Figure 2: Sacrifice under the *Thamkhunda* inside *Shamadi* *(Credit, Lakeshwar Doloi)*

Figure 3. Animal Sacrifice at *Bor-Chongkhong* Ceremony *(Credit, facebook.com)*

Figure 4. Cremation ground of Amsai Village *(Credit, Tilok Thakuria)*

Figure 5. Megaliths of Chongkhong Sal, Amsai Village *(Credit, Raktim Patar)*

Figure 6: A *Chu-lao (Credit, Facebook.com)*

Notes and References:

[1] Bronislaw Malinowski, *Magic, Science and Religion and Other Essays*, The Free Press, Illinois, 1948, p. 1.

[2] Lewis H. Morgan, *Ancient Society*, Charles H. Kerr & Company, Chicago, 1877, p. 5.

[3] James G. Frazer, *The Golden Bough*, The Macmillan Company, New York, 1925.

[4] John Lubbock, *The Origin of Civilization and the Primitive Condition of Man*, D. Appleton & Company, London, 1898.

[5] *Ibid.*, p. 206.

[6] *Ibid.*, p. 210.

[7] Bronislaw Malinowski, *op. cit.*, p.6.

[8] Emile Durkheim, *The Elementary Forms of Religious Life* (new translation), The Free Press, New York, 1995, pp. 2-3.

[9] B.K. Gohain, *Continuity and Change in the Hills of Assam*, Omsons Publications, 2006, p. 142.

[10] P.C. Choudhury, *The History of Civilization of the People of Assam to the Twelve Century A.D.*, Spectrum Publications, Guwahati, 1987, p. 388.

[11] B. C. Allen, *Administrative Report on the Census of Assam*, 1901, Shillong, 1902, p. 58.

[12] Julia Elliott (ed.), *Oxford Dictionary and Thesaurus* III, New York, 2008, p.26.

[13] James G. Frazer, *op.cit.*, pp. 111-112.

[14] The *Wasirawa* ceremony marks the beginning of the collection of bamboo and other forest products for the repair and construction of new dwellings. The Tiwa do not procure wild bamboo and thatch without performing this ceremony.

[15] R.B. Pemberton, *Report on the Eastern Frontier of British India* (3rd edn.) DHAS, Guwahati,, 1991, p.221.

[16] E.B. Taylor, *Primitive Culture*, Vol. II (6th edn.), John Murray, London, 1920, p. 113.

[17] B.K. Gohain, *The Hill Lalungs*, ABILAC, Guwahati, 1992, p.65.

[18] *Kobiya* is a resident son-in-law in traditional Tiwa family. Tiwa were originally a matrilineal society though currently they follow the bilateral descent system which allows both matrilineal and patrilineal descent. The majority of hill Tiwa follow *Kobai Kona* or *Kobai*. In this system the husband formally goes to live with his wife at her mothers house and the descent is traced through the mother.

[19] This appears to be a recent phenomenon, because a *Loro*, needs to devote a lot of time in public affairs. Recently the *Loro* of Bormarjong who belonged to the Madar clan gave up his position of *Loro* on account of personal issues.

[20] This story is translated from Maheswar Pators, *Fera*, Tiwa Sahitya Sabha, 2004, pp.3-4.

[21] Collected from Horsing Kholar, age 50 years of Chikdamakha village.

[22] The boundary of Palakhongor is extended to a large area in the Amri area of West Karbi Anglong district of Assam. There are twelve border landmarks or the *nima* mentioned in the oral traditions of the Tiwa. These *nima* are not only

a landmark that demarcates the boundary of Palakhonger but the hill Tiwa also considers it to be an animate deity. Every year at the time of the *Chongkhong* and *Pakhukara* ceremony twelve fowls are sacrificed in their name. The twelve *nima* of Palakhongor are Wadarmakha, Khanimuji, Sondrophali, Miran Khai, Umpanai Baro, Khusa Makha, Sinani, Seraseri, Dundumia Makha, Nungthunguri, Laisari Khunguri and Tikrum.

23 W.W. Hunter, *Statistical Accounts of Assam,* Vol. I, (reprint), B.R. Publishing, Delhi, 1975, p.167

24 *Toloi* or *Doloi* is the second most important position in the council of village elders called the *Pisai*. His main duty is to assist the village priest, the *Loro* in discharging religious functions.

25 Maheswar Pator, *op. cit.,* pp.5-6.

26 *Borjela* is the head of a family/clan.

27 Maheswar Pator, *op. cit.,* pp. 7-9

28 Other than the *Moinarikanthi* festival no girls are allowed to take part in dancing. It is the boys who perform dances in all the religious festivals except *Monarikanthi.*

29 The informant is a resident of Magro village.

30 B.C. Allen, *op. cit.*

31 R.B. Pemberton, *op. cit.*

32 He is one of the members of the village council and the principal assistant of the village priest, the *Loro.*

33 The hill Tiwa called the Khasi -Jainntia people as "Melang".

34 *Dewri* is a priest.

35 The original name of this place was *mindai sal,* meaning the abode of god. Subsequently, it was sanskritised to *Deosal.* Earlier the chief of the Gobha principality used to offer sacrifices at this place. Now it has been converted into a Siva temple.

36 S.K. Bhuyan(ed.), *Jayantia Buranji*(3rd edn.), DHAS, Guwahati, 2012.

37 P.R.T. Gurdon, *op. cit.,,* p. 103

38 *Ibid.*

39 Sahari was an important principality under the Gobha chieftainship. The rituals of the Gobha chief were also practiced in the Sahari principality.

40 P.R.T. Gurdon, *op. cit.,* p. 124.

41 Bronislaw Malinowski, *op. cit.,* p. 29.

42 The story about the Malang clan was collected from Phulson Kholar, 50 yrs, of Amsai village on 07/07/2016.

43 A *Phamari* is an expert shaman. It is believed that she can communicate with the spirits of the dead. Among the Tiwa the *Phamari* are generally a woman.

44 *Mahar* means mother and *Sha* means one: it denotes members belonging to one mother, grandmother or mother's sisters.

45 Cited in Bronislaw Malinowski, *op. cit.,* p.4.

46 Sigmund Freud, *Totem and Taboo,* Taylor and Francis e-library, 2004, p. 3.

47   Bronislaw Malinowski, *op. cit.* p. 4.

48   Khyrim as pronounced by the Khasi.

49   N.K. Syamchaudhury, M.M. Das, *op. cit.*, pp.58-59

50   Mary Douglas, "Taboo", in Richard Cavendish (ed.), *Man, Myth and Magic*, London, 1979, pp. 2767-71

51   Sigmund Freud, *op. cit.*, pp. 21-22

52   N.K. Syamchaudhuri, M.M. Das, *op. cit.*

53   Referred in the tour dairy of A.E. Heath, the Sub-Divisional Officer of Jowai in 1882, Assam State Archives, Guwahati.

54   Mary Douglas, *op. cit.*

55   Hunaki Amsi age 80 years, a resident of Tharakhunji village.

56   B.K. Gohain *op. cit.* (1992), p.66.

CHAPTER IV

Religion and Belief System: The Plain Tiwa

This chapter deals with the religious practices of the Tiwa living in the plain districts of Assam. In view of the changes in the religious beliefs and practices of the Plain Tiwa, it is necessary to discuss separately. S.K. Bhuyan[1] contended that,

> The Aryan population of the Brahmaputra Valley has grown out of the nucleus which had come to this part of India in very ancient times and which has expanded by fresh influxes from western India through the progress of the centuries. Among them, there are various forms of veneration which include Sivisim, Saktisim and Vaishnavism. Each of these categories of followers has distinct way of offering and sacrifice which forms the greater Hindu religious identity.

There are a number of tribes in the Brahmaputra Valley which has adopted and following the Vedic Hindu tradition alongside their traditional ancestral belief system. One such group is the Plain Tiwa. Some of the popular Hindu traditional festivals celebrated among them are *Durga Puja, Lakhi Puja, Sivaratri, Saraswati Puja, Biswakarma Puja* etc. Similarly, the purification ceremony after the birth and death of a Tiwa individual in line with Hindu religious norms clearly indicates the incorporation of Vedic Hindu traditions. However, despite being impacted by Hinduism a large section of Plain Tiwa still continues to adhere to their traditional belief system. Our fieldwork suggests that the religious beliefs of the Plain Tiwa are an admixture of Hindu practices and traditional religion/ancestral religion.

The religious beliefs of the Plain Tiwa can be classified into two broad categories: a) those that follow elements of the traditional religion as well as those of Hinduism and b) those that follow Neo-Vaishnavism.[2] An interesting aspect of the religious belief system of the Plain Tiwa is that those who follow the traditional religion have also incorporated Hindu rituals in birth, death and marriage ceremonies. They have incorporated the worship of popular Hindu deities as well as veneration of ancestor spirits in the form of occasional sacrifices. One of the examples that we would like to cite is that of the Gobha *Raja's* way of worship. During our fieldwork at Gobha village, one of the villagers informed us that at the beginning of the annual agriculture cycle they offer sacrifices to their ancestor spirits and invoke their blessings for the safety and wellbeing of their family members. Nevertheless, they would also offer *puja* at the small temple within the compound of their house to invoke the blessings of Siva and Ganesh whose idols are placed inside the temple.

From our observation at Tiwa villages of Meruwagaon, Bhurbandha, Domal, and Matiporbat in Morigaon district of Assam, it appears that the Plain Tiwa adhere to their old customs and habits of eating and drinking. Like their counterparts in the hills, they also have a *Nobaro*[3] or *Borghor*[4] where sacrifices are offered to the clan deities/ancestral spirits on important occasions such as the *Bihu*[5] and *Nokhuwa*[6]. During these occasions, clan deities are offered with various edibles such as rice, meat of various animals, areca nut, *pan* leaf, rice beer etc. All the important members of the clans are invited. They also worship various Hindu deities such as Siva, Krishna, Ganesh and Kuber who are given equal importance while propitiating. Similarly, temple visits and celebration of popular Hindu festivals like *Holi, Diwali, Ras, Sivaratri, Biswakarma Puja, Sarawati Puja, Durga Puja* are also significant among them.

The followers of Neo-Vaishnavism among the Plain Tiwa are guided by the virtues and principles of Neo-Vaishnavism propounded by Sankardeva and Madhavdeva which advocate the invocation of only one god, Vishnu. On account of exclusive devotion to Vishnu, Neo-Vaishnavism is also known as *ekasarana nama dharma* meaning the invocation of one and only Vishnu. For them, the traditional religion does not hold any significance and they have completely abandoned the rituals and religious ceremonies of their traditional religion. They consider Tiwa traditional religious practices like animal sacrifice and invocation of dead ancestors as irrelevant and refrain from eating pork and drinking rice beer, which is otherwise considered to be an important facet of traditional Tiwa religious practices.

Traditional Belief System:

Among the Plain Tiwa, there is a large section of people that still adhere to their traditional religious beliefs and customs. Among the followers of the traditional/ancestral faith birth and death rituals are performed in a manner similar to their hill counterparts. They also observe religious ceremonies like *Chongkhong, Langkhon* and *Wanchuwa* etc. Their rituals are marked by animal sacrifice and the offering of rice beer to the spirits. The community religious ceremonies are performed at a designated place called *thaan* or *mindai sal*. Ancestor spirits are propitiated at their main dwelling house, *borghor (nobaro)* under the sacred pillar called *thuna*. For them, it is a place of worship and they consider it as an important part of their belief system. They propitiate Tiwa deities such as Sharipahai, Palakhongor, Silikhongor, Nashuni, Baguni, Bodolmaji, Kantha Boroi, Kalikha etc. This section of Tiwa believes that Sharipahai is identical to Mahadeo and he is the creator and protector of this world. Another significant facet of their belief system is that they are strongly attached to their ancestral spirits and regular sacrifices are made to invoke their blessings. They consider that after the death of a person, the soul goes to another world but always keep an eye on their living family members and expect sacrifices and offerings. Thus they offer sacrifices to their ancestors on important occasions such as *Bihu* celebration, eating of the first meal prepared from fresh harvest etc. Among them, offering pork and rice beer (*chumagra*) is considered to be an indispensable part of their religious life. Like their hill counterparts, they also believe that the soul of the deceased reincarnates among the close relatives of the family.

The census report of 1881[7] conducted primarily in the present Nagaon and Morigaon district of Assam recorded that, the manner of Lalung (Tiwa) worship was similar with all other 'wild' tribes of Assam. It states that the Lalung (Tiwa) sacrifice a fowl, pig, or goat on common religious ceremonies but on big occasions they sacrifice a buffalo and the prayers are aimed at imploring their deities to protect them, their cattle, rice fields and farmyards. The report further commented that the Lalungs (Tiwa) make sacrifices at *thaan* or earthen platform and the *dao* or bill-hook was a sacred weapon and attract adoration. The report observed that the prayers to the *mindai* were often a mixture of Assamese with Lalung (Tiwa) words bearing Assamese inflection and there were many Hindu influences in their religious beliefs. It mentioned that Sharipahai-Sharikora is a Hindu rendering of primitive Lalung (Tiwa) origin. After twenty years, the census report of 1901[8] described the Lalung (Tiwa) religion as Animism and mentions the practice of human sacrifice for their god in the past. The *District Gazetteers of Nowgong*[9] in 1905 described the Lalung (Tiwa) as strong believers of their ancestral faith and that only a few people identified themselves as Hindu. It further stated that their beliefs were an ordinary animistic type and that they were chiefly concerned with the propitiation of evil spirits with sacrifices to ensure prosperity. Subsequently, the census report of 1911 recorded a considerable number of animistic believers among the Tiwa. It recorded only 496 followers of the Hindu faith against 38723 who were identified as animists. The census report of 1921 also records a good number of animists among the Tiwa population of Assam with a minor increase in Hindu followers as compared to the previous census. It mentioned 37679 Tiwa individuals as followers of animism and 3354 persons as Hindu. The census reports suggest that the Tiwa population in the plains of Assam were primarily followers of their ancestral faith during the pre-independence period which the colonial enumerators placed under the category of animism. At the same time, the reports also recorded a gradual increase in the number of Hindu followers among this tribe in the subsequent years. It appears that the colonial administrators were concern about the growing influence of Hindu tradition among the tribal communities and wanted to separate them at least in their policy documents from the larger Hindu communities. The colonial policy to segregate the tribal communities on the basis of language and culture from the rest of the communities was essentially intended to divide the people of Brahmaputra Valley and to strengthen British rule.

The Plain Tiwa considers Mahadeo or Siva as the supreme god. He is depicted as a benevolent deity who showers blessings upon those who worship him with devotion. They begin every important social and cultural ceremony with an invocation to Mahadeo. Interestingly most of the tribes in the Brahmaputra valley consider Siva as their supreme god.[10] We do not have concrete evidence to show how Siva worship or Saivism became a part of the belief system of these tribes. According to Maheswar Neog,[11] the worship of Siva seems to have been in vogue in ancient Kamarupa from great antiquity. B.K. Kakati[12] states that "Saivism in some gross form, associated with wine and flesh, was prevalent among the aboriginal Kiratas and that the Aryanised colonists held it in great disdain". The Tiwa strongly believe that Mahadeo created this universe and is the master of every creation in this world. He provides food, shelter and protects humans from every danger, and looks after their cattle. The Kailash Mountain is considered to be the holy place for the Plain Tiwa as it is the abode of Mahadeo. They consider their deity Sharipahai as identical to Mahadeo. According to the Tiwa tradition, Sharipahai is the creator of this world. Thus it is easy to identify Sharipahai with Siva because of similar beliefs attributed to them. During our fieldwork, it was found that the popular Siva temple at Deosal near Jagiroad along National Highway no 37 is a Tiwa traditional place of worship. Before the erection of the present Siva temple in the 1960s, it was a thickly forested sacred grove dedicated to Bodolmaji, the clan deity of the Gobha *Raja*. According to our informant,[13] before 1960 only Tiwa people used to visit this place during the annual ritual hosted by Gobha *Raja*. They call this place *Gobha Rajane mindai sal* meaning Gobha *Raja's* Sacred Place. In the olden days, the Tiwa chief of Gobha used to offer sacrifices in the name of their god, Sharipahai and Bodolmaji on the occasion of *Phidri Chongkhong* ritual.[14] During this ceremony there was a tradition of erecting a pair of flat stones. *Deosal* is the present name of the former *mindai sa* of the Gobha *Raja*. The word *Deo*[15] is an Assamese word meaning lord/god. It is possible that the word *midai* must have been replaced by the word *deo* in the early part of 17th century invariably after the establishment of the Ahom suzerainty across the Kolong- Kapili valley. In the 1960's a temple dedicated to Siva was built where regular offerings are made by devotees belonging to different Hindu communities.

Nevertheless, an interesting feature of this temple is that it retained some of the earlier traditions associated with propitiation. Generally in Hindu temples, the priest has to be a Brahmin and invocations are made in Sanskrit. However, the practice associated with *Deosal* Siva temple is quite different from that of any other Siva temple. According to Anil Konwar, the assistant priest of Deosal temple, the god Sharipahai or Siva can be propitiated only by a Tiwa priest and the hymns should be chanted only in Tiwa language.

Birth Ceremonies:

There have been some new additions to the ceremonies associated with childbirth among the Plain Tiwa in contrast to their hill counterparts. The purification ceremony followed in the Hindu tradition has gained importance among the Plain Tiwa. During the birth of a baby, except for the husband of the expectant mother, no males are allowed to come inside the room. Generally, an experienced elderly woman of the village belonging to a different clan is called by the family members to attend to the expectant mother at the time of the birth of the baby. The expert midwife is called *ujani*. She cuts the umbilical cord with a thin bamboo sliver called *sesuli* which is generally extracted from a bamboo post of the house. If the house is made of concrete, then any piece of bamboo may be used. But the use of an iron blade or any other metal is forbidden. A similar practice is also observed among their hill counterparts. After cutting the umbilical cord, the *midwife* looks at omens for the future health of the baby. If the cord is straight enough, it is believed that the baby will have good health in the future but when the cord is curved or twisted then it is assumed that the baby will have health-related problems in the future. The umbilical cord is placed in a deep pit dug at a considerable distance from the house. This they believe increases the child-bearing capacity of the mother. After birth, if the baby is found to be motionless then a bell metal plate and bowls are used to create noise to awaken the baby. They believe that the sounds can make the baby responsive. Unlike their counterparts in the hills, the Plain Tiwa clean the house with mud plaster mixed with cow dung soon after the baby is born. It is the part of the purification process which ends with the *aukhush kheda*[16] ceremony performed soon after the fall of the navel cord of the baby. Similar to their hill counterparts, soon after the baby is born, the Plain Tiwa observe a small thanksgiving ceremony by sacrificing a fowl or an egg offered to ancestral spirits. This ceremony is performed by the eldest maternal uncle of the family, the *borjela*,[17] and in his absence it is performed by the eldest member of the family. After this ritual, the midwife can come out of the room where the baby was born.

From the day of birth of a baby till the purification ceremony (*aukhush kheda*), the clan members observes some taboos during this period. They do not touch the granary and no other religious ceremonies are performed. After the baby is delivered, the mother also has to observe some taboos. According to tradition, till the falling off the navel cord of the baby, the mother must not sleep with her back to the child. In order to fasten the process of fall of the navel cord, a paste made of sap of the basil leaf and mud collected from the hearth is applied on the navel of the baby. After its fall, the navel cord is carefully preserved in a proper place. It is believed that if the baby suffers from stomach ache, the water dipped in its navel cord could cure the problem. When the baby refuses breast feeding and continues to cry, it is believed that the baby is the reincarnation of one of the recently dead family members. Hence, a small divination ceremony is performed to determine the reincarnated family member. This divination ceremony is also performed by their hill counterparts.

The purification ceremony is a religious one and involves the invocation of ancestral spirits. It is generally observed on the following day just after the fall of navel cord of the baby. This ceremony is known as *auskara* or *aukhush kheda*.[18] On this occasion, some senior members of the village are invited and the *bojela* invokes the ancestral spirits with the sacrifice of one fowl. After that, the father shaves the head of the baby. In the absence of the father, a close relative may perform the job. After this, the *Hari Kongri*,[19] shoots six arrows aiming towards the east, west, north, south as well as towards the sky and on the ground in the case of a male child. Then the seventh arrow is fixed on the bow and placed in the hands of the infant. In case the baby is a female, a sickle and cotton yarn is placed in the hands. Gurdon[20] recorded a similar ceremony among the Khasis. He mentioned that during the naming ceremony of a child, a bow and three arrows are placed near a male child. In the case of a female child, a *dao* and *u star* or cane head-strap is placed near the child. However, there are some differences between the Khasi and Tiwa rituals. One important difference is that the Khasi place the bow and arrow on the occasion of the naming ceremony whereas the Tiwa does it on the occasion of the purification ceremony. Another divergence is the variation in the number of arrows that are used on the occasion. Ganesh Senapati[21] contended that the shooting of six arrows in six directions signifies the popularity of the child which spreads far and wide in the future. It also indicates the hunting skills of Tiwa males in the past as the bow and arrow was an indispensable part of life. Similarly, the sickle and cotton yarn signifies the weaving and agricultural skills of a woman. The choice of object is indicative of the most desirable characteristics of the two sexes in the minds of the early Tiwa- the ideal man was a warrior and hunter and the ideal woman a tough industrious field worker and housewife. Meanwhile, the *hari konwari* draws seven vertical lines on the ground near the altar made for the purification ceremony. With her middle finger, she picks a pinch of soil from the middle line and puts it on the forehead, chest, ears, and both shoulders of the baby. The earthen mark on the body of the baby symbolizes the close connection of the Tiwa with mother earth and nature. After the ceremony, the baby is blessed by the village elders one by one while holding the baby in their hands. Rice beer (*chumagra*) and *khaji*, a special curry made of arum leaves and chicken meat is served to the guests. This curry is served regularly to the mother until she recovers from the weakness and other troubles associated with childbirth. It is believed that this curry helps the mother of the newborn baby to recover from pain and blood loss suffered during the delivery. Probably the early Tiwa knew the fact that arum leaves are highly nutritious and it helps to regenerate red blood cells in the body.

Funerary Rituals:

As soon as information about the demise of an individual is received, the senior members of the village gather at the house of the deceased and make decisions regarding the cremation procedure. The entire cremation rituals are done under the supervision of a couple of locally appointed priests called *gyati*[22] and *gyatini*.[23] The senior members of the village (*khel*) select a male member of their village belonging to a different clan (other than that of the deceased) as *gyati* and one female as *gyatini* to perform the rituals associated with the cremation of the deceased. The male *gyati* is responsible for setting up of the funeral pyre and the performance of rituals associated with cremation. On the other hand, the female *gyatini* looks after the arrangements before the deceased is taken to the cremation ground. Both individuals are responsible for the proper conduct of rituals associated with death ceremonies. Their role and presence are indispensable during the funerary rituals. However on completion of rituals they are released from their temporary role of the priesthood.

Under the guidance of the *gyati,* the place for the funeral pyre or the *hatham* is selected. It is to be noted that like their hill counterparts, the Plain Tiwa also have a separate cremation place assigned for every clan in the village within the designated cremation ground called the *mangkhor* or *makor*. According to Ganesh Chandra Senapati,[24] *hatham* is a place where the bones of the deceased clan members are deposited after cremation. It implies that even after death the clan members remain together. He further mentions that the cremation of an individual at the *hatham* of his clan is a tradition that has been following by their ancestors since time immemorial. It is considered to be a matter of pride to reunite with their clan members at the *hatham* after the death of an individual. The Plain Tiwa forbids cremation of dead bodies in places other than its *hatham*. Generally, the place for setting up the funeral pyre for a particular clan is identified with the help of a senior member of the clan of the deceased. However, if it becomes untraceable due to undergrowth then a small divination ceremony is performed by the *gyati* by breaking a chicken egg known as *tutikawa*. It is believed that the egg will break only in a place where the ancestors of the deceased were cremated earlier. After the identification of the spot, the *gyati* with the help of other individuals of the village set up the funeral pyre.

The corpse is kept inside the house before it is taken to the cremation ground. Preparation for the cremation begins with a symbolic bath in which a paste made of turmeric and pulses is applied over the body of the deceased. With the arrival of all the relatives and clansmen, the preparations for washing the corpse starts under the direction of the *gyati* and *gyatini*. All the members of the family of the deceased take part in the bathing ritual. Similar rituals are also practices by the other Assamese community. Gurdon also recorded a similar ritual among the Khasis[25] and W. Crook among the Ollar Gadaba tribe of Orissa.[26] The ritual of bath before cremation is an important Vedic Hindu ritual which is has been incorporated among the Tiwa.

After the bathing ceremony, the deceased is offered food by the family members cooked by the *gyatini*. The food for the deceased generally contains rice and a curry made of dry jute leaf and dry fish, egg and rice beer. Nowadays, other items enjoyed by the deceased when alive, are also offered during the rituals. The food offering rite is called *maikhutaina or bhatkatiwa* in Assamese. The offering of food and bath ceremony symbolises the preparation of the soul of the deceased for the journey to the next life. During this ritual, family members and others offer money to the deceased. The Tiwa believe that the money which is provided in the rituals is used by the deceased as ferry fees to cross the river of death.[27] Frazer commented that "many people have been in the habit of supplying their dead with money or its equivalent to enable them to defray the expenses of the journey to the other world.[28] A similar tradition is also prevalent among the Kakhyens of Burma who places a piece of silver in the mouth of a corpse to pay ferry dues over the streams the spirit may have to cross.[29]

To transport the corpse to the cremation ground which is generally located at some distance or outside the village settlement, the bier is an essential part of the funerary ritual. On the morning of the funeral day, a bier is prepared by expert bier- makers of the settlement. The bier is made of bamboo. Because of the importance of bamboo during a person's life time as well in the funerary rituals, the Tiwa prefer to have the bamboo groves in their bacyards. While making the bier, no one is allowed to cross over the bamboo poles that are used for bier making. It is believed to be a bad omen if someone crosses the bamboo poles. Soon after the corpse is placed on the bier, a chicken egg is sacrificed by the *gyati*. It symbolizes the end of life for the deceased in this world.

While transporting the corpse to the cremation ground, the female *gyatini* carries the remaining portion of the food that was offered to the deceased along with the uncooked rice donated by co-villagers and relatives. She also carries white thread to be tied to trees by the side of the road leading to the cremation ground. It is believed that the thread acts as a bridge over the river of death which the deceased has to cross while going to the other world. [30] A similar ritual is also practiced by their Hill counterpart.

At the *hatham* the corpse is placed on the pyre pointing its legs towards the east. There are various studies regarding the orientation of the body concerning cardinal directions. E. B. Taylor remarked: "Orientation of the body in death with respect to cardinal directions seems to be the working out of the solar analogy, on the one hand, is death at sunset… a new life at sunrise."[31] Rose, who studied celestial and terrestrial orientation of burial, says that, Celestial orientation is related to a belief in a continued life of the dead man at a celestial land of the dead, orientation being in the direction the deceased must travel in their journey to the land of the dead. The terrestrial orientation is, related to a belief in reincarnation since the body is aligned toward the location where the soul must reside before being reborn.[32] Gurdon mentions that the Khasis place their deceased on the pyre with the head to the west and the feet to the east.[33]

While cremating the corpse, if fire sets easily then it is considered to be a good omen for the family of the deceased. If the fire takes time to consume the wood on the pyre, it is believed that the deceased had unfulfilled desires when alive. Hence food, other edibles, and rice beer are offered in the name of the deceased. It is the duty of the *gyati* to ensure that nothing is left unburnt on the pyre. If he fails to perform his duty properly, then it is considered to be a serious offence. He may be heavily fined for his carelessness by the village elders and stern warnings may be served to be remembered in the future.[34]

The Tiwa believe in the existence of evil spirits and therefore take precautions particularly when the funeral party returns from the cremation ground. While returning no one looks behind as it is considered to be a bad omen. After reaching the house of the deceased, they have to cross over a small fireplace kept at the entrance. It is believed that the crossing of fire keeps the members of the funeral party safe from the evil spirits which cannot chase them beyond the fireplace. After entering the house of the deceased, purified water mixed with cow dung, basil leaf and barmuda grass (*bubori bon*) are sprinkled upon the members of the funeral party. They are offered few grains of rice, areca nut, and *pan* leaf by the family members of the deceased. Before entering their respective houses the members of the funeral party have to remove their clothes outside the house and take bath. They drink purified water dipped in basil leaves and golden ornaments to ward off the evil spirits. The practice of purification after returning from cremation ground has been incorporated from the Hindu tradition.[35]

Unlike their counterparts in the hills, the Plain Tiwa observe three days of mourning after the demise of a family member. According to tradition, all the near relatives of the deceased should refrain from consuming salt, oil, ginger, chilli, and other spicy food during the period of mourning. However, they can consume boiled rice and vegetables once a day during the three days of mourning. The family members are also forbidden to use soap or any cosmetic items during those days. On the third day, a purification ceremony called *tiloni* is performed by the *gyati* and *borjela* of the family to purify the living members of the deceased. After this ritual, the family can take a vegetarian meal. However they have to refrain from non-vegetarian food until a ceremony called *kharmass luwa* is performed on the seventh day.

Though the purification ceremony is completed with the *kharmass luwa,* a special funerary ritual called *karam* is performed within a year or several years after the demise of a person depending upon the financial condition of the family. Sometime, this ceremony is performed together for several deceased family members of a lineage. Sharma Thakur observed that "the *karam* is a purification ceremony after the death of an individual in which the pending death ceremonies of a few families of the same *bangsha* or clan are solemnised jointly."[36] The *karam* is performed jointly for several dead members of the clan. It is an expensive ritual where the co-villagers also contribute to the family in kind which includes rice, pulses, vegetables, and rice beer for the ceremony. Maneshwar Dewri[37] commented that the *karam* is equivalent to the Vedic death ritual of *shardha.*

Rituals Associated with Agriculture:

The main objective of the rituals associated with agriculture is to seek the protection of crops and livestock from evil spirits. The prayers are simple and are mainly concerned with the well-being of human, animal, and paddy fields.

In the Brahmaputra Valley the first ritual associated with agricultural activities is the spring festival called the *Bohag Bihu*. Like many other Assamese communities, the Plain Tiwa also observe the *Bohag Bihu* with pomp and gaiety. However, the celebration is a little different from that of the other Assamese communities. The *Bohag Bihu* is celebrated in the Assamese month of *Bohag* which falls in mid April. On the first day of the *Bihu*, the head of the family performs a ritual in front of the cowshed. On the occasion, two bamboo sticks are stuck with a small piece of homespun cotton yarn, tied on the top of each stick. The yarn on the stick left of the propitiator is soaked in mustard oil and right stick is decorated with flowers. This decorated stick is the deity called *malthakur*, who is considered to be the guardian of livestock. It is believed that he resides in the cowshed. The ritual begins with the burning off the yarn soaked in mustard oil. Meanwhile, the propitiator sacrifices a red fowl after depositing some of its feathers at the altar. The blood of the fowl is smeared on the stick covered with flowers and incantations are chanted for the protection and good health of livestock. The process comes to an end before the yarn is burnt out.

The ceremony described above is unique to the Plain Tiwa so far as the celebration of *Bohag Bihu* is concerned. It is aimed to protect the livestock especially the cow and ox which are important assets for the families. Wet paddy cultivation is labour intensive work and the ox has been an integral part of the agricultural cycle from ploughing to harvesting. In the plains, the ox is also required to remove the paddy grains from the stalks after it is harvested. Not surprisingly among the Hill Tiwa, this ceremony is unknown as keeping of the cattle is forbidden in their traditional belief system. Since the Hill Tiwa practice *jhum* cultivation which is dependent on the expenditure of human energy and the use of simple implements such as the hoe and *dao*, it is reasonable to assume that the keeping of cattle was unnecessary.

In some of the Plain Tiwa villages[38] *Chongkhong Puja* (*Phuja*) is celebrated soon after the *Bohag Bihu*. Unlike in the hills, the Plain Tiwa does not have a particular place for this ceremony. It is performed anywhere near the paddy field. On the day of the ceremony the village elders led by the village priest (Dewri) goes to a place near the paddy field where a small rectangular shaped altar is made. In this altar, the priest pilled up one hundred and ten *tara* leaves (a wild variety of cardamom, scientific name *hedychiumcoronarium*). On the heap of some rice a silver ring and a chicken egg is placed. He also plants seven bamboo twigs and two tiny pieces of reed on either side of the altar. After sprinkling water kept in a brass pot dipped in basil leaves, the priest reads the omen by tossing two small pieces of bamboo sticks on the altar and cuts one chicken egg. If the omen is good, it is believed that the harvest will be good for that year. After the divination, the priest sacrifices four chickens and blood is smeared on the altar. Subsequently, the viscera of these birds are taken out one by one to see if there are any black spots in them. It is believed that the black spots will bring bad season of cultivation in the coming year. After observing the omens, the viscera are placed on the altar. After that, a small piece of meat cut from the breast and the wings are strung together in a thin bamboo stick for roasting. After offering the meat roasted on a bamboo stick to the deity, the ceremonial meal is served to the participants of the ceremony. The Plain Tiwa believes that by performing the *Chongkhong puja* the villagers and their paddy field will be protected from the malevolent spirits.

After one week of the *Chongkhong Puja*, another ceremony called the *Phidri- Chongkhong* ceremony is performed. In this ceremony, every household of the village contributes rice and rice beer. On the occasion, a special session of the village council is held to review all the pending penalties imposed by the village elders on individuals for various offences. According to tradition, all penalties should be paid before the *Phidri-Chongkhong* ceremony. Generally, penalties are paid in cash as well as in kind. Rice and money realised as penalty goes for the preparation of a ceremonial meal. Meanwhile, the priest (*Dewri*) carries out the rituals and builds four earthen altars for four deities namely, *Bagh Raja* (tiger god), *Jol-thol Devota*(god of land and water), *Mahadeo* or *Hajaidew* (god of the mountain) and *Sharipahai* (high god). On each of these altars, grains of rice, one chicken egg, areca nut and betel leaves are put on a banana leaf. On the altar made for Sharipahai, two hundred and ten *tara* leaves are stacked. Next a silver ring and a chicken egg are placed on the top of the stack of leaves. According to the Plain Tiwa offering of a silver ring signifies purity of the ceremony as well as honour to their deity. Subsequently, four fowls are sacrificed in the name of the four deities, and prayers are offered for the well-being of livestock and humans. After two months when the crops have grown considerably, a propitiatory rite is performed at the same place where the *Chongkhong* ceremony was held. It is performed for the protection of the crops from insects, birds, and wild animals.

The special offering of *tara* leaves and the greater number of sacrifices on the altar made for the deity Sharipahai indicates that he is considered to be a high god among the deities worshiped by the Tiwa. Both the Hill and Plain Tiwa consider Sharipahai as their creator and protector of the world. During our fieldwork, we have found that the *Chongkhong* ceremony is gradually disappearing from the traditional belief system of the Plain Tiwa. The reason may be ascribed to a lack of interest and knowledge about the traditional religious ceremonies among the younger generations of the Plain Tiwa.

Suni Puja:

The *Suni Puja* is observed during May/June. This *puja* is performed by the villagers to get rid of the the evil spirit, the *Suni*. It is believed among the Plain Tiwa that *Suni* comes to the village during the celebration of *Chongkhong* and takes shelter in the peacock flower tree (*ponicianapulcherrima*). Hence fourteen small branches of this tree are used in this ceremony. This ceremony is performed at the far end of the village. Here the village priest (*Dewri*) makes an earthen pyramid-shaped altar where one chicken egg is placed. He then sets up branches of the peacock flower tree around the altar. Subsequently, the priest sacrifices the chicken egg and reads the omen. The main purpose of this ceremony is to chase away the *Suni* from the village as its presence in the village may cause sickness and epidemics to the people.

Hogora Puja:

Hogora Puja is observed by the Tiwa living at the village near the foothills celebrates this annual festival. This *puja* is performed to obtain good harvest. It is performed at the *Shamadi* (the bachelor's dormitory) of the village. On the occasion, sacrifices are made in the name of *Sharipahai* for bumper crop. Interestingly, with the gradual disappearance of the *Shamadi* system among the Plain Tiwa, the *Hogora Puja* has also becoming a thing of the past. The new generation of Tiwa youths hardly knows about this ceremony.

Mal Puja:

The *Mal Puja* is celebrated during June/July corresponding with the Assamese month of *Jeth* and *Ahar* which is considered to be an auspicious time to perform the *puja*. It is observed at the gap of two or three years depending upon the financial condition of the village. 'Mal' is the bamboo and wooden poles specially designed for the occasion. The place where these *mals* are prepared is called *mal sasa*. There are two types of *mals*, one is called the *bor mal* or the bigger *mal* and other as *saru mal* or the small *mal*. The *bor mal* is made of bamboo while the stem of a small tree is used for the *saru mal*. The ceremony starts on a Tuesday and ends on the following day. On the first day, the *mals* are decorated with various floral designs and coloured in yellow and black using turmeric juice and charcoal. After the offerings, the *mals* would be kept in a designated place called *mal puta*. Generally, a mature person is selected to carry the *bormal* and a young man is selected to carry the *saru mal*.

On the following day, the villagers again gather at the *mal puta* and they would pick up the *mals* and proceed in small groups towards different directions of the village. While visiting every house they would repeatedly beat the roofs and make a loud noise. The family of the household would offer their regards to the *mal* and serve rice beer and specially prepared curry (*khaji*) made of the tender banana trunk to the members of the group. Sometime this process would continue for the whole day. In the evening, all the groups carrying the *mals* gather in the outskirts of the village and plant them under a big tree. On the following day, all the villagers gather at the place where the *mals* were prepared and conclude the ceremony with a feast. According to the people, this *puja* was performed to protect the village from various epidemics and natural calamities. Presently the *mal puja* is no longer celebrated among the Plain Tiwa. According to our informant,[39] this *puja* disappeared from the Tiwa villages during the 1980s on account of lack of interest among the younger generations and introduction of Neo-Vaishnavism among the Tiwa, leading to the discontinuance of this important ritual.

An interesting observation of *mal puta* ritual is that it has a resemblance with the *behdeinkhlam* festival of the Jaintia. This festival is celebrated by the Pnars of the Jaintia Hills district in Meghalaya in June. Gurdon[40] recorded that, *khlam* is the Khasi word for plague or pestilence and *beh-dieng* signifies the act of driving away with sticks.

Tusuma:

Tusuma is performed to propitiate the *Bagh Raja*(tiger god). They also called it as *Khor Raja* and *Bon Raja*. It is performed during September/October. In this ceremony fowls are sacrificed in the name of the tiger god and prayers are made for the well-being of the people of the village and the standing crops. The villagers go to the forest to collect wild bamboo for basketry and house construction only after the *Tusuma* ceremony.

Deo Sewa:

Deo Sewa is an annual ceremony held during October/November. This ceremony is performed by every clan at their *nobaro* or *borghor* to receive blessings from the clan deity to ensure prosperity of the clan. This ceremony marks the beginning of the consumption of the fresh areca nut (*tamul*) by the Plain Tiwa. It is to be noted that areca nut is considered to be an important article not only among the Plain Tiwa but also among all the communities of the Brahmaputra valley because of its significance in all socio-cultural affairs. However, this ceremony is hardly observed now among the Plain Tiwa. This is due to a lack of interest and knowledge on this ceremony among the younger generation and decreasing attachment to their traditional belief system. Moreover as a result of the commercialisation of the areca nut, Tiwa families no longer have to wait for this ceremony for the harvesting and consumption of the crop. They prefer to sell off their areca nuts in advance to earn good profit, to the local agents of *pan masala*/ tobacco companies. Once it is sold, then there is no question of observing any traditional rituals associated with the areca nut.

Borot Ceremony:

The word *Borot* originated from the Sanskrit word *"brata"* which means penance observed to pacify the god. The *Borot* is a community festival of the Plain Tiwa celebrated especially in the Tetelia area of Morigaon district in December corresponding the Assamese month of *Puha*, on a full moon night (*purnima*). This festival is observed to purge the village of pestilence, epidemics and aggression of wild animals. On the occasion, a special dance called *borotnitya* is also performed by the youth. An interesting facet of this festival is that the songs are obscene and vulgar containing an essence of sexuality. Though this festival was unique to Tetilia region, it now has become one of the most popular festivals of the Plain Tiwa.

Thaan Worship:

Thaan is an Assamese word meaning a place of worship. It resembles Hill Tiwa's concept of *sal* meaning the abode of god or sacred place. The *sal* is an open space or a patch of forest dedicated to different deities. There is no raised structure such as a temple or shrine at the *sal*. However, in the *thaan* there could be temples dedicated to a particular god which is not found in the *sal*. In our opinion, the *thaan* system is different from that of the Hindu concept of the temple. Unlike the temples which are generally located within the village, the *thaans* are established in the periphery of the village. Similarly, *thaans* are generally visited by people only during certain occasions but there is no specific time or period for a temple visit. Moreover, unlike temples, there is no priest stationed at the *thaans*. The *thaan* system among the Plain Tiwa can be termed as the continuity of the *mindai sal41* system practiced by their hill counterparts. An interesting feature of the *thaans* is the presence of vertically placed standing stone or menhirs ranging from two to four feet tall. It is sometimes linked with the Siva *Linga* by the Plain Tiwa and their neghbouring communities as they look identical. Hence many of the *thaans* are now converted to Siva temples and have become a commonplace of worship for both Tiwa as well as other communities.

The Plain Tiwa consider the Deosal (in which a popular Siva temple is now located) and Basundori as the most important *thaan*. The Deosal *thaan* is located along national highway 37 near Jagiroad. According to tradition, the annual offerings at Deosal were held at the direction and guidance of the Gobha *Raja*. Now this place has been converted into a popular Siva temple where many people visit to offer *puja*. The Basundori *thaan* is located on the bank of Kapili River in Raha revenue circle of Nagaon district. The Sahari *Raja* performs annual *puja* at the Basundori *thaan* in mid April. A traditional fair or *mela* is also held at Sahari coinciding with annual *puja*.

Besides the above-mentioned *thaans,* Saripahai, Bura Gosain, Uttar Khola, Nelli and Kalikha *thaan* are also considered to be important *thaan* by the Plain Tiwa.

Gosain Uluwa Utsav:

One of the outstanding features of religious festivals which reflect the close association of Tiwa with the Ahom kingdom is the *Gosain Uluwa Utsav. Gosain* is an Assamese word meaning lord or deity, *uluwa* means to take out and *utsav* means festival. In this festival, the principal deities of the twelve minor principalities established by the Ahoms are displayed and taken in procession. This festival is celebrated between the Assamese month of *Bohag* and *Jeth* corresponding to April and May. An interesting aspect of this festival is that it is celebrated under the patronage of the twelve minor principalities collectively known as *Pasu-Raja* or five *Rajas*/chiefs and *Satu-Raja* or seven *Rajas*/chiefs, collectively known as *Puwali-Raja* (minor or tributary *Raja* of the Ahoms) located in the Nagaon and Morigaon districts of Assam. It is a major socio-religious event in this part of Assam. During this festival, Krishna the tutelary deity of these principalities is taken out from the prayer hall in a procession followed by dance and music.

There are three legends[42] associated with the origin of this festival. According to one legend, this festival began during the reign of Koch king Naranarayan as a mark of friendship between the principalities of *Pasu-*

Raja and *Satu-Raja*. The story further narrates that when Chilarai, the Koch general and brother of Naranarayan was imprisoned by the sultan of Gaur after a failed campaign against the latter, Naranarayan planned to invade Gaur with a joint army consisting of soldiers supplied by Tiwa chiefs of *Pasu-Raja* and *Satu-Raja*. In response to the call, the chiefs offered all possible help. However, the proposed invasion was aborted on account of Chilarai's release from captivity by the sultan apparently because he saved the kings mother from a snake bite. However, to mark the effort of the *Pasu Raja* and *Satu Raja* in the proposed campaign against the king of Gaur, King Naranarayan decided to organise an annual festival.

The second popular theory about the origin of this festival is that it is another form of *Daul Utsav* where the image of Lord Krishna is publicly worshiped and a procession is taken out while performing *nama* and *kirtan*(devotional song). It is believed that this festival began after some of the chiefs of these principalities embraced Neo-Vaishnavism in the late 17th century.

According to another legend, this festival was started by Aai Kanaklata, the granddaughter-in-law of saint Sankardeva in 1669 to celebrate her successful pilgrimage to Barduwa, the birthplace of Sankardeva presently in Nagaon district.[43] The story narrates that during her pilgrimage she was assisted by the chief of Mikirgoya principality who eventfully converted to Neo-Vaishnavism after taking initiation from Aai Kanaklata. He then decided to organise an annual festival where the idol of Lord Krishna would be worshipped in public with pomp and gaiety.

The first legend associated with the Koch King Naranarayan has no historical base as the *Satu Raja* and *Pasu Raja*, or twelve principalities did not exist during the reign of Naranarayan. According to the *Deodhai Asam Buranji*[44] the process of installation of these minor principalities began during the reign of Ahom King Jaydhwaj Singha (1653-63), whereas king Naranarayan (1540-84)[45] ruled the Brahmaputra valley long before the establishment of these minor principalities in the Kolong and Kapili Valley.

As far as the second theory is concerned, it is highly unlikely that the festival is another form of *Dol Utsav* because its celebration time does not match with the *Gosain Uluwa Utsav*. The *Dol Utsav* is celebrated on the occasion of *Dol Purnima* during the month of March but this festival takes place between April and May after the *Bohag Bihu*.

The festival where the deities of twelve minor principalities known as the *Pasu- Raja,* the five chiefs and the *Satu-Raja,* the seven chiefs, collectively known as *Puwali Raja* is located in the present Nagaon and Morigaon districts of Assam. King Jaydhwaj Singha(1653-63 CE) created three Tiwa principalities Topakuchi, Baropujia, and Mikirgoya after the subjugation of the influential Gobha chief.[46] Subsequently during the reign of Ahom King Rudra Singha (1696-1714 CE) another seven principalities namely Hukunagug, Boghora, Tetelia, Ghoguwa, Torani-Kolbari, Kumoi and Mayong were established and placed under the supervision of the head of the Jagi post, Jagial Gohain. He was followed by Rajeshwar Singha (1751-69 CE) who established another two principalities namely Khora and Khaigarh as tributaries to the Ahoms and placed them under the officer-in-charge of the Raha post, the Rohial Baruah.[47] The chief of the seven principalities established by Rudra Singha were collectively called as *Satu-Raja* or the group of seven chiefs and the five principalities established by Jaydhwaj Singha and Rajeshwar Singha was known as *Pasu-Raja* or the group of five chiefs. As a symbol of the Ahom suzerainty, the chief of these principalities who were recognized as *Rajas* had to pay a compulsory visit to the Ahom king on the occasion of *Magh Bihu.*[48] They also had to offer one piece of rhino horn, two pieces of elephant tusk and eight pieces of the buffalo horn as an annual tribute.[49] Besides they started a tradition of annual display and procession of their tutelary deity on a specific day in the month of *Bohag*(April-May) in presence of the head of the Raha *chokey* (post), the Rahial Baruah and Jagial Gohain who were entrusted with the responsibility to collect the annual tribute from the *Pasu-Raja* and *Satu-Raja.* A popular saying related to the *Gosain Uluwa Utsav* mentioned that "*Pasu Rajar mah saul Rohial Baruar bor hobah*" meaning psauRajas or five kings/chiefs (Topakuchi, Baropujia, and Mikirgoya, Khoraand Khaigarh) feast at the Rohial Baruah's(officer-in-charge of Raha post) annual assembly. According to this legend, the Rahial Baruah used to conduct an annual assembly where the five kings (*Pasu-Raja*) had to offer a feast. Tiwa scholar Maneshwar Dewri mentions the *Gosain Uluwa Utsav* is a symbol of feudalism in Assam as it was begun by the minor Tiwa principalities to satisfy their Ahom masters where the common people had to pay taxes out of their hard-earned produces.[50]

The presence of Rahial Baruah during the festival indicates that Ahoms wanted to assert their supremacy on the Plain Tiwa population both politically as well as diplomatically by having a religious dimension to the annual gathering. It appears that initially, the festival was a political gathering but subsequently with the conversion of the chiefs of *Pasu-Raja* and *Satu-Raja* to Neo-Vaishnavism, it transformed into a religious festival.

From the above discussion, it appears that the essence of religious beliefs of the Plain Tiwa lies at the junction of two belief systems: one group that practices the traditional alongside the Hindu religious practices and the other group that professes only Neo-Vaishnavism or *ekasarana nama dharma*.

Notes and References:

1   S.K. Bhuyan, *Studies in the History of Assam* (2nd edn.), Omsons Publications New Delhi, 1985, p.43.

2   Vaishnavism was introduced by Sankardeva in the 15th-16th century in the Brahmaputra Valley. It transformed into a religious movement in the latter part of the 16th century because of its liberal outlook which attracted many tribal groups.

3   A detailed discussion on the *Nobaro*, the traditional Tiwa house and its religious significance has been given in Chapter III.

4   *Borghor* is an Assamese term for *Nobaro* meaning the main house.

5   The *Bihu* is an important cultural festival of the Brahmaputra Valley. It is celebrated thrice in a year under different names. These are *Bohag Bihu* or *Rongali Bihu* celebrated in the Assamese month of *Bohag* corresponding to the month of April, *Kati Bihu* or *Kongali Bihu* is celebrated in the Assamese month of *Kati* corresponding to the month of October and the *Magh Bihu* or the *Bhugali Bihu* celebrated in the Assamese month of *Magh* corresponding to the month of January.

6   *Nokhuwa* is a popular family ritual practiced in the Brahmaputra Valley. It marks the beginning of the consumption of newly harvested rice.

7   E.A. Gait, *Census of India,1891, Assam*,Shillong, 1892.

8   B.C. Allen, *Administrative Report on The Census of Assam, 1901*, Shillong, 1902, p. 58

9   *Idem, Assam District Gazetteers, Nowgong,* Part VI, City Press, Calcutta, 1905, pp. 83-84

10 The tribes of Brahmaputra Valley such as the Bodo, Dimasa, Rabha, Sonowal, Thengal etc. consider Siva or Mahadeo as high god.

11 MaheswarNeog, *Religions of the North-East*, Publication Board Assam, Guwahati, 2008, p. 1

12 B.K. Kakati, *The Mother Goddess Kamakhya*, Lawyer's Books Stall, Guwahati, 1948, p. 17

13 TamsingDewri, age 59 years is one of the priests at the Deosal Siva temple interviewed on 13/09/2015.

14 A similar ceremony is still observed among the Hill Tiwa

15 In Assamese *deo* means god. This word is closely associated with the Ahom rule in Assam. They consider their kings as *Swargadeo* or the god of heaven. Similarly the word *deo* has also been used to show respect in kinship relations among the Ahoms, for example, *baideo* or elder sister, *mahideo* or aunt, *puthadeo* or maternal grandfather, *mumaideo* or maternal uncle etc.

16 *Aukhush Kheda* means driving away the impurity. It is performed soon after the falling of the navel cord of a new born baby.

17 *Jela* in Tiwa language means an individual. *Bojela* means the senior most member of the family, especially from the women's family such as maternal uncle or elder

brother can became the *borjela* of the family. His main responsibility is to look after the religious activities of the family as a priest of the family and to assist his niece, nephew and sisters' family in times of marriage, inheritance, birth and death related ceremonies etc. among the hill Tiwa he also known as *borjela* or *jelaraw*.

[18] This ceremony is a not practiced by the Hill Tiwa. This purification ceremony is specifically observed by the Plain Tiwa which reflects the influence of Hindu concept of purity and pollution.

[19] *Hari Kongri* is the senior most woman of a family. The Tiwa being originally a matrilineal society recognizes the oldest living woman of the family as the *Hari Kongri*. She could be the grandmother or the aunt of the baby.

[20] P.R.T. Gurdon, *The Khasis* (reprint), Low Price Publication, Delhi, 2010, p. 124

[21] Ganesh Chandra Senapati, "Tiwa Samajor Akhush Bidhi", *Ringchang*, Tiwa Mathonlai Tokhra, Amsoi, 2004, pp. 106-120.

[22] *Gyati* is a male individual who is specially chosen to act as a priest for the conduct of the funeral ceremony. His clan should be different from that of the deceased. He takes care of the entire funeral ceremony.

[23] *Gyatini* is female individual who is selected for the funeral ceremony. She is responsible for the cooking of food to be offered to the deceased at home as well as at the cremation ground.

[24] Ganesh Chandra Senapati, "Tiwa Jatir Mankhor Stapon aru Sa-Dah Pratha", in *Tiwa Sampradayar Parichay*, Asom Sahitya Sabha, Jorhat, 1975, p.43.

[25] *Ibid*

[26] William Crook, *Popular Religion and Folklore of Northern India*, Vol. I, Oxford, 1926, p. 37

[27] Ganesh Chandra Senapati, *op. cit* (1975).

[28] J.G Frazer, *Fear of the Dead in Primitive Religion*, Vol. 11, London, 1934, p. 193

[29] Anderson, *Mandalay to Momeien*, London, 1876, p. 143, cited in J.G. Frazer, *op. cit*, pp. 193-194.

[30] Lokeshwar Gogoi, *Tiwa Sanskritir Ruprekha*, Vol II, Tiwa Sahitya Sabha, Silchang, 1987, p. 36

[31] E.B. Taylor, *Primitive Culture*, London, 1871, p. 508.

[32] H. J. Rose, "Celestial and terrestrial Orientation of the Dead", *Journal of the royal Anthropological Institute of Great Britain and Ireland*, 52, 1922 pp. 129-133.

[33] P.R.T. Gurdon, *op. cit.*, p. 133.

[34] Ganesh Chandra Senapati, *op. cit.*(1975)

[35] Lokeshwar Gogoi, *op. cit.*

[36] G.C. Sharma Thakur, *The Lalungs(Tiwas)*, Guwahati, 1985, p. 57.

[37] Maneshwar Dewri, *Tiwa Sampradayar Parichay*, Asom Sahitya Sabha, Jorhat, 1975, pp. 80-81.

[38] Nambor, Silchang, Nokhola etc.

[39] The informant is a resident of Kathiatoli village in Nagaon district.

40   P.R.T. Gurdon, *op. cit.* p. 158

41   *Mindai Sal* is an important place of worship for the hill Tiwa. Every village reserves a patch of land generally a small hill near the village for the worship of the village deity. All the community worship and sacrifices are made in these*mindaisal*.

42   Maneshwar Dewri, "Mela (Gosain Uluwa Utsav)", *Ringsang*, Tiwa MathonlaiTokhra, 2004, pp. 359-368

43   Lokeshwar Gogoi, *op. cit.*, p. 146

44   S.K. Bhuyan (ed.), *Deodhai Asam Buranji* (4[th]edn.), DHAS, Guwahati, 2001, p. 99.

45   Edward Gait, *A History of Assam* (reprint), Lawyers Books Stall, Guwahati, 1997, p. 47.

46   S.K. Bhuyan (ed.), 2001, *op.cit.*

47   *Ibid.*, p. 121

48   *Magh Bihu* is a popular harvesting festival of the Brahmaputra valley that takes place in the month *Magh* corresponding to the month of January.

49   Lokeshwar Gogoi, *op. cit.*, p. 120

50   Maneshwar Dewri, *op. cit.*(2004)

CHAPTER V

Social Institutions and Traditional Polity Formation

According to the *Oxford Dictionary of Sociology*,[1] social institution is a cluster of specialised normative expectations and consist of all the structural components of a society through which the main concerns and activities are organized and social needs such as those for order, beliefs, and reproduction are met. It is an important component of any society. Every human group has developed their social institutions for the smooth functioning of the society through imposition of social norms to an individual member of the society.

Family and Clan:

A traditional Tiwa family consists of parents, unmarried sons/daughters and married daughters and their children. The husband of one of the married daughters selected by the parents as the resident son-in-law (*kobiya*) is also a member of the household. Ideally *Shodya*, the youngest daughter lives with her parents and inherits the parent's house and a major share of the parental landed property. The sons after marriage go and stay with their wives in their in-laws' households. In cases where the wife is not the inheritor or the youngest daughter of the family, the husband constructs a house at his mother-in-law's property which is inherited by his wife and children. The matrilineal system of the Tiwa is called *kobai kona* or *kobai* and the male after marriage is called *kobiya*. In this system, the sons of the family go to their wives' house as resident sons-in-law (*kobiya*) and cannot inherit their parental property. When there is more than one daughter in the family, generally the youngest daughter (*shodya*) inherits the parental house trand other daughters are given land for construction of a house within their parent's homestead land. In case there is no daughter in the family and sons, if any, go to live with their respective in-laws the household becomes extinct after the death of the couple. Among the Tiwa, there is no system of adoption of girls to carry forward the lineage. So a daughter in the family is necessary to continue the lineage. In other words, the core of the Tiwa family is always a female. In case of the death of the husband in the family, a widow with her children may constitute a household though not an ideal one until the grown-up daughters marry and the *kobiya*, the resident son-in-law becomes the head of the family in absence of his father-in-law (*hu*). It is to be noted that the male in the Tiwa society becomes head of a family only after marriage when he goes to his wife's house. Hence a Tiwa woman is the core of the household, she inherits the property of her parents and her husband becomes the manager of the property and master of the house after the death of her parents. In this regard, S. Karotemprel[2] contended that the Tiwa matrilineal system does not endow the women with any special ascendency over their male counterparts as in other matriarchal societies where the man used to be reduced to the status of a chattel. Both man and woman have equal status, even though the boy customarily goes to live in the house of the girl after marriage.

Until the 1980s bringing a daughter-in-law or *pohari* was not very common among the Hill Tiwa. Even if a Tiwa boy brings his wife to his house, his daughters and sons continue the tradition of matrilineality by bringing a resident son-in-law and sons going to their wife's residence as the *kobiya*. B.K. Gohain[3] recorded that Oba Amsong was the first person of Bormarjong village who brought his wife from a nearby Karbi village as *pohari* and got her adopted into the Mithi clan. However, his daughters continued the tradition of matrilineal descent system by bringing resident son-in-law.

A traditional Tiwa village consists of several individual clans called *khul*. According to oral tradition, there were twelve original clans which have descended from twelve sisters, who lived in Makha Koja (the red mountain). The story tells that when these sisters grew up, they did not find any young men to marry. As time went by and remained unmarried, they were depressed and disheartened and decided to end their lives by throwing themselves into a river. However, the god of water took pity on them and sent twelve young men who eventually married these sisters. These twelve sisters are said to be the progeny of the twelve original Tiwa clans. These are the Mothrong-wali, Madur-wali, Maloi-wali, Lumphui-wali, Hukai-wali, Agar-wali, Mithi-wali, Amsong-wali, Kholar-wali, Darphang-wali, Malang-wali and Lorom-wali. Today these clans have several sub- clans. According to our informant, the suffix *wali* denotes a girl or a woman. It connotes a clan for woman or a race in general4 which suggests that the Tiwa trace their descent through the female line. The following are Tiwa clans that are known: Agari, Amphi, Amsi, Amsong, Hukai, Khajar, Khamli, Khargol, Kholar, Khorai, Kraikho, Ladur, Ligra, Lumphui, Madar, Malang, Markhang, Maslai, Melang, Mithi, Mothrong, Muni, Phamjong, Puma, Borong, Puru, Tamlong, Sagra, Somsol, Talung, Tarphang (Darphang), Tilar(Dilar), Radu, Lorom, Maloi, Kosrong and Solong.

Kinship:

Kinship is a system of social organization based on real or putative family ties. According to thoughtco.com[5] "It is one of the most important organizing components of society…this social institution ties individuals and groups together and establishes a relationship among them". The kinship relationships are based on consanguineal and affinal bonds. The consanguineal kinship is based on blood, the relationship meaning the relationship between parents and children, grandparents and grandchildren and also among immediate siblings. It is said to be the basic and universal in relationships. However, consanguineal relation is not only based on actual blood relation but may be based on supposed blood relation. Affinal kinship is based on marriage. The relationship between husband and wife is the basic kin relations. The consanguineal kins of the husband are the affinal kin of the wife and vice-versa. The father-in-law, mother-in-law, brother-in-law, sister-in-law etc., are affinal kin. Their kinship includes the kin related through both the father's side and the mother's side. *fa* (father), *ayong* (father's elder brother), *tadai* (father's younger brother), *ani* (father's sister), *ayong* (father' elder brother's wife), *asi* (father's younger brother's wife), *asa* (father's sister's husband) etc. are the kin related through the father's side and *ma* (mother), *mamai* (mother's brother), *asi* (mother's sister), *ani* (mother's brother's wife), *asa* (mother's sister's husband) etc. are the kin related through the mother's side. Thus, both descriptive and classificatory kinship terms are found among them. *Fa* (father) and *ma* (mother) are descriptive terms and *ayong* (father' elder brother), *tadai* (father's younger brother), *mamai* (mother's brother), *asa* (father's/mother's sister's husband),*asi* (father's younger brother's wife/ mother' sister), *ani* (father's sister/mother's brother's wife) etc. are classificatory terms. An interesting aspect of the Tiwa kinship terms is that both father's elder brother and his wife are addressed as *ayong*. Similarly, reciprocal term of address is seen between grandparent, *ajo/abi* and grandchildren *shutabla*. The siblings of brothers and sisters without distinction of sex are designated by a single kinship term called *pagen*. This term also includes the cross cousins of the second order. Thus there is no cross cousin marriage among the Tiwa. It may be attributed to the consanguine and structural unity existing between the male and female siblings born of the same mother.

Joking behavior between grandparents and grandchildren, elder sister's husband and wife's younger sister, elder brother's wife and husband's younger brothers and sisters are common amog the Tiwa. Similarly, the kinship relation between the mother-in-law and sons-in-law and father-in-law and daughters-in-law, between younger brother's wife and husband's elder brother, wife's elder brothers and sisters and younger sister's husband etc. are the avoidance behavior. The following table describes the kinship relationship, term of reference and terms of address among different kins among this tribe.

Tiwa Kinship Terms:

Table: IV

Primary Kin:

Kinship Relationship	Terms of Reference	Terms of Address
Father	*pha/paba*	*paba/pha*
Mother	*Ma*	*Ma*
Son	*Sa*	by name
Daughter	*Sajao*	by name
(e) Brother	*Khai*	*Khai*

Kinship Relationship	Terms of Reference	Terms of Address
(y) Brother	*Kojal*	*Kojal*/ by name
(e) Sister	*Pai*	*Pai*
(y) Sister	*Nanao*	*nanao*/by name
Husband	*Soi*	By name of eldest son/daughter with the suffix *pha/fa*
Wife	*si/ margi*	By the name of eldest son/daughter with the suffix *ma*

Secondary Kin:

Fa Fa	*Ajo*	*Ajo*
Mo Fa	*Ajo*	*Ajo*
Fa Mo	*Abi*	*Abi*
Mo Mo	*Abi*	*Abi*
Fa(e)Br	*Ayong*	*Ayong*
Fa(y)Br	*Tadai*	*Tadai*
Fa(e)Si	*Ayong*	*Ayong*
Fa(y) Si	*Ani*	*Ani*
Mo(e)Br	*Mamai*	*Mamai*
Mo(y)Br	*Mamai*	*Mamai*
Mo(e)Si	*Ayong*	*Ayong*
Mo(y)Si	*Asi*	*Asi*
(e)Br Wi	*Pawji*	*Pawji*
(y)Br Wi	*Pohari*	*Pohari*/by name
(e)Si Hu	*Punsi*	*Punsi*
(y)Si Hu	*Kabi*	*Chongai*
Br So	*Pagen*	*Pagen*/by name
Si So	*Pagen*	*Pagen*
Br Da	*Pagrai*	*Pagrai*/by name
Si Da	*Pagrai*	*Pagrai*
Wi Fa	*Hu*	*Paba*
Wi Mo	*Niw*	*Ma*
Hu Fa	*Hu*	*Paba*
Hu Mo	*Niw*	*Ma*
Wi(e)Si	*Nanisha*	*Pai*
Wi(y)Si	*Sali*	by name
Wi(e)Br	*Chelaraw(jelaraw)*	*Khai*
Wi(y)Br	*Sali*	*Kojal*/by name
Hu(e)Br	*Jothal*	*Nabur* if not married/if married by first Childs name with the suffix *pha/fa*

(Contd)

Hu(y)Br	*Sali*	*kojal/by name*
Hu(e)Si	*Nanisa*	*Pai*
Hu(y)Si	*Sali*	*nanao/by name*
So Wi	*Pohari*	*Pohari*
Da Hu	*Saraw*	*Chongai*
So So	*Shu*	*Ajo/by name*
So Da	*Shu*	*Abi/by name*
Da So	*Shu*	*Ajo/by name*
Da Da	*Shu*	*Abi/by name*
So So So	*Shutabla*	*Ajo/by name*
Da Da So	*Shutabla*	*Abi/by name*
So Da Son	*Shutabla*	*Ajo/by name*
Da Son Da	*Shutabla*	*Abi/by name*

Tertiary Kin:

Fa (e) Br Wi	*Ayong*	*Ayong*
Fa (y) Br Wi	*Asi*	*Asi*
Fa Si Hu	*Asa*	*Asa*
Fa Br So	*Khai/kojal*	*Khai/kojal* or by name
Fa Br Da	*Pai/nanao*	*Pai/nanao* or by name
Fa Si So	*Khai/kojal*	*Khai/kojal* or by name
Fa Si Da	*Pai/nanao*	*Pai/nanao* or by name
Mo Br Wi	*Ani*	*Ani*
Mo Si Hu	*Asa*	*Asa*
Mo Br So	*Khai/kojal*	*Khai/kojal* or by name
Mo Br Da	*Pai/nanao*	*Pai/nanao* or by name
Mo Si So	*Khai/kojal*	*Khai/kojal* or by name
Mo Si Da	*Pai/nanao*	*Pai/nanao* or by name
Wi Br So	*Pagen*	*Pagen/ mamai/* by name
Wi Br Da	*Pagrai*	*Pagrai/by name*
Wi Si So	*Pagen*	*Pagen/mamai* by name
Wi Si Da	*Pagrai*	*Pagrai/by name*
Hu Br So	*Pagen*	*Pagen/* by name
Hu Br Da	*Pagrai*	*Pagrai/by name*
Hu Si So	*Pagen*	*Pagen/by name*
Hu Si Da	*Pagrai*	*Pagrai/by name*
Hu Fa Fa	*Ajo*	*Ajo* (reciprocal)
Hu Mo Fa	*Ajo*	*Ajo*(reciprocal)
Wi Fa Fa	*Ajo*	*Ajo*(reciprocal)
Hu Mo Mo	*Abi*	*Abi*(reciprocal)

Wi Mo Mo	Abi	Abi(reciprocal)
Wi Fa Mo	Abi	Abi(reciprocal)
So Wi Fa	Beyai	Beyai(reciprocal)
So Wi Mo	Biyai	Beyai(reciprocal)
Da Hu Fa	Biyai	Biyai(reciprocal)
Da Hu Mo	Biyai	Biyai(reciprocal)

The data presented above were collected from the Tiwa villages of Amsai, Borrongkhoi, Magro and Makhaguri and concerns a *Kobai* situation (matrilocal Marriage). The terms applied to affines (in-laws) shed some light on the structure, revealing some symmetry between the paternal and maternal sides. Most remarkable is between father's sister's husband (*asa*) and mother's sister's husband (*asa*) and symmetrically between mother's brother's wife and father's sister (*ani*). The only exception is that the father's younger brother is not call *asa*, like the mother's younger sister's husband, but *tadai*. The implications of the use of Indo-Aryan terms like *mamai, sali, pohari, beyai*, etc. and Bodo-Garo terms like *ayong, ajo, asi, abi* etc. needs to be studied in greater detail which is beyond the scope of the present study.

Marriage:

In every society, marriage in many respects is one of the most important social institutions. The stability of society, to a great extent, depends upon this universal and primary institution. Marriage occupies a significant place among the social institutions of the Tiwa society. Tiwa marriages are called *lo churi*. Marriage is not allowed between members of the same clan who are grouped in one cluster called the *maharsha*. 'Mahar' in Tiwa means mother's relatives/kin and 'sha' meaning one.[6] Literally, *maharsha* means a kin group descended from one mother. According to B.K. Gohain[7] a *maharsha* usually consists of those kins who can trace their common descent through the female line, but in a more comprehensive sense, it also means a single clan or includes a cluster of clans. Among the Tiwa there are six *maharsha* namely Amsi, Khorai, Mothrong, Sagra, Puma, and Kholar.

The following table indicates the *Maharsha* and the clans that fall under each one.

List of Six *Mahars* and Clans:

Table: V

Maharsha	Clans
Amsi	Amsi, Amsong and Amphi
Khorai	Khorai, Hukai, Malang and Muni
Mothrong	Mothrong, Kosrong and Solong
Sagra	Sagra, Agari, Maslai, Melang, Tarphang/Darphang, Tamlong, Somsol, Kraikho, Lorom, Maloi, Tilar/Dilar, Khamli, Borong
Puma	Puma, Phamjong and Puru
Kholar	Kholar, Madar, Khajar, Madur, Radu, Ladur, Mithi, Lumphui and Markhang

The main function of the clan or the cluster of clans is to regulate the matrimonial relations; no marriages can take place between members of a clan or between members of the same cluster of clans (*maharsha*). For example Amsi and Amsong are two different clans but they represent one *marharsha*. Similarly, Maslai, Melang, Tamlong, Borong and Agari are five different clans but marriages between members of these clans are forbidden as they belong to the same *maharsha*. Thus, the Tiwa follow the rule of exogamy[8] in marriage and the members of the same clan and *maharsha* behave as brothers and sisters hence marriage between them is a serious offence. The rule of exogamy of clan cluster is strictly followed in the Tiwa society. Its violation is considered to be the highest offence a person can commit. In the olden days, this kind of offence was punishable by death or ex-communication from the village. Identification of members of the *maharsha* is one of the primary responsibilities of every parent. Children are made aware of their *maharsha* through their parents and other kin members.

B.K. Gohain[9] recorded three kinds of marriage among the Tiwa. They include (a) marriage through negotiation (b) marriage by mutual consent and (c) marriage by force. In the olden days the first type of marriage was very rare. The general residence pattern followed in Tiwa society is matrilocality, in which a Tiwa man after marriage relocates either to the parental house of his wife or at least to someplace in the vicinity of his wife's parental house. However, cases of a man bringing his wife to his parental home are not unknown among the Tiwa. This kind of marriage takes place only when a boy marries a girl from another village and brings her to his parental home. In this case, the boy's parents have to pay a bride price to the parents of the girl. The eldest maternal uncle of the boy, the *jelaraw* goes to the girl's house with *chu-lao*,[10] gourds of rice beer, areca nut, and betel leaves and fixes a date for the marriage. On the day of the marriage, the boy goes as a groom with his maternal uncle, elder brothers and some friends to the bride's house where the marriage takes place. The girl's parents provide a sumptuous meal to the bridegroom's party with rounds of *chu-magra* or rice beer. The bride price is paid to the girl's mother and the mother gives bell-metal plates and bowls to the girl. After the arrival of the bridegroom's party at the boy's house, the *jelaraw* asks for the blessings of their clan deity/ancestral spirits and explains to the bride about the rituals of the clan deity.

Marriage by mutual consent is a common practice among the Tiwa. The village festivals are an occasion for the young men and women to meet each other and to choose their future partners. When both the boy and girl take a fancy to one another and if they do not belong to the same cluster of clans (*maharsha*), the girl informs her parents about their intention of getting married. Then the boy is allowed to stay one night at the girl's house by her parent. In the following morning, the girl's parents inform the villagers that the boy has married the girl and will stay as a resident son-in-law (*kobiya*). In the evening the girl's parent invites the villagers and the friends of the son-in-law for the *ratey chiniwa*[11] ceremony. In this ceremony the elder maternal uncle of the girl, the *jelaraw or borjela* introduces the son-in-law (*saraw*) to the family members and informs him about the clan deities of the family. He then sacrifices a fowl in the name of the clan god (*khule mindai*) and advises him that to be respectful of family deities and to integrate with the family and be ready to play his role in the new family. After that, he is given a piece of cloth called *thenas*[12] from the bride's family. It is obligatory on his part to wear it on his first visit to his parent's house after marriage. When he moves about with the *thenas* on his body, people distinguish it as the boy's acceptance of uxorial residence in his bride's family. In case the boy comes from a different village, the information of his marriage is intimated to his parents through his friends and members of the *Shamadi* (bachelor's dormitory) of the girl's village. After one year the boy visits his parental home along with his wife and mother-in-law (*miw*) with *chu-lao,* areca nut and betel leaves and takes a meal there. Later in the evening, he goes back along with his wife and mother-in-law to his newly adopted home.

Although after marriage a boy goes to stay in his wife's parental house, he never severs his ties with the family of his birth. After the marriage, he becomes a *jela* or the representative of his family and the clan. He can not change his clan deity and continues to worship the clan deity in his parental home. His presence is essential in all the ceremonies associated with birth and death in his family of birth.

Another kind of marriage that used to be practiced among the Tiwa is marriage by force. In this kind of marriage, the boy is taken by force by young men from the girl's village and forced to enter into wedlock with the girl and to become a resident son-in-law in the girl's house. This happens when a boy develops intimacy with a girl of another village through meetings at different festivals or in the market and frequently visits the girl's house in the evening. In such cases, if the young men of the girl's village find that the boy is not serious about marrying the girl even after such intimacy, they forcibly take him to the girl's house and make him marry the girl. The boy has to accept his fate and later his parents are informed about the marriage. Separation and divorce in this kind of marriage cannot be denied as the marriage takes place without the full consent of the boy and the girl. Hence nowadays this type of marriage has declined among the Tiwa. In the case of divorce, usually, it is the male who takes the initiative. But divorces are generally rare,[13] and no compensation is paid to the woman and she remains in the house of her mother.

Child marriage or marriages at an early age are not practiced by the Tiwa.[14] Generally Tiwa boys marry between the age of twenty and twenty two years and a girl between sixteen to twenty years. Marital union is generally stable and monogamous.[15] Observations from our fieldwork at Amsai, Bormarjong, Morten and Tharakhunji village revealed no instances of divorce. Marital bonds last till the death of a partner. A.E. Heath[16] recorded that there have been no instances of a divorce from two to three generations among the Tiwa (Lalung) and consequently there were no rules related to divorce. From the foregoing discussion, we can assume that family life between husband and wife is quite stable among the Hill Tiwa.

Inheritance:

In the *Kobai* system, after marriage, a Tiwa couple constitutes a single household. The youngest daughter is called *shodya*. Normally she stays in her mother's house and looks after her parents. She is given a larger share of the family land than her elder sisters. While dividing the share of property among the daughters, the mother consults with her elder brother. Inheritance is strictly in the female line. The *Deodhai Asam Buranji*[17] recorded laws of the inheritance among the Tiwa in the mid-17th century during the time of the Ahom king Jaydhwaj Singha (1648-63). It states that among the *datiyalia*[18] (frontier people), women inherit the property and the king's son cannot become king, only the daughter's son can become king. The king's son has to work as a servant. Subsequently, in 1882, A.E. Heath[19] recorded that among the Lalung (Tiwa), in case, a man dies leaving behind his wife and mother then his wife inherits the acquired property and his mother inherits the ancestral property. In case a man dies and is survived by his mother and son, then all the property goes to his mother. If a man dies and leaves his mother, son and one daughter then the mother takes the hereditary property and the daughter inherits the acquired property, but the property remains with the mother till marriage. If a man dies and leaves two daughters and two sisters, then the sisters inherit the hereditary property and daughters share his acquired property. Similarly, if a woman dies and leaves behind a husband and mother, then the mother takes all the property. If a woman dies and leaves one son, one daughter and mother then the daughter inherits everything. In case a woman dies and leaves two sons and two daughters and two sisters, then the daughters divide the property among themselves.

In all the cases described above by A.E. Heath, we find no instance where a son inherits his father's or mother's property. In all circumstances, it was found that property was inherited either by mother, wife, daughter or sister. It is an indication that the Tiwa was a matrilineal society where women inherited property. During our fieldwork, we have found that generally, the youngest daughter (*shodya*) inherits the major share of the property in the family. However, if she decides to move away from her ancestral house, any daughter who lives in the parental house gets the major share.

In a traditional Tiwa family, the husband has no claim to the property. His main responsibility is to bear the economic responsibility of the family and to manage the household as an integrated economic unit. Though he becomes a member of the matrilineal family of his wife and lives in the house which belongs to his mother-in-law or his wife, his consanguine identity of birth is not merged in the clan of his wife. In his relationship with the parents-in-law, he is not equated by them with his wife's siblings. He is distinguished by them as *saraw*, which means the male who has married in the family and living as the husband of the daughter. The *saraw* refers to his mother-in- law as *niw* and father-in-law as *hu*. One of the important features of the *Kobai* system is that a resident son-in-law (*kobiya*) does not take any important responsibility in the rituals connected with his wife's clan deities. It is the *jelaraw* i.e. the wife's brother or maternal uncle or some other male member of her clan who performs the rituals associated with clan deities of the family.

Village Administration:

The study of village administration as a part of traditional institutions has attracted the attention of policymakers, researchers, and social scientists. It may be difficult to define and categorize traditional institutions into social, cultural, political and economic institutions since tradition in any given society is a composite whole. Traditions stand for time-honoured customs and respected beliefs.

According to a legend current among the Hill Tiwa that, in the olden days, the Tiwa people consisted of twelve clans who lived together for several centuries at Nukurikhunji.[20] They had village priests called the

Loro under whom the religious ceremonies were performed. During their stay at Nukurikhunji, they often fought among themselves over the right in the selection of the Pisai or the village elder's council and to gain dominance in village administration. Over time such internecine feuds caused organisation of clans into different groups. Subsequently, these groups moved out of Nukurikhunji and settled at various places. In this process, twelve villages came into existence. These villages were Amsai, Marjong, Amni, Rogkhoi, Makro, Lumphui, Mayong, Amkha, Amri, Sagra, Ligra and Amjong. It is important to note that, when the Tiwa meets their fellow tribesmen they generally identify themselves by the root village to which they belong. Even in case, they form a new village away from their root village, they would identify themselves by their original village. They use the suffix *wali* to denote their place of descent such as the Amsai-wali, Marjong-wali, and Rongkhoi-wali etc. signifying the particular root village. The Tiwa called these twelve villages as *krai binnung* or the root/original village. It has found that out of the twelve root villages, Amri and Ligra is no more in existence.[21] During our fieldwork, we traced a village by the name Bor-amri in the Kapili valley near Chapormukh under the Raha revenue circle in Nagaon district. Our informants told us that, according to an oral tradition the ancestors of Boramri had come down to the present area from the hills of West Karbi Anglong. From the description, we can assume that the present Boramri is an offshoot of the now-extinct Amri village. Presently the Assam government has created a development block in West Karbi Anglong after the lost village of Amri. As far as Ligra is concerned we could not find any village by this name. However, we could trace an oral tradition shared by the Tiwa people of Bherakuchi, Nibera, Bahtola and Bamfor village in Demoria area of the present Kamrup district which indicates that they are the descendants of the *Ligra-wali* people.

Presently four root villages namely Mayong, Amjong, Makro/Magro and Lumphui are located in the Ri-Bhoi district of Meghalaya under the traditional Khyrim chieftainship. Every year the representative of these villages offer their annual tribute in the form of a he-goat to the Khyrim chief at his official residence in Smit village near Shillong on the occasion of the Nongkrem festival held in November. The tradition suggests a cordial and age old socio-political relationship between the Tiwa and the Khasi.

Many of the Tiwa villages in the hills of Karbi Anglong, Nagaon, Morigaon and Kamrup district in Assam and Ri-Bhoi in Meghalaya, are the branches of the twelve root villages mentioned above. The Tiwa call the branches of the root villages as *phams*. The *phams* traditionally owe allegiance to the root village and identify themselves as a part of it. The *phams* must participate in all the important festivals of the root village and contribute both physically and financially. The following are the root villages and their offshoots identified in the course of fieldwork. However, there are many other villages both in the hills and plains that need to be studied on their affiliation with the root villages.

Table: VI

Root Village (*Krai Binnung*)	State/ District	Branch Village(*Phams*)
Amsai	Assam/West Karbi Anglong	Moro, Amsai Pisa, Chukuri Amsai, Mawlen and Punduri Makha
Bormarjong	Do	Sukuri Marjong, Khawra Krai, Mobai, Silangkhunji, Natral, Hadaw, Umbormon, Uthangkhunji, Murji Khunji, Deosal, Dabarghat, Pumakhunji, Khaplangkhunji, Bhulaguri, Sanisor, Amdoba, Mugaguri, Bhongraguri, Singum, Satpani and Kyanbat
Amkha	Do	Amdoba, Maslaikhunji, Amkhalam, and Kothiyatoli
Amri	Do	Boramri
Borrongkhoi	Do	Balikhunji, Tharakhunji, Rongkhoisa, Gomnasal, Gorkhunji, Andari Krai, Amsikhunji and Ashukhunji
Amni	Assam/West Karbi Anglong and Morigaon	Amnisa, Silchang
Ligra	Assam/Kamrup	Bherakusi, Nibera, Bahtola and Bamfor
Magro	Meghalaya/Ri-Bhoi	Phatmagro, Ulukhunji, Tiwa Jungthung, Silaguri, Khromkhunji, Khumrain Khora and Orlongshadali,
Amjong	Do	Amdubighat, Markongduba, Panbari and Tiami-Amjong
Lumphui	Do	Phitrisal, Dapsal, Krombaro and Tiami
Sagra	Do	Amphreng
Mayong	Do	No branch identified

S. Karotemprel stated, "…a Tiwa village is among the most closely-knit village set-ups that one can find among the tribes of Northeast India".[22] It is the centre of socio- religious and economic activities. It closely controls, monitors and determines every act of the Tiwa individuals. In a traditional Tiwa village, the village elders (*Pisai*) play a very important role. Their support and consent are necessary to undertake anything other than what is laid down by Tiwa customary laws and tradition. Without the consent of the *Pisai,* practically nothing can be done in a village.

The *Loro* along with eleven members of the council of elders in a village are collectively known as the *Pisai.* Other than the *Loro,* the members of the *Pisai* are selected from among the senior members of the village. Once selected the members of the *Pisai* continues to hold office till they die or get too old to do any work. If any member of the *Pisai* dies, his place is not filled until the next *Khelchawa*[23] festival that takes place once every five or six years. Being the head of the *Pisai* the *Loro* is also known as the *Pisai Mul.* The following are the twelve members of the *Pisai: Loro, Toloi, Phador, Shangot, Maji, Hadari, Barika Baro, Barika Pisa, Phayak Mul Kra, Phayak Mul Majowa, and two Phayak Mul Jokha.* According to tradition, each of the positions in the *Pisai* system except the *Loro* is distributed equally among the clans of a village.

Apart from discharging secular responsibilities such as the settlement of disputes and conferring punishments to offenders, the *Pisai* also actively takes part in all the religious functions of the village. They decide the date of ceremonies and carry forward the process of celebration. During the religious ceremonies, the *Toloi* oversees the preparation of the place of sacrifice. The *Phador* oversees the preparation of the place of sacrifice along with the *Toloi.* The *Sangot* is an important member of the *Pisai* who prepares the materials required for various religious ceremonies. On the other hand, the *Maji* and *Sangot* are responsible for the procurement of the animals and birds required for a religious ceremony. The *Hadari* is the personal assistant of the *Loro.* He has to assit the the *Loro* in the preparation of animal sacrifice and provide all other manual help to the *Loro* during religious ceremonies. Among the *Pisais,* there are four positions of *Phayak Muls.* They are appointed by the *Loro* to act as helpers during the religious ceremonies. According to tradition, anyone who is offered rice beer in a bronze bowl in the *Loro's* house is thereby appointed to the post of *Phayak Mul* and has to accept the responsibility.[24] They are responsible for cleaning, cooking, serving rice beer and curry during the religious ceremonies. The *Pisai* also includes two *Barikas* or messengers. They are responsible for conveying messages and collecting donations/contributions from the village. Thus appointed, the members of the Pisai need to be well acquainted in their given responsibilities and discharge them according to time-honoured tradition.

Besides the *Pisai*, another important person in a Tiwa village is the *Sarkari Gangbura* or the village headman. He is not a part of *Pisai* but occupies a significant position as he is appointed by the government. In the hills of Karbi Anglong, he acts as an agent of the Karbi Anglong Autonomous Council. Though he is not allowed to take an active part in any of the religious ceremonies, nevertheless his status is considered to be higher than that of a common villager. The main functions of a *Sarkari Gangbura* are to assist visiting government officials during the general census, election purposes, implementation of government schemes etc.

In a branch village or *Pham* the *Pisai* is composed of the village headman, the *Gangbura*, the *Tewri*, the *Barika* and the *Randhuni*. There can not be a *Loro*, *Toloi* or *Shangot* in a *Pham* as these offices are exclusively reserved for the root village. It is mandatory to inform the *Loro* of the root village when someone is appointed as a *Pisai* of its branch village.

The main function of the *Pisai* of the root villages is to conduct religious ceremonies. They also act as the overall in-charge of village administration. They not only look after the religious needs of the people but also act as an institution to maintain social harmony and peace. Under the leadership of the *Loro*, the *Pisai* disposes a majority of disputes both civil and criminal according to the customary law of the Tiwa society. Different types of punishments are awarded to the offenders. Fine is imposed in cases of disobedience of village social customs and rule. On many occasions, the *Pisai* acts as a jury to resolve petty criminal cases and disputes associated with land and property. The *Pisais* are the custodian of Tiwa customary law. While pronouncing judgments on different cases the *Pisai* may ask the advice of the *Sarkari Gnagbura*.

The Shamadi:

Studies on the bachelor or youth dormitory system occupied a significant place in clonial ethnography in North East India. Shakespear[25] studied the Mizo youth dormitory. Gurdon[26] talked about the dormitory system among the War clan of the Khasi tribe. He observed that the bachelor dormitory system is a Tibeto-Burman trait.[27] Endle[28] comented that once the bachelor dormitory system was prevalent among the Kachari in the past but all traces have disappeared. Hutton[29] also opined that this system was prevalent among the Kachari in Assam but it was discontinued due to cultural change.

Among the Tiwa, the youth group or *panthai khel* is a moving force behind the governance of a village. The *panthai khel* is centered on the village youth dormitory called the *Shamadi*. It is the most important socio-religious institution which is still prevalent among the Hill Tiwa.[30] The *Shamadi* system provides an opportunity for the Tiwa youth to develop a spirit of cooperation, responsibility and skills essential in all the stages of an individuals life. It is an indispensable part of the social and religious life of the Hill Tiwa. It is a seat of learning for the younger generation. They learn music, dance, handicraft and other essential facts of life at the *Shamadi*. The youth join the *Shamadi* at the age of twelve and remain as members of the institution until they attain the age of twenty-five years, that is, till they get married. The *Shamadi* is a rectangular hall of around 40/50 feet long and 25/30 feet wide. It is constructed on a wooden and bamboo platform raised five to six feet above the ground. The *Shamadi* is built in the centre of a village to facilitate easy access to villagers. Both the entry and exit points of the *Shamadi* have no walls. Floors are covered with split bamboos. Unmarried youth of the villages generally spend the night at the *Shamadi*. There is no restriction on married men sleeping in the dormitory. However, entry of the women is prohibited in the *Shamadi*. A managing committee known as *panthai khel* is formed to look after the affairs of the *Shamadi*. The three main functionaries of the *panthai khel* are named after the three main posts of the *Shamadi*, the *Shangdoloi, Shangmaji,* and Huruma. These three posts are collectively called as *Thamkhunda.* The entire *Shamadi* is divided into four un-demarcated parts, each with a specific purpose. The area in front of the *Shangdoloi* is called *Nomaji*. It is used for performing different ceremonies. The portion behind the *Nomaji* is called *Nukthi*. It is used for important discussions. There are two fire-places, the one which is meant for the village elders and guests and the other one is for the officials of the *Shamadi* (*panthai khel*). The firewood is stored under the raised platform in large quantity so that it lasts throughout the winter and the rainy season. The cross beam of the *Shamadi* is decorated with carvings of developed female breasts or *sho*. According to our informant[31], as the physical entry of women is restricted inside the *Shamadi*, the female breasts symbolises their presence in the *Shamadi*. Besides, geometrical designs, forms of animals and birds are inscribed on the posts of the *Shamadi* to signify their close association with nature.

Membership of the village *Shamadi* was compulsory for every boy of the village. A Tiwa boy enters the dormitory at the age of twelve and remains as an active member for the next twelve or thirteen years. During the *Khelchawa* festival, the leader of the *panthai khel* goes to the house of every eligible boy and informs about new recruitment to the *Shamadi*. Later in the evening, the mother of the boy goes to the village chief's (*Loro*) house where all the *Pisais* gather. She presents her son to the assembly and recites:

> *Respected village elders in compliance with your order which is the code of conduct of our tribe that the Shamadi should continue, I have come to present you one of your helpers, to whom you will give the necessary training and understanding in upholding our glory. I pray that you will always run the Shamadi with strict discipline and keep high its cause, do justice to all and extend help to the villagers, so that we may live and prosper in peace.*[32]

This procedure is repeated by the mother of every boy and may take a long time to complete. It shows the commitment of the boys' family towards the dormitory institution and its significance to the community life of the Tiwa society. The newly enrolled members are placed under the junior group known as *korkhiya-panthai*. He has to stay in this group for at least six years. During this period, he works under the strict supervision of the senior group known as the *khra-panthai*. He needs to bring water, firewood and take care of the requirements of the *Shamadi*. The junior boys sometimes arrange the beds for the seniors and do odd jobs that may be required of them in the *Shamadi*. The seniors make sure that the juniors strictly maintain the decorum of the *Shamadi*. The three most important leaders of the *panthai khel* of the *Shamadi* are the *Shangdoloi*, *Shangmaji* and *Huruma* selected from among the senior group. The main function of the leaders of the *panthai khel* is to maintain discipline among the boys. As the head of the *Shamadi*, the *Shangdoloi* is responsible for the overall supervision of the institution. He always takes the lead in all community work. The *Shangdoloi* is assisted by a deputy called *Shangmaji* who is in charge of the ceremonial attire and musical instruments used by the boys on various festive occasions. The next most important official of the *Shamadi* is the *Huruma*. He is responsible for the maintenance and cleanliness of village paths. He also needs to look after the water sources from where drinking water is obtained. Moreover, the *Huruma* has to keep a watch on the maintenance of decorum in the entire village during festive occasions. He is assisted by a deputy, the *Hurumaphali* in discharging various duties.

Among the Tiwa, the boys must not sleep outside the dormitory. One may stay at home on account of illness but must return to the *Shamadi* soon after recovery. In case a boy refuses to come to the *Shamadi* without any sickness or valid reason, the leaders of the *panthai khel* goes to the boy's house and ask him to rejoin. If he disobeys the leaders of the *panthai khel*, the case is forwarded to the *Pisai* of the village. Generally, the parent of the boy is fined even after the boy agrees to go to the *Shamadi* for violation of social norms. However, if they refuse to send the boy to the dormitory, then it is considered to be a serious offence for which the whole family is ostracized and forced to leave the village.

After spending six years in the junior group, a Tiwa boy becomes eligible to enter into the senior group. This promotion is an important event in the *Shamadi* system as it is also the time of retirement of the senior group and selection of a new *panthai khel*. It is also the time to demolish the old *Shamadi* and construct a new one. The Tiwa can marry only when they are in the senior group. In case a senior boy continues to remain unmarried, he merely sleeps as usual in the *Shamadi* but lives a retired life keeping himself aloof from the other boys. He also does not receive any respect and services from the junior boys.

According to traditional belief, the *Shamadi* is the place where the Lampha Raja resides. Among the Hill Tiwa, the Lampha Raja is considered to be one of the benevolent deities. Hence the *Shamadi* is no less than a holy shrine for the Tiwa. The prayer (*khruma*) chanted at the ceremony held before procurement of the main post for the *Shamadi* is noted below:

> *oi' pha deuri hadari ta'*
> *etha porlena*
>
> *tao konong oi Sharipahai Sharikora*
> *lampha Rajane pale chinge etha*
>
> *jella lanina ta' porlena porbena oi deu*
> *Sharipahai Sharikora...*

Free Translation

> (Oh father *Dewri*, *Hadari* (village elders)! Today we all pray for Sharipahai Sharikora (Tiwa deity) and request permission to construct the *Shamadi*; the residence of Lampha *Raja*(deity) and to select the village elders).

The above prayer shows the significance of the *Shamadi* in the socio-religious life of the Tiwa people. In the *Shamadi* the Tiwa boys receive training and motivation essential for a traditional way of life at a crucial age. Dormitory life makes them understand and acquire knowledge about community life. It enables them to take part in social activities, thereby allowing them to improve their personality and leadership quality. The *Shamadi* also provides security to the village. The presence of the youth in the middle of the village provides a sense of security to the villagers. Moreover, the *Shamadi* is a common meeting place for the villagers where important decisions regarding socio- religious issues are taken. Hence, the above discussion indicates that the *Shamadi* system among the Tiwa emerged to maintain the spirit of community life and to prepare and train the youths for their future life. The *Shamadi* has contributed towards social integration and group solidarity and streghthened social control among the Tiwa.

The Origin of the *Shamadi* System:

The exact origin of the Shamadi among the Tiwa is not known. However, according to the traditional beliefs, it is the place where the Lampha *Raja* resides.

In the prayer, mentioned above we find that the villagers asking permission from their high god Sharibai Sharikora to construct the house of Lampha Raja where village elders will be selected. It is worthwhile to mention that the council of elders or pisai of a Tiwa village are selected and installed at the *Shamadi*. It indicates the importance of the *Shamadi* in socio-religious matters. Hence the *Shamadi* system can be attributed to the society formation and religious beliefs of the Tiwa. The *Shamadi* system may be as old as the Tiwa society itself.

Shyamchoudhuri opined that the avoidance of incest could be a cause of the origin of the *Shamadi* system. He referred to Sinha's suggestion about the Garos tribe where the main aim of the dormitory system is to safeguard against the probable incest, as in their cultural development the unconscious oedipus and incest feeling are comparatively strong. But it is not possible to say that the avoidance of incest or keeping down the unconscious oedipus by separating the boy from the night stay at his home is the main motivation behind the dormitory organization among the Tiwa. As avoidance of incest is not a peculiar psychological phenomenon of the tribal society. It is a common social trait in all societies. The carvings of the developed female breasts on the crossbeams of the dormitory perhaps emanate from sex repression. But it may also be argued that frank and bold displays of sexual parts of the female body in these carvings are intended to free the inmates from inhibition. Hence the theory of incest cannot be approved altogether.

If we look at the main aim and objective of the *Shamadi* system we discern that, it is a place where all boys get training and motivation essential for a traditional way of life at an important age. The dormitory life makes them understand and acquire knowledge about the community life of the village. It enables them to take part in social activities thereby exposing themselves for improving personality and leadership quality. The *Shamadi* also provides security to the village. The presence of the youths in the middle of the village provides a sense of security to the villagers. Moreover, the *Shamadi* is a common meeting place for the village where important decisions regarding socio-religious aspects are taken. Hence, the above discussion indicates that the *Shamadi* system among the Tiwa must have evolved to maintain a spirit of community life and to prepare and train the youths for their future life.

Traditional Polity Formation:

According to Surajit Sinha,[33] "...chiefdom is a development of the segmentary tribal system to a higher level of integration. It provides a centralised direction to a hitherto tribal society and gives greater productivity without necessarily any change in technological methods."

The Tiwa considers the Gobha *Raja* as their traditional chief and his influence among this tribe is discernible on the occasion of the annual fair called *Jonbil* held near Jagiroad. On the occasion of this fair, the Tiwa of both the hills and plains gather on a certain date in January every year and pay tribute to their chief and offer nominal tax in the form of agricultural products such as turmeric, chili pepper, yam, arum etc. Moreover, on special occasions such as the *Sogra, Yangli, Wanchuwa, Khelchawa* festivals, it is customary to take permission from the Gobha *Raja* before its commencement. The Gobha *Raja* also validate the selection of the politico-ritual chiefs of the root villages (*Loro*) by offering them turbans (*Phaga*), ceremonial jackets (*tagla*) and purification water (*ti- khumur*). The above description about the Gobha *Raja* suggests that he bears a significant position in the socio-political life of both hills and the plain Tiwa.[42] Today Gobha *Raja* is still a major figure in the socio-economic and cultural set up of Kolong and the Kapili valley. His importance can be gauged from the fact that the Jonbil festival which has been held over many centuries at the initiative of the Gobha *Raja* considers being a binding factor for the Tiwa people.

The Gobha principality which took its name from a place called Gobha or Kova is located in the submontane area of central Assam.[34] The Tiwa people still owe allegiance to the Gobha *Raja*. He is still considered to be an important figure in the socio-cultural setup of the Tiwa society.[35] In the Ahom chronicles (*Buranji*), the Gobha *Raja* is described as the Garo[36] chief under the Jaintia *Raja*. In the *Jayantia Buranji*[37], the Gobha *Raja* repeatedly appears as a facilitator of the diplomatic relations between the Ahom and Jaintia state. Francis Hamilton reported that "the 'Jayantia' territory up to the river Kolong was under the petty chiefs of the Garo nation, who still maintained their ancient custom."[38] He must have been referring to the Tiwa chiefs of Gobha, Nelli, and Khola which were very influential during the pre-colonial period.[39]

A.J. Moffat Mills[40] recorded that a small *'pergunnah'* close to the hills of the 'Jayantia' state was ruled by *Salung Rajas*. The report further states that these *Salung Rajas* belong to the 'Cossiah' (Khasi). He also observed that these *Rajas* had severed their relationship with the Khasis by the time he came to know about them. From Mill's observation, it is clear that he was referring to Gobha, Nelli and Khola principalities which were ruled by the Lalung or *Salung Raja*.

Since the early 17th century, Gobha is mentioned as an important center of trade between the Ahom and the Jaintia kingdom.[41] Moreover it was an important transit point used by the Ahom and the Jaintia for diplomatic purposes. On some occasions, the Gobha *Raja* had to act as the special envoy of the Jaintia state to restore friendly relations with the Ahom.

From the 17th to 19th century, the Gobha principality played an important role in the politics of Kollong and Kapili valleys before it was finally annexed to the British Empire. For these three centuries, two major powers the Ahoms in the plains of Brahmaputra valley and the Jaintia in the present eastern Meghalaya plateau competed with each other to extend their political control over the kingdom of Gobha. During the early part of the 19th century, even the Khyrim *Raja* tried to establish authority over it. R.B. Pemberton[43] recorded that there was a feud between the *Raja* of 'Khyram' and Jaintia for political control over the Gobha principality which had a serious impact on the latter's prosperity. The reason behind the endeavor to win over the Gobha principality by the Ahom, Jaintia and Khyrim *Raja* to their respective sides shows the strategic importance of this kingdom. Multiple factors encouraged the competing powers to exercise their control over this kingdom. Gobha was one of the passes kwnon as '*Nauduar*'[44] on the southern side of the Brahmaputra valley. It was marked as a strategic location and transit point between the Jaintia hills and the Assam plains. Hence it was extensively used not only to maintain diplomatic relations but also as a trading point between the hills and the plains. It has also significant commercial importance because of its strategic location. The Ahom envoys had travelled through Gobha to Jaintiapur, the capital of the Jaintia state to accomplish various diplomatic missions for several centuries.[45] During the early years of British colonization in North East India this route was extensively used to maintain an effective line of communication between Assam and Bengal. David Scott, the first British agent in North-East India marched through this route in early April 1824, from Sylhet to Assam, with an escort of three companies of the 23rd Native Infantry regiment under captain Horsburgh.[46]

According to R.B. Pemberton[47] the Gobha division of the Jaintia territory was under the supervision of the *Raja* of Nurtung (Nartiang). The area of this division was about 860 square miles, bounded on the north by the river of Kullung (Kolong). The total population was roughly estimated around one lakh which according to him was too much exaggeration of actual numbers. He further recorded that this area was inhabited by a race of unarmed low-landers, similar in every respect to those who occupy the adjoining districts of Assam.

Presently, Gobha is a revenue village under the Morigaon district of Assam. There are four villages in Gobha proper namely, Khamar Khunji, Sonai Khunji, Gorong Khunji and Gaolia Khunji. Local traditions tell that at Kharmar Khunji, the local blacksmith used to make weapons for the Gobha *Rajas* soldiers and they also knew the art of making canons. At Sonai Khunji, the local goldsmith used to design ornaments for the royal families and at Gorong Khunji there were many quarries from where the miners used to extract iron ore. In Gaolia Khunji the Gobha *Rajas* palace was located where soldiers used to guard it against external enemies.[48]

The Assamese *Buranjis*[49] and the British reports[50] suggest that Gobha was a vassal principality under the Jaintia King. The *Jayantia Buranji* gives an account of the Gobha as a transit point for the exchange of diplomatic correspondence between Jaintia *Raja* and the Ahom kingdom. Hence, due to its strategic and economic importance, the Gobha territory had been a bone of contention between the Ahom and the Jaintia kingdom.

The *Asam Buranji*,[51] recorded that Gobha was attacked by the Jaintia prince Pramata Rai in 1658 and destroyed four of its villages for refusing assistance against his grandfather Jasamanta Rai, the king of Jaintia. After this incident, the Gobha Raja sought protection from the Kachari king Jaso Narayan Deb but the Ahoms intervened and demanded that since they are the paramount power and hence they should seek their help. Eventually, the Gobha chief took refuge under Ahom king Jaydhwaj Singha who settled his people at Khagarijan in the present Nagaon district of Assam.[52] Subsequently, during the reign of the Ahom king Rudra Singha, the Ahom army used the Gobha territory as their base camp to launch attacks against the Jaintia kingdom.[53] During this invasion with the active logistical support of the Gobha Raja, the Ahoms defeated the Jaintia kingdom and captured Ram Singha, the king of Jaintia. He was kept as a prisoner at Gobha by the Ahom soldiers for several days before taking him to the Ahom capital at Gargaon. This territory was extensively used as a strategic point both by the Ahom and the Jaintia to gain political advantages. On one hand, the Jaintia territory in the hills centered at Nurtung(Nartinag) was very dependent on the market[54] located in the Gobha area which was well connected with both the Kolong and Kapili valleys and on the other hand the Ahoms needed to have the Gobha territory for their advances into the Jaintia Hills.

According to B.K. Gohain,[55] Gobha was an important and large state of the Tiwa founded by Langbar. In a later period, it was divided into several smaller principalities, namely, Nelli, Khola, Sahari, and Mayang etc. He also stated that the over landtrade route to Jaintiapur via Sylhet to Bengal lay through Gobha and because of this, it commanded a very important position in the internal and external trade of Northeast India.

During the initial periods of British rule in North East India, Gobha played an important role in resisting the British domination over Assam. 'Chuttur Sing'[56] the contemporary Gobha chief posed a serious threat to the British designs by waging war against them. In 1832 after deafeating a company of British forces, his men captured four British officials and used them as prized victims for sacrifice at his traditional place of worship. The British reports mentioned that out of the four officials, three were immolated at the shrine of Kali situated within the boundaries of Gobha.[57] The capture and killing of the three British officials had a profound impact on both Gobha and the Jaintia state. Soon after the incident, the British authorities demanded to surrender the persons responsible to the Jaintia *Raja* Rajendra Singh as the Gobha chief was considered to be under his political control. However, even after two years of constant pressure from the British authority, the Jaintia king refused to entertain the demand and claimed that he had no control over the chief of Gobha.[58] Rajendra Singh repeatedly claimed his innocence and denied any involvement in the issue. After the failure of constant bargaining and pressure tactics, on 15th March 1835 the Sylhet Light Infantry under the command of Captain Lister, took formal possession of Jaintiapur, the capital of the Jaintia Kingdom and annexed it to the British Empire.[59] A few weeks later Gobha was also annexed by the British in April 1835 by a detachment of the Assam Light Infantry.[60] Gait, recorded that after the annexation of Gobha territory in the plains, the Jaintia *Raja* was unwilling to retain the hill areas and the British placed it under the political officer of Khasi Hills.[61] The plain territory was placed under the Dantipar *Mahal* in the newly created 'Nowgong' district. Later it was converted into a revenue village and the deposed chief of Gobha was made the Mauzadar. After independence, Gobha remained as a revenue village. However, the Gobha chiefs who used to be the Mauzadar during the British rule were removed.

The Gobha king even after losing the political authority soon after its annexation to the British Empire continued to maintain its traditional political influence over the Tiwa population both in the plains and the hills. The Tiwa people continued to offer their annual tribute to the Gobha chief in the form of one he-goat from each village, agricultural produce and firewood for annual religious ceremonies. According to the chief priest[62] of the *Deosal Thaan,* at the time of the creation of Meghalaya state in 1971, the Khyrim *Raja* requested the Gobha chief Konsing Deo Raja to join the Meghalaya state. He was invited by the Khryrim *Raja* for a discussion on the issue. However, the king put a condition that Gobha Raja should be recognized as the legitimate head of the Tiwa people and all the officials of the Gobha *Raja* should be given a government job. He also claimed that fifty percent of the revenue earned by the Khyrim state should share with Gobha *Raja.*

The Tiwa believe that the chief of Gobha has a divine connection. The legend regarding the birth of the first Tiwa king has found in two different versions. According to one version as recorded by G. C. Sharma Thakur,[63] the war between Drikpati and Dakshin resulted in the loss of their king. The depressed Tiwa prayed to Lord Mahadeo for a king. In response, Mahadeo along with his consort Parvati visited the Earth. During the visit but one drop of Siva's bodily fluid fell on a lake near the Tiwa habitation. Soon it was swallowed by a *mali* fish (*lebeo calabasu*) and in course of time, a male baby was born from the fish. The Tiwa took care of the boy and later made him the chief. This same story was recorded by L. Gogoi[64] with a slight variation. According to this version, a baby girl was born who came out of the womb of a fish, the ancestress of Gobha lineage (*Hari Kongri*). Both these stories are popular among the Plain Tiwa regarding the origin of the Gobha king. The story mentioned above no doubt was created to give the Gobha king a divine origin. According to Philippe Ramirez[65] beyond the classical Hindu model of Siva's semen engendering a royal or divine figure, a particular pattern that needs to be kept in mind is the Gobha *Raja's* origin from a princess born out of a fish. Interestingly a similar legend is also recorded in the *Jayantia Buranji*[66] which talks about a fish caught by a Garo from where a young girl emerged and married 'Nortengia Garo'. Subsequently, a boy was born from their union who became the first Jaintia king.

According to the second version, the ancestor of the Gobha *Raja* was born out of a stone at a place called Thinimoslong or Timowflong. He was born in the Malewa Khul(Clan) and named *Soddonga Raja*. His successor was also known by the same name. According to the story, after staying for several years at Thinimoslong the Tiwa king moved to Amsai and settled there. The legend further states that at Thinimoslong the Jaitha *Raja* (Jaintia) was born from the ground and the Khrem[67] *Raja* (Khasi king) was born from a hollow tree and thus these three political figures are considered as brothers. In this version of the story, there is some similarity with the origin myth of the Jaintia king. The reference to *Soddonga/Suttanga* as a prominent figure in both the Tiwa and Jaintia story undoubtedly tells about the parallel origin of both the Jaintia and Gobha *Raja*. The exact location of Thinimoslong is uncertain. However, from the story, it must certainly be a place where the Tiwa and Khasi-Jaintia people once coexisted. Sharma Thakur[68] recorded that this place is a natural lake in the present West Karbi Anglong district of Assam. However, according to the Hill Tiwa, Timowflong/Thinimoslong is a hillock situated between the ancient borders of the three (Tiwa, Khasi and Jaintia) kingdoms. It is believed to be a triangular in shape where the source of the river Killing is situated. The Hill Tiwa believe that the twelve megaliths at 'Kutusi Mokoidharam' not far from Thinimoslong, standing right on the trail down from Nartiang (Jaintia Hills) show the significance of political relationship between the ruler of Khyrim and Gobha. Some Hill Tiwa explained that in the olden days whenever the "Khrem Raja" (Khyrim) pay a visit to the Gobha *Raja*, he used to a take rest at this place where a market was held.[69] It is believed that via this trail the Khyrim *Raja* used to travel to attend the *Jonbil* fair hosted by the Gobha *Raja* every year in January. Until recently the Khyrim Chief was the chief guest on the opening day of the *Jonbil* fair. A documentary[70] produced by the Tribal Research Institute, Assam in 1985 filmed the incumbent of Khyrim state Balajied Sing Syiem as the chief guest of the *Jonbil* fair of 1984. Such a narrative shows the close socio-economic and political relationship between the Tiwa and Khasi-Jaintia people.

From the above discussion, it appears that the ancestors of the Gobha principality were born in the present Jaintia Hills district of Meghalaya. According to the Hill Tiwa, the Gobha *Raja's* ancestors lived at Amsai before one of them decided to migrate to the plains. There is a tradition among the Tiwa of Amsai to offer sacrifices and invocation to the ancestors of the Gobha *Raja* on the occasion of the annual *Sogra* ritual. They called the former courtyard of the Gobha Raja as *phujasal*. According to an oral tradition still current among them, Botsing *Raja* moved the capital of Tiwa kingdom from Amsai to Gobha apparently because of an omen. The story furthers narrates that there was a tall tree in front of the palace *(Rajano)*[71] at Amsai. One morning the *Raja* noticed that a crow made a very unfamiliar noise which sounded like *Kova..Kova*. From then onwards, the *Raja* heard the same noise every morning. The *Raja* was so swayed by the unusual sound that he thought it was a prediction about a place where he must go. Accordingly, he decided to leave Amsai and settled at Kova. In course of time, the name *Kova* became Gobha. According to the priest (*Loro*) of Borrongkhoi village, the ancestors of their village came along with Botsing *Raja* from Amsai while he was going down towards the plains. During this journey, some people settled at Balikhunji and Sukuri Amsai (now called Sahari Amsoi). These villages are on the east of Amsai on the trail towards the Kapili valley. The *Jayantia Buranji* referred to the Gobha principality several times as an important transit point during the reign of Ahom King Pratap Singha(1603-1641 A.D.) which suggests that Botsing *Raja* must have migrated from Amsai to Gobha several centuries before the 17th century.[72]

Even after migrating to the plains, the Gobha *Raja* continued to govern the Tiwa in the hills. As a mark of solidarity between the people of hills and the plains, an annual fair was initiated by the subsequent Gobha chiefs on the bank of *Jonbil* (the Moon Lake) near Jagiroad. A significant aspect of this fair is that, on the first day, the people of hills and the plains exchange their agricultural products such as yam(*thagong*) turmeric(*huldi*), ginger(*hajing*), chili(*chalu*) tuber(*tha*), pumpkin(*khumdai*)etc. with dry fish (*naflang*), sweet pan cake (*pitha*), rice powder (*wanguri*). Philippe Ramirez,[73] who has worked extensively on the ethnography of the Assam-Meghalaya borderlands states that the *Jonbil* fair is famous among the Assamese as being one of the last places where the system of barter was done. During the fair, the Gobha *Raja* along with his nobles collects nominal taxes in kind from the participants who come for bartering. According to the Hill Tiwa, the exchange of goods between them and their counterparts in the plains strengthens the age-old relationship. Thus the *Jonbil* fair has a very important historical significance. According to the present incumbent of the Gobha principality Deepsing Deo-Raja, their ancestors had begun this fair in 15th century to bring the people of the hills and plains together to celebrate their bond of brotherhood.

Figure 1. Present *Raja* Gobha, Deepsing Deo Raja (first in the line) *(credit, Facebook.com)*

Figure 2. Barter of Commodities at Jonbil *mela* *(credit, facebook.com)*

Figure 3. Members of *Panthai Khel* (*Credit, Leander Lumphui*)

Figure 4. Members of *Pisai*, the Village Elders Council (Amsai Village)
(Credit Leander Lumphui)

Figure 5. A Tiwa woman initiating the process of weaving *(credit Raktim Patar)*

Figure 6. Tiwa women during Wanchuwa festival *(credit, Bipul Bordoloi)*

Notes and References:

[1] John Scott, *Oxford Dictionary of Sociology*(4th edn.), Oxford University Press, 2014, pp. 357-58

[2] S. Karotemprel, *A Brief History of the Catholic Church among the Tiwa*, Shillong, 1981, p. 7.

[3] B.K. Gohain, *Continuity and Change in the Hills of Assam*, Omsons Publication, New Delhi, 2006, pp. 88-89.

[4] V. Len Kholar, *Tiwa Matpadi* (1st edn.), Tiwa Sahitya Sabha, Jagiroad, 1995, p. 207

[5] www.thoughtco.com/kinship online access on 15/07/2017

[6] V. Len Kholar, *op. cit.*, p.104.

[7] B.K. Gohain, *op. cit.*, (2006), pp. 82-83.

[8] According to www.merriam-webster.com (access online on 12/01/2017), marriage outside of a specific group especially as required by custom is called exogamy. Such groups are usually defined in terms of kinship rather than in terms of politics or territory.

[9] B.K. Gohain, *The Hill Lalungs*, ABILAC, Guwahati, 1992, p. 43

[10] *Chu-lao* is an important vessel which bears a lot of significance in Tiwa socio-religious life. It is made of dry bitter gourd. Serving rice beer in the *chu-lao* is considered to be an honourable act among the Tiwa. In all the religious ceremonies the *chu-lao* is indispensable.

[11] In this ceremony the bride groom is introduced by the maternal uncle of the girl to village elders.

[12] *Thenas* is a long piece of cotton fabric. It is wide and richly embellished with motifs. The decorative patterns which adorn the cloth are intricate in terms of design and execution. *Thenas* are regarded as a status symbol of the wearer. It is obligatory to wear *thenas* during festivals.

[13] B.K. Gohain, *op.cit.*(1992), p. 44

[14] A.E. Heath, *Tour Dairy of the Sub-divisional officer of Jowai for the month of November and December 1882*, Assam State Archives, Guwahati, p. 24

[15] S. Karotemprel, *op.cit.*, p. 8

[16] A.E. Heath, *op.cit.*, p.24

[17] S.K. Bhuyan(ed.), *Deodhai Asam Buranji* (reprint), DHAS, Guwahati, 2001, pp. 96-98

[18] *Datiyalia* is an Assamese word meaning frontier/border. The Ahoms used this word to denote people living on the fringes of their kingdom. The Ahom chronicles referred to the Tiwa as *datiyalia*.

[19] A.E. Heath, *op. cit.*, pp. 23-24

[20] According to the Hill Tiwa Nukurikhunji was a village inhabited by one-hundred and eighty families. They say that, it was located on a hill near Bormarjong village

around 40 kilometers from Jagiroad in the Amri development block of West Karbi Anglong district of Assam.

21   Exact reasons for the disappearance are not known. Many people believe that due to short distance migration to escape from epidemic and shifting cultivation might have contributed for the disappearance of the village. During our fieldwork we found that in the recent past some Tiwa village have shifted to new locations to escape sickness and unnatural death that had occurred in their previous location.

22   S. Karotemprel, *op. cit.,*,p.8

23   The *Khelchawa* festival marks the demolition of the old youth dormitory and inauguration of a new one. It is the time when the youth body or the *panthai khel* gets its new leaders to manage the *Shamadi*, the youth dormitory of the Tiwa. In the past the *Khelchawa* festival was held after a gap of five or six years. But due to the expenses involved and paucity of resources, some villages take up to twelve years to have a *Khelchawa* festival.

24   U.V. Josh, *Tiwa-English Dictionary,* Don Bosco Centre for Indigenous Culture, Shillong, *2014,* p. 418

25   J. Shakespeare, *The Lushei Kuki Clans,* Macmillan, London, 1912, p. 52

26   P.R.T. Gurdon, *The Khasis*(reprint), Low Price Publication, Delhi, 2010,p. 32

27   *Ibid.,* p. 194

28   S. Endle, *The Kacharis,* Macmillan, London, 1911, p. 11

29   J.H. Hutton, *The Sema Nagas,* Macmillan, London, 1921, p. 121

30   The *Shamadi* system among the Plain Tiwa has disappeared on account of social and cultural changes.

31   The informant is a resident of Amsai village.

32   N.K. Shyamchaudhury, N.N. Das, *The Lalung Society,* Anthropological Survey of India, Calcutta, 1973, p. 29

33   Surajit Sinha(ed.), *Tribal Polities and State Systems in Pre-colonial Eastern and North Eastern India,* K.P. Bagchi and Company, Calcutta, 1987, pp. x-xi.

34   On several occasions the *Jayantia Buranji* describes about the meeting of Ahom officers with the Garo living near the Kolong and Kapili valley. However there are no traces of Garo in that area. Therefore, the people whom the Buranjis recorded as Garo were the Tiwa people who have been occupying the Kolong-Kapili Valley for the last several centuries.

35   The Hill Tiwa still considers the Gobha Raja as a respected personality. In order to get rid of any sins that are committed in the villages they go to the Gobha *Raja* to collect holy water or *ti-khumur* in order to purify the sin.

36   The term 'Garo' has been defined by Philippe Ramirez in his book *People of the Margins,* Spectrum, Guwahati, 2014, p. 149, in the following words, "…Garo in ancient Assamese/ Bengali means 'up-lander." the Ahom *Buranjis* referred to those living in the uplands or in the hills as 'Garo'. Perhaps the term 'Garo' was used by

the Ahom chronicles to denote the people living in the hill areas in the southern part of their kingdom.

37 S.K. Bhuyan(ed.), *Jayantia Buranji*, DHAS, Guwahati, 2012

38 Francis Hamilton, *An Account of Assam*, (3rd ed.), DHAS, Guwahati, 1987.

39 In the *Jayantia Buranji*, Gobha, Nelli and Khola are mentioned as minor principalities under the Ahoms on the Ahom-Jaintia border. The Raja of these three principalities played a significant role in maintaining diplomatic relations between the Jaintia state and the Ahoms in the pre-colonial era.

40 A.J. Moffat Mills, *Report on the province of Assam*, Guwahati, (2nd edn.), 1984, p. 207.

41 *See* S.K. Bhuyan (ed.), *Jayantia Buranji* and *Deodhai Asam Buranji, op. cit.*

42 S.K. Bhuyan (ed), *op.cit.* (2012), pp. 78-79.

43 R.B. Pemberton, *Report on the Eastern Frontier of British India*, DHAS, Guwahati, 3rd impression, 1991, p.229.

44 The term '*Nauduar*' was collectively used to imply the Nine *duars* or the passes in the south of Brahmaputra.

45 S.K. Bhuyan(ed.), *op. cit.*, 2012.

46 Alexander Mackenzie, *The North-East Frontier of India* (reprint), Mittal Publications, Delhi, 1979, p. 218.

47 R.B. Pemberton, *op. cit.*, 229.

48 Sarbananda Rajkumar, *Itihase Soaura Chakhata Bachar*,Banlata, Dibrugarh, 2000, p. 486.

49 *See,Jayantia Buranji, Deodhai Asam Buranji, op. cit.*

50 Alexander Mackenzie, *op. cit.*, p.219

51 S.K. Dutta(ed.), *Asam Buranji*(1648-1681) 2nd edn., DHAS, Guwahati, 1991, pp.12-13

52 Edward Gait, *A History of Assam* (7th edn.), Guwahati, 1997, p. 119

53 *Ibid.*, 166-67

54 During our field study we have recorded a story associated with the Gobha megaliths that suggests that the Gobha Raja used to have a market at that place.

55 B. K. Gohain, *op. cit.*(2006), p. 60

56 Chattro Sing as pronounce by the hill Tiwa.

57 For further details, *see* R.B. Pemberton, *op. cit.* p. 221, E.A. Gait, *op. cit.*, pp. 306-307, Alexander Mackenzie, *op. cit.*, p.219.

58 E. Gait, *op. cit.*, pp. 290-291.

59 R.B. Pemberton, *op. cit*, p. 229.

60 Alexander Mackenzie, *op. cit.*, p. 219.

61 E. Gait, *op. cit.*

62 Anil Konwar, age 55 yrs, the assistant priest of the Deosal Siva temple.

63 G.C. Sharma Thakur, *The Lalungs (Tiwas)*, Guwahati, 1985, p. 3.

64 Lokeshwar Gogoi, *Tiwa Sanskritir Ruprekha*(Pratham Khanda), Tiwa Mathonlai Tokhra, Nagaon, 1986,

65 Philippe Ramirez, *op. cit.*, p.145.

66 S.K. Bhuyan, *op. cit.* (2012), pp. 1-8.

67 The hill Tiwa pronounce Khyrim as '*Khrem*'.

68 G.C. Sharma Thakur, *op. cit.*, p. 4.

69 Philippe Ramirez, *op. cit.*, p.146.

70 Documentary on *Jonbil Mela*, directed by Upakul Bordoloi, produced by Tribal Research Institute, Guwahati, 1985.

71 Traces of the *Rajano* or Gobha Raja's palace are still visible on a hill adjacent to Amsai village. According to the village elders, earlier their village was located under the slopes of the king's palace. Later, it was abandoned due to the migration of their chief to Gobha. As a mark of respect to their king the Tiwa of Amsai begins the annual *Sogra* and *Langkhun* ceremony at the former courtyard of *Rajano*. Until recently the Gobha Raja used to visit Amsai to meet the council of elders (*Pisai*) once in a year.

72 See Jayantia Buranji op. cit., for details about the role of Gobha Raja and his envoys in maintaining diplomatic relationship between the Ahoms and the Jayantia state.

73 Philippe Ramirez, *op. cit.*, p.141

CHAPTER VI

Traditional Economy

Agriculture has been the principal means of livelihood of the Tiwa since the pre- colonial period. Paddy is the main crop of Tiwa agriculture both in the hills and plains. The distinctive eco-cultural features of the Tiwa economic organisation lie in its corporate activities and inter-dependence between the families living within a village for the satisfaction of basic needs of food, clothing and housing.

In the hills of North East India, *jhum* or shifting cultivation is not merely a slash and burn method of agricultural practice; it encompasses all aspects of a community life. For the Tiwa this method of cultivation has been woven into the fabric of their life-style and cultural milieu.[1]The calendar for shifting cultivation starts with '*Mahak*' (January/February) when the plots are selected for cultivation by the households. The Tiwa called their *jhum* field, *maiha* (*mai*-paddy, *ha*-field). The households have their plots occupied with the consent of the village council of elders (*Pisai*) for shifting cultivation and the head of the family decides which plot is to be selected for that particular year's cultivation. Selection of the plot depends on the *jhum* cycle as rejuvenation of the soil is necessary after a plot has been cultivated and left fallow for a period of four to six years. The land left fallow for regaining the fertility of the soil is called *hagari* (*ha*-land, *gari*-left over). At the end of the *jhum* cycle the family returns to the same plot of land cultivated by it at the beginning of the cycle. If the household decides to clear a fresh plot of land unoccupied before, then the head of the family approaches the head of the village council of elders (*Loro*) with rice beer in *chu-lao*.[2] Subsequently, the matter is discussed among the elders and permission is generally granted if the desired plot of land falls within the jurisdiction of that village. In case of dispute over the occupation of a desired plot of land by two different families, settlements are made through discussion among the maternal uncle or elder brother of the claimant of the families. The outcome of the discussion depends on the evidence of the previous record of cultivation on a disputed plot of land. If both the families fail to resolve the issue, then they approach the *Loro* and the *Pisai* of their village for a final resolution. The *Pisai* pronounce their judgment based on arguments forwarded by both the contesting parties. While taking a decision, the *Pisai* follows the Tiwa customary laws on land disputes as a precedent.

In the following month of '*Phagun*' (February/March) and *Chit* (March/April), the jungle is cleared before the monsoon starts. The trees and shrubs are cut down and the entire plot is allowed to dry for thirty to forty days. Just before the rain starts, the plot is set on fire on a day fixed by common consent of the co-villagers. Great care is taken to avoid the spread of fire in the jhum fields of the neighbouring villages. After firing, ash-covered burnt soil is thoroughly hoed and the soil is mixed with the ash so that it is not washed away by the initial rains. In mid-April after the *Phidri-Chongkhong* ceremony takes place the sowing of seeds is done. Carefully preserved seeds (*khodya*) of paddy and other vegetables are selected for sowing. Usually eight to ten grains of paddy are put in a hole dibbled with a pointed stick (*khadi*). Both men and women work together while sowing the seeds. Men dig the holes starting from one end of the plot, followed by women who drop the seeds and cover them with earth. The Hill Tiwa grow several crops simultaneously in a plot of land. Chili, cucumber, gourd, egg-pant, sesame, arum, sweet potato and yam are grown in a common plot. Sowing activities takes about a month to complete. Shoots of yam and arum are generally planted at the end of the sowing season. During our fieldwork, the Hill Tiwa informed that before the 1970s, they used to cultivate cotton for weaving varieties of cloth for both men and women. However, with the growth of markets in the vicinity of their villages, they have abandoned the practice of cotton cultivation as the machine-made yarns are comparatively cheaper than the cotton yarns produced domestically.

Mixed cultivation requires more sustained and greater attention and care than the wet rice cultivation in the valleys. The crops are weeded twice, in July and late September. A watch has to be kept over it day and night. Two huts are built for this purpose; a bamboo hut on treetops (*thunggi*) and a small shed on the ground (*maru*), used for guarding in the day. At night a small fire is lighted near it. The man who guards the jhum field at night stays on the higher hut from where he can easily observe elephants, wild pigs, deer, or porcupine.

The Hill Tiwa also practice wet paddy cultivation on the narrow valleys of Umswai, Morten, Bormarjong and Ulukhunji. They called their wet paddy field as *fadar*. Unlike their plain counterparts, the Hill Tiwa does not use ox driven iron ploughs. Rather they use hoe for preparing the soil which begins by the end of March and continues for about a month. After hoeing and irrigating the soil, water buffalo are allowed to tread on the soil to make it smooth; when there is no buffalo loosening of the soil is done by hoeing only which is very strenuous. The process of wet paddy cultivation is more labour intensive than the *jhum* cultivation as both men and women need to hoe the field in the absence of a plough. Although the normal practice is to transplant seedlings from the seed-bed (*thuli*) which is prepared well ahead of transplantation, some varieties of seeds are planted directly in the irrigated fields. Direct sowing of seeds is undertaken on the onset of the monsoon in June. But transplantation is done from June onwards and continues till September. The following are the verities of paddy grown by the Tiwa in their wet paddy fields (*fadar*); *Pathisara, Tiningrimai, Chngnimai, Jogamai, Maikhara, Paramai, Mikhirmai, Choloukkuthimai* and *Labramai*. In our opinion, they must have learned wet rice cultivation from their plain counterparts at a much later period. This can be authenticated by the fact that when William Griffith, visited the Umswai valley while he was going to Upper Assam in the early 1830s, he did not record anything about wet rice cultivation there. He mentioned that 'onswye' (Umswai) valley was a marshy land and full of wild elephants that trod up the land.[3] However when, A.E. Heath, the Sub-Divisional Officer of Jowai visited Umswai in 1882, he did record the extensive use of the valley for rice cultivation. He commented about the high rate of rice production over that valley by the Tiwa inhabitants.[4]

Paddy is harvested in November and December. Unlike their plain counterpart, the Hill Tiwa do not use the ox or human feet for separating the grains from the stalks of paddy. Rather they use a three to four feet long wooden or bamboo stick to separate the seeds by threshing which they called *maipothala*. For this purpose, a small plot of land is selected in the paddy field. Men and women in separate groups of seven or nine, take turns at separating the grains from the stalks with the sticks. The process continues till the entire paddy has been threshed. The grains are then gathered in a heap and fanned with a winnow to blow away broken stalks. After this, the paddy grains are collected in baskets of straw called *maipur*, each containing 30/35 kilograms of paddy. The Hill Tiwa does not construct a separate granary to preserve their paddy. Instead, they keep the *maipur* or the straw basket inside the *nukthi* (part of the traditional house *nobaro*) along the walls.

Bamboo is another useful economic commodity. During our fieldwork, we have observed almost every household growing a bamboo grove in the backyard. It is an all-purpose material equally useful in house building, basketry, fencing the homestead etc. once a grove has been raised, it thrives by itself. The homestead groves supply bamboo for the repair and building of small sheds for storing firewood, piggery, and fences around the huts and garden. With the establishment of a paper mill in the 1980s at Jagiroad, bamboo became a profitable commodity. Because of the growing demand for bamboo, they have started growing bamboo in the *jhum* fields. With the opening of the *jhum* field, they would plant bamboo saplings in the periphery and it would transform into a bamboo grove within three to four years. Another important commercial crop that the Hill Tiwa produces is the broomstick. Because of its high demand outside North East India, the people of the West Karbi Anglong have been growing broom sticks since the early 1990s. It yields a good amount of money to the farmers. According to our informant,[5] they would plant the broom saplings along with the paddy and other vegetables on the same plot of land used for *jhum* cultivation. These saplings become small grove from the second year onwards and can be harvested for the next five to six years. At present, each Hill Tiwa household cultivates broomstick which has become the major source of income.

Besides these perennial crops, seasonal vegetables such as gourds, arum, legume, ginger, sweet potato, cucumber, chilli and fruits like pineapple, pears and jack fruit are grown in the homestead land for domestic consumption. In recent years, some Hill Tiwa have started selling these crops on a commercial basis in the weekly markets. During our fieldwork, we have observed the cultivation of cinnamon and betel leaf (pan) for commercial purpose in the Tharakhunji, Borrongkhoi and Hadaw villages.

Apart from the *jhum* and wet paddy cultivation, the rearing of *eri*-larva has been a major household work till the 1980s. The Tiwa use the *eri*-cocoon to produce traditional clothes, *thanese, thana, phaga* etc. in the loin looms. *Lac* was another important material that was produced in large quantities. *Eri*-cocoon and *lac* were the most important products that were in high demand in the plain markets. The Hill Tiwa used to barter these commodities in the weekly markets at Phuloguri and Nelli in exchange for dry-fish, salt and iron implements until the 1960s. The Ahom *buranjis*[6]recorded that the Phuloguri market was established in the early 17[th]century by the Jaintia king under the supervision of the Gobha chief to facilitate trade between the people from the hills and the plains. During the pre-colonial period, Phuloguri, Demoria and Gobha were centers of trade between the people of the plains and the tribes of the southern hills like the Tiwa, Karbi and Khasi-Jaintia.[7]

Corporate activity:

Both men and women play a significant role in the traditional Tiwa economy. *Jhum* cultivation involving the slashing and burning of fields, sowing of seeds, weeding and harvesting, is a joint activity with both the sexes working in tandem. Their oral tradition indicates the equal participation of both male and female in agricultural activities. According to one legend, the twelve male and female progenitors of the Tiwa cultivated for twelve years day and night with hoe and spade at Langrathuli, Makha Koja, Bortongkhara, Tumra Mathi and Sera Siri.

Among the Tiwa, there are two types of corporate activity; the *hadari khel* and *kil*. In the Tiwa language, *hadari* means volunteer and *khel* means a working group. It can be termed as a volunteer working group. *The hadari khel* is a group of individual volunteers who help out in collective activities of the village as well as those of individual families in agriculture activities such as hoeing, seeding, and harvesting. There are two types of *hadari khel*, one a male group called *mewa khel* and a female group called *margi khel*. Membership is open to any adult male and female in the *hadari khel*. It has no group leader and every member share equal responsibility within the group. There is no specific rule regarding the number of members in a *hadari khel* and there may be several groups in a village. Membership may vary from five to fifteen depending upon the individuals willing to work. These groups offer their physical labour to needy families in exchange of paddy. On the day of work, the host family needs to offer lunch and a lot of rice beer (*chu-magra*) to the *hadaris* while at work. At the end of the year, the paddy collected by the *hadari khel* is sold, and the profits are held in reserve. After three years, the money is utilised for procuring bell-metal plates which are distributed equally among the members of the *hadari khel*. On the day of distribution of these plates, the members celebrate the closing ceremony with a feast. With this celebration, the group is disbanded and new groups are formed and individuals are free to join any group.

The *kil* is a system of reciprocal help at the individual level. According to this system when a villager works in the field of his/her co-villager then in return the co-villager also reciprocates with an equal amount of labour. No wages are paid in this system. The only requirement is that the host family offer lunch and rice beer on working days.

The *hadari khel* institution which has played a significant role in the corporate activities of the village has now disappeared from many villages. Both the *hadari khel* and *kil* systems were once important socio-economic institutions that strengthened the bonding of Tiwa villages as one unit. However, with the entry of the market economy and cash transactions, now-a-days instead of calling the *hadari khels*, families hire individual labourers on a daily wage payment system for undertaking agricultural or other kinds of work.

Traditional Land Measurement System:

The Tiwa follow their traditional system of land measurement to calculate the area of cultivation both for the *jhum* field (*maiha*) as well as wet paddy fields (*fadar*). This land measurement system is popularly known as *Jari* system. The unit of measurement is given below;

> *Kawling = It is a 12 feet long bamboo pipe. Khadisha = 2 Kawling (2x 12 = 24 feet)*
> *Tanglenger = a rectangular area covering 1 Kawling (12 feet) x 7 Kawling (84 feet) = 1008 square feet.*
> *Tangsha= A rectangular area of 6 Kawling (72 feet) x 2 Kawling (24 feet) =1728 square feet.*
> *Jari= 12 Tangsha (12x1728 =20736 square feet)*

The traditional land measurement system is still in practice. However, most of the people now prefer to measure their land on basis of the *bigha*[8]system as it has been the standard unit of land measurement in Assam. With the privatisation of land holdings and the issue of land documents, the traditional *jari* system is gradually disappearing.

Measurement of Time:

According to our informant[9] before the introduction of the modern watch, the Tiwa used the Sun to measure time. They divided the whole day from sunrise (*salnawa*) to the sunset (*salkowa*) into different parts. Each part has a specific name and function. The period between sunrises to sunset is called *tinsha*. Half a day from sunrise to noon is called *salphungsha* and quarter of the day is called *salikhensha*. There are two *salikhensa* in a day, one in the morning and another in the evening before sunset. *Salikhensha* is considered as a resting time for the farmers working in the *jhum* field. Wages are measured according to the amount of work accomplished within the specific time.

Plain Tiwa Economy:

In the plains, the Tiwa share a common agricultural pattern with other Assamese communities. For the cultivation of paddy, the land is utilised during the wet months between April and September. On the first April shower, a summer variety of paddy called *ahu* which takes about three months to ripen is sown. But it is not cultivated extensively because it thrives in pre-monsoon rain on lands generally lower in elevation than those on which the winter paddy commonly known as *sali/hali* is grown. According to Sharma Thakur,[10] *hali* or *sali* paddy cultivation was introduced by the Bodo groups of people. In the Tibeto-Burman Bodo-Garo language, *ha* means soil and *li* mean wide. Thus paddy grown in wide land is called *hali/sali*. There is another variety of summer paddy, called *bao* which is grown on low lands where water accumulates during rains or floods.

Hali is the principal winter crop that requires a longer time than the other varieties of paddy cultivation. The seedlings are transplanted from the seedbed in the high monsoon for two months from late July to early September. The ears come out after the monsoon and the crop is ready for harvesting in winter. It is reaped before the *Magh Bihu* festival sometime in the middle of January.

Harvesting is done from November to late December. For separating the grains from the stalks, the Plain Tiwa applies a different technique from their hill counterpart. They spread the paddy out in the open courtyard of the house and bullocks or cows tied in pairs with loose loops at the end of the rope, are made to tread upon the paddy stalks until the grains are separated from it. The empty ears and stalks are then collected and heaped on one side of the house compound. The Plain Tiwa store their paddy in a separate granary built on stilts. Its walls and floor are thickly plastered on the inside to protect from moisture.

Food and Drink:

Rice is the staple food of the Tiwa. They eat non-vegetarian food which includes meat, fish and egg. Pork and chicken are their special delicacies. Dry fish procured from the weekly markets in the plains are used in almost every curry. The chrysalis of the *eri* silkworm is also a delicacy for both the Tiwa group. They do not eat beef and consider its consumption as unethical thus forbidden. Similarly, cow milk is also not a popular drink among the Tiwa. According to our informant[11] in the olden days they used to cook in bamboo tubes and banana leaves and small bamboo tubes were used for drinking water and rice beer. Subsequently, they used earthen pots for cooking. Now-a-days they use steel made utensils for cooking as well as eating and drinking.

Rice beer is as important as food in Tiwa society both in the hills and plains. The popular drink of the Tiwa is called *chu-magra* or rice beer. Every Tiwa household in the hills as well as in the plains brews rice beer mainly for domestic consumption and to entertain guests. Now-a-days some families sell rice beer to co-villagers which have become a subsidiary income for the family. The *chu-magra* is made by fermenting broken rice grains which they get as a by- product. Since only broken rice is used in brewing beer, it does not affect the householder's requirement of rice as a staple food. The *chu-magra* has both social and religious significance. *Chu-magra* offered in *chu-lao* is considered to be the most honoured act. In every social gathering such as marriage, birth or death ceremonies it has the most significant place. Among the Tiwa, it is customary to use *chu-magra* in all religious functions. Without its offering no religious ceremony is complete. Its importance can be gauged from the fact that every village has a plot of community land where paddy is cultivated for brewing rice beer during religious functions. According to Sharma Thakur,[12] any guest whoever visited a Tiwa house during the 1950s had to drink *chu-magra* as the act of refusal was considered as disrespect to the host. The Christian Tiwa does not brew rice beer at their house but most of them consume it.

Animal Husbandry:

Besides cultivation, animal husbandry is one of the important components of traditional Tiwa economy. Among the Hill Tiwa, except cattle, other animals like pigs, goats, and fowls are reared for domestic consumption and religious ceremonies. They build separate shelters for pigs, goats and chickens within the house compound. It provides a good source of protein as well as a means of income in times of need by selling them in the market. In the course of fieldwork at some villages of Umswai and Morten area, water buffalo herds were seen. The Hill Tiwa use the water buffalo to tread the soil for cultivation in narrow valleys at Morten, Umswai and Bormarjong.

During our fieldwork, we have not found any Hill Tiwa village where cow is reared. There may be two reasons for this: 1.Unlike other animals like the pig, fowls and goat the cow is not a part of religious sacrifice. 2. Cows are not an important component of *jhum* cultivation. Absence of the cow among the Hill Tiwa implies that they were primarily *jhum* cultivators who have adopted wet rice cultivation from their plain counterparts in the recent past. It is to be noted that the Hill Tiwa instead of using ox driven ploughs, use water buffalo to tread the soil for wet rice cultivation. A. E. Heath recorded in 1882, that the Tiwa does not rear cows because their religion forbids it. Besides religion, other factor that may explain the absence of cow among them is probably because the consumption of milk is not an integral part of their daily diet. During our fieldwork, we have found that milk is not a popular drink among the Hill Tiwa.

Fishing:

Fishing is an important economic activity of the Plain Tiwa. Collective fishing expiditions has become a part of their social life. Fish provides a healthy diet and it is an everyday delicacy for them. However, fishning is not a popular economic activity among the Hill Tiwa. It may be because there are no big water bodies such as rivers and marshy areas in the hills to procure freshwater fish. In place of fresh fish they prefer fermented or dried fish (*naflang*) in their daily diet. It is used in every recipe of traditional food of the Tiwa both in the hills and the plains. It has also found an important place in the funerary rituals.[13] Both men and women take an active interest in fishing especially during the slack season when agricultural activities are reduced. Community fishing at different ponds during the *Magh Bihu* and *Bohang Bihu* festivals is a significant event among the Plain Tiwa. They use various implements and traps for fishing. These implements are made of bamboo and wood. Some of the fishing implements that are used by the Plain Tiwa are *jakoi, khaloi, sepa, polou, juluki, khoka,* etc.

Hunting:

Hunting wildlife or feral animals is most commonly done by humans for food, recreation, to remove predators that are dangerous to humans or domestic animals or for trade.[14] Hunting of wild animals has been an important economic activity of the Tiwa. According to our informant, the main purpose of hunting in the olden days was to procure food and to protect their *jhum* fields from wild animals especially the wild boar and monkey. He stated that hunting was never done as a recreation activity as the Tiwa considers wild animals as important as humans. It can be gauged from the fact that Mithi and Hukai clan consider the Tiger as their totem. Besides the Tiwa give special offerings to tigers which they call as *Misa-Raja* or *Bag-Raja* before the commencement of the agriculture cycle and invoke them not to harm humans and domestic animals.

The Tiwa has developed several implements to catch different wild animals. These hunting tools are made of bamboo, wood and locally available materials. Horsing Kholar[15] has listed eighteen hunting tools that were used by the Tiwa. These include *Shikta*, a kind of trap to hunt deer, *Musi Chele* a trap made of bamboo and cotton thread to catch small animals like rabbit and mongoose etc. *Rangthap* is a trap to catch rodents; *Morong Kodar* is a cage type trap used for catching fox and leopard. The Tiwa used *Tingri Morong* to trap monkeys. Some other traps are, *Sibar, Tandal Sumu, Sanggu Sumu, Thagap Sawa, Hada Sawa, Tohola Sawa, Kat Chuwa, Hagri Sawa, Chal, Pathuli and Warap.* The design and trigger mechanism in these hunting tools suggest their technical knowledge of using naturally available materials for hunting. Our informant further stated that hunting has considerably reduced among the Tiwa in the last few decades on account of the government ban on the hunting of wild animals. He also commented that the younger generation hardly know much about the manufacture of hunting tools as it is no longer in practice.

The following are the type of tools used by the Tiwa for hunting wild animals:

List of Hunting Tolls:

Table: VII

Name of the Tool	Materials for Manufacturing	Animals
Shikta	Bamboo, wood and cotton thread	Deer
Musi Chele	Bamboo and bark of *odal* tree (*Sterculia Villosa Roxb*)	Rat, Wild Cat, Mongoose, Water Hen,
Pla Chele(bow and arrow)	Bamboo, bark of *odal* tree, Iron	Any animal and bird
Rangthap	Bamboo, wood	Deer and Rabbit
Morong Kodar	Bamboo, wood	Wild boar, leopard, bear and fox
Tingri Morong	Bamboo	Monkey
Sibar	Bamboo, wood and vine	Rabbit, wild cat and Mongoose
Tandal Sumu	Wood and bamboo	Monkey
Sanggu Sumu	Wood and Bamboo	Monkey
Thagap Sawa	Wood, bamboo and vine	Monkey
Hada sawa	Bamboo	Wild birds
Tohola Sawa	Wood and bark of *odal* tree	Rabbit, rat
Kat Chuwa	Bamboo	Deer and other antelopes
Chal	Nylon	Leopard, deer and monkey
Khangri Sawa	Iron	Fox and deer
Chathhi	Wood and iron	Deer, wild boar and other small animals
Pathuli	Bamboo, *eri* silk thread	Wild birds and other small animals
Warap	Bamboo	Rodents

Weaving:

Weaving is an essential part of the household activities of Tiwa women. S.K. Chatterji commented, "Weaving of cloth on simple loom is one of the main characteristics of the tribes belongs to Indo-Mongoloid". The Tiwa women are expert weavers; they prepare their garments at their residences on loin looms. It is also referred to as back strap or body tension loom. They also use natural dyes to colour their dresses. Women of both the hills and plains produce cloth domestically. The Tiwa has a specific dress both for men and women. The main dress of a Tiwa woman is *kasong, phaskai, joskai, thanes,* and *nara* and for men *tagla* and *thana*. According to our informant, till the 1970s, the weaving of cloth was done by women with *eri* yarn and locally produced cotton yarn. During our fieldwork, we have witnessed a few households in Amsai village where women still rear *eri* cocoon and produce *eri* yarn for weaving. However, production of cotton has been abandoned due to the emergence of machine-made yarns in the local weekly markets. According to N.K. Syamchaudhuri & Das[16], weaving of *eri* silk is common among all Bodo (Tibeto-Burman speaker) tribes of Assam. It is an ethno-cultural speciality by which they can be distinguished from almost all other tribes of Assam. They state that, the whole process of rearing the cocoon, spinning and weaving is a laborious and long-drawn one. It takes a woman about six months to make a wrapper, *Kachong* of *eri* silk from the spinning of the yarn, to the weaving of the cloth which she has to do along with her other domestic work.[17] S. Endle[18] writes that *eri* rearing and manufacture of *eri* cloths was one of the chief industries and a profitable one among the Kachari. For the Tiwa *eri* was not only used for weaving cloth but was also an important item of trade. According to our informant, the Hill Tiwa exchanged *eri* cocoon, castor seed, and sesame for pottery and iron implements such as hoe, sickle, knife etc. in the markets located in the plains until the 1960s.

Improvement of communication and easy access to cheap yarns in the markets has drastically reduced the use of hand-spun cotton yarn. Earlier cotton was cultivated in the hilly slopes for domestic use. The emergence of markets in and around their habitation has led to the extinction of cotton cultivation. Initially, it was two Plain Tiwa girls from Nagaon district of Assam who came to the Bormarjong village as daughters-in-law (*pohari*) who introduced the use of the modern hand loom and taught its usefulness to other women. During our fieldwork, we have observed both handlooms and loin looms at Tiwa houses in Bormarjong, Amsai, Borrongkhoi and Ulukhunji villages. However, they are not using the hand made cottonj yarn. All the yarns used in these looms are procured from the weekly markets at Umswai and Nelli.

In the olden days the Tiwa men wore only two pices of cloth. They used to shave above their forehead high up and the remaining hair was gathered into a knot at the back of the head. The upper body was covered by *tagla* and the lower part was covered with a small piece of white cotton cloth called *thana* to cover their male genital parts. The *thana* is a loin cloth that covers the male genital parts. The cloth is allowed to pass between the legs and coming up behind it wraps around the waist with the end tucked in under the folds at the back. The other end is allowed to hang in front like a small apron. The normal length of a *thana* varies between 330 c.m. and 350 c.m., while the breadth varies between 30 c.m to 35 c.m. or more. The length of the fringe is around 11 and 15cm. Both the ends of a *thana* are adorned with few strips of coloured threads. The *Thana* protects their private parts and gives agility to move faster in the hills. During our fieldwork, we have observed a few old Tiwa individuals that use the traditional dress (*tagla* and *thana*) in daily life in different villages. The younger males do not wear *thana*. They prefer to use the wrapper (*phali*) around their waist and shirts on the upper body while performing day to day activities. Now-a-days jeans and cotton trousers have also become a part of their everyday dress. The *tagla* in the old days was different from that of the modified one. It was a sleeveless coat weaved in such a manner that it leaves the neck and the arms of the wearer bare. It was very short and could cover only up to the ribs of the wearer. However, the long warp threads constituting the fringe were allowed to swing so loosely in front and back that the garment did not appear too short to reach the buttock of the wearer. It protects their chest from excess heat and cold. From the 1990s the traditional *tagla* has undergone changes in terms of shape and size. Nevertheless, according to Tiwa custom, it is mandatory to put on the traditional dress consisting of *tagla* and *thana* during festive occasions.

Notes and References:

1. B.K. Gohain, *The Hill Lalungs*, ABILAC, Guwahati, 1992, p. 30
2. *Chu-lao* is made of dried bottle gourd and integral part of all social and religious ceremonies.
3. William Griffith, *Journals of Travels in Assam, Burma, Bhootan, Afghanistan and the Neighbouring Countries* (ebook), reproduced by Les Bowler, 2005, p. 30
4. A.E. Heath, *Tour Dairy of the Sub-divisional officer of Jowai for the month of November and December 1882*, Assam State Archives, Guwahati p. 23.
5. He is a resident of Hadaw village in West Karbi Anglong.
6. See S.K. Bhuyan(ed.), *Jayantia Buranji*, DHAS, Guwahati,2012
7. *Ibid*, pp.17-18
8. According to www.easycalculation.com (online access on 12/12/2017), *Bigha* is a traditional term used in the measurement of land in India. It does not have a standard size and varies from state to state. In Assam one *Bigha* is equal to 43560 square feet surface area.
9. The information on the traditional way of calculating time was collected from Ton Maslai, age 55 years, a resident of village Pundurimakha.
10. G.C. Sharma Thakur, *The Lalungs (Tiwas)*, Guwahati, 1985, p. 23
11. The informant is a resident of Amsai village
12. N.K. Shyamchaudhury, N.N. Das, *The Lalung Society*, Anthropological Survey of India, Calcutta, 1973, p.22.
13. Curry mixed with dry fish is offered to the deceased before the funeral takes place.
14. www.wikipedia.org online access on 17/10/2017 at 10.30.pm.
15. Horsing Kholar, *Tiwa Rawe Sikgarune Sonjuli*, Tiwa Sahitya Sabha, Jagiroad, 2006.
16. N.K. Shyamchaudhury, N.N. Das, *op. cit.*, p. 17.
17. *Ibid*.
18. S. Endle, *The Kacharis*, Macmillan, London, 1911, p. 19.

CHAPTER: VII

Continuity and Change

In the previous chapters, we have discussed issues related to the origin, migration and settlement patterns of the Tiwa. We have also brought out the religious aspects of both the Hill and the Plain Tiwa and have dealt with various socio-political institutions. This chapter will examine aspects of continuity and change in the socio-cultural and economic facets of Tiwa society.

It is generally held that whenever changes are taking place in culture, the material aspects of life change at a faster rate, than the non-material aspects.[1] Change is the law of nature; like most things in the world, society also undergoes changes of various types and seldom remains static. There are three basic theories of social change: evolutionary, functional and conflict theories. The main propounder of the evolutionary theory such as Auguste Comte, L.H. Morgan, Emile Durkheim and Herbert Spencer believed that human societies evolve in a unilinear way.[2] According to them, social change meant progress towards something better. They saw changes as positive and beneficial. According to them, all societies pass through the same sequence of evolutionary stages to reach the same destiny. To them, the evolutionary process implied that societies would necessarily reach new and higher levels of civilization.[3] The structural-functional theory of social change has been strongly advocated by several sociologists, particularly by Tallcott, Parsons and Merton.[4] According to them, every social system has two aspects, one structural and the other functional. A structure is an arrangement/unit for the performance of functions. The function is the consequent of the activities of structures. All the structures are closely related to each other and all the functions are interrelated and interdependent. Change in one leads to changes in others. Each structure serves its function and at the same time helps others to function. Functional theorists are concerned with the role of cultural elements in preserving the social order as a whole. Functionalists see society as a system in equilibrium. If some external force disrupts the equilibrium of the society, there takes place a counter force for maintaining the social equilibrium.[5] Conflict theorists maintain that, since a society's wealthy and powerful ensure the status quo in which social practices and institutions favorable to them continue, therefore change plays a vital role in remedying social inequalities and injustices.[6]Although Karl Marx accepted the evolutionary argument that societies develop along a specific direction, he did not agree that each successive stage presents an improvement over the previous stage. Marx noted that history proceeds in stages in which the rich always exploit the poor and weak as a class of people. Only by socialist revolution led by the proletariat (working class), explained by Marx in his 1867 *Das Capital*, will any society move into its final stage of development: a free, classless, and communist society.[7]

In *English Social History*,[8] Trevelyan writes "Social change moves like an underground river, obeying its own laws or those of economic change, rather than following the direction of political happenings that move on the surface of life." It is a fact that all societies are characterised by both continuity and change. Continuity is maintained by social controls particularly by the methods used in child-rearing and education which transmit the accumulated social heritage to the new generation. M.N Srinivas[9] provided a social anthropologist's view of social change in modern India. He gave theoretical bearings as to how social changes have been brought about through 'Sanskritisation', 'westernization' and 'secularization' and their connectedness. On the issue of social change, Ember writes[10],

> Some of the shared behaviors, beliefs and values that were common at one time are modified or replaced at another time. In every society, there are some conditions that pave the way for social change. Most important are the growth in knowledge and occurrence of social contact and social conflict with other groups. The impetus for change may come from within the society or from

without. From within, the unconscious or conscious pressure for consistency will produce culture change if enough people adjust old behavior and thinking to a new one. Change can also occur if people try to invent better ways of doing things. Changes in a society may also be stimulated by the change of external environment and contact with other societies. Migration may also contribute towards the change of food habits and way of life in a new habitat.

Haimendorf,[11] analysed the process of change among the tribes of Arunachal Pradesh and Andhra Pradesh that had occurred due to their contact with people who migrated to their areas. He gave the example of the Gond tribe who become the worshiper of the Hindu deities rather than their tribal deities due to the teachings through schools. It was influenced by contact with government officials and traders from outside their territory. Moreover, educational development and information/ knowledge about new things may also generate changes in a society. Other factors that influence and stimulate changes in a society may include modernization, technological development and government policies. Any society that exists today consists of traditions that have been handed down from one generation to another and the changes that have occurred with the progress of time to cope with the changes in time and space. In this context, Eric Hobsbwarm stated, "The belief that 'traditional society' is static and unchanging is a myth of vulgar social science".[12] As he rightly pointed out that up to a certain point of change a society can remain 'traditional' because the mold of the past continues to shape the present.[13]

Factors of Change among the Tiwa:

Several factors have contributed to the socio-cultural changes among the Tiwa. One of the factors is the growth of transport and communication in the Hill Tiwa area. Construction of roads connecting Ulukhunji, Umswai, Morten etc. in the West Karbi Anglong district during the 1960s brought about a lot of change in many aspects of Tiwa society. It facilitated the easy movement of Tiwa people and frequent interaction with other communities. Before the setting up of the Public Works Department (PWD) office at Umpanai there was no market in the Hill Tiwa area. According to Bangthai Bordoloi,[14] the Hill Tiwa used to visit Umsning along the Guwahati-Shillong road at a distance of 45 kilometers and the weekly market held at Nelli[15] once in a week at a distance of about 35 K.M. from Amsai. The Hill Tiwa would go to Nelli located in the plains along the National Highway No. 37 on Sunday and spent the night in the makeshift sheds. Next morning they would exchange their produce such as lac, castor seeds, sesame *eri-* cocoon, vagetables for pottery, iron implements, salt, dry fish, kerosene oil etc. with the local traders. As there was no introduction of money economy in the Hill Tiwa area before 1960s, they had to depend wholly on the mercy of the plains traders for getting the proper value of the commodities exchanged.[16] The establishment of the Assam government's Public Works Department office at Umpanai in1965 resulted in the setting up of a weekly market at Umswai by some Bengali traders from the plains which in turn opened the flood gates for free interaction of the Hill Tiwa with the people of the plains. The introduction of a market around their habitation not only brought changes in the social system but also heralded a transformation of their economic life following the change from barter to the money economy. The introduction of government offices brought better road communications and made the traditional Tiwa villages' more accessible. It facilitated frequent and easy contact with the outside world.

Another factor that contributed to social change is the growing economic condition. Before the 1960s, the Tiwa economy was largely dependent on *jhum* cultivation and limited trade through the barter system. However, the introduction of a market economy and the cultivation of bamboo and broom during the 1990s on a commercial basis largely improved the economic condition of the Hill Tiwa. It encouraged the Tiwa youth to procure motorbikes and cars that facilitated travel and communication with other areas. Subsequently, during the early part of the 21st century, the entry of modern gadgets like television and mobile phones in the Tiwa villages brought about new ideas among the new generation of youth. With access to Bollywood movies and TV serials, new ideas and philosophies are influencing the youth and the traditional way of life.

Another very important factor that has a considerable impact on the Hill Tiwa society is modern education. Till the 1960s there were very few lower primary schools in the entire Tiwa inhabited areas in the West Karbi Anglong district. According to our informant, during the 1960s there were very few Tiwa who had a school education as there were few schools in and around Tiwa villages. The few that existed were located at a considerable distance from most Tiwa villages. Hence the number of students enrolled in schools was very poor. Only a few Christian Tiwa studied in schools run by missionaries. He further stated that the children would learn their basic life skills, like making of various bamboo products, hunting traps, musical instruments and *jhum* cultivation under the guidance of the village youth dormitory (*Shamadi*). The oral accounts indicate that formal education was not a necessity for the Tiwa as the learning process for survival was institutionalised in the *Shamadi* system. Moreover, limited number of schools and the distance between school and village also contributed to the under-development of education among the Tiwa during that period. However, since the 1980s, under government initiatives, a good number of schools were established in almost all the major Hill Tiwa villages. Nevertheless, there was limited enrollment in these schools as most of the parents were illiterate and they never realised the importance of modern education. According to our informant,[17] during the 1980s the Hill Tiwa could hardly speak the Assamese language and as the medium of teaching was in Assamese, therefore the parents were unwilling to send their children to school. Those who went to school had difficulties in learning as it was quite challenging to follow the Assamese language for the Tiwa speaking children. He further stated that, when he was a student, they had to struggle a lot to acquire the reading and writing skills in Assamese which eventually affected their results. Most of the students would drop their studies because of the language issues. Subsequently, the need for educational qualifications to get government jobs encouraged some of the parents to send their wards to school. Gradually with the growing number of schools, the enrollment of students has also started increasing.

Trends of Change in Marriage and Descent:

Presently the Tiwa follow a bilateral descent system. This descent system is recognized culturally as taking place more or less equally in both the male and female line and is called bilateral descent.[18] However, the Tiwa oral tradition suggests that their progenitors were females and the descent was traced from them. According to oral tradition maintained by the Hill Tiwa, twelve sisters were the progenitors of twelve original clans of the Tiwa, suggesting that the Tiwa were originally a matrilineal society. The *Deodhai Asam Buranji*[19] also refers to an incident that took place during the reign of Ahom King Jaydhwaj Singha(1653-1663 CE). It narrates about an interaction between the Ahom soldiers and some Hill Tiwa regarding the descent system of the Tiwa. During this conversation, the Hill Tiwa reported that, according to their custom, the son was debarred from succession and property was inherited by a daughter, and that the son of a chief had to earn his bread by serving under another person. Both the oral tradition and the Ahom chronicles suggest that the Tiwa were a matrilineal society.

The Tiwa matrilineal marriage system is called *Kobai* and the married males are called *kobiya* who live in the wife's house with her kin as the resident son-in-law (matrilocal marriage). In the *Kobai* system, the children take their mother's clan name and daughters inherit the parent's property and a major share is given to the younger daughter called *Shodya*.

Until the 1980s bringing a daughter-in-law (*pohari*) into the boy's residence was not very common among the Hill Tiwa. Even if a Hill Tiwa boy brings his wife to his house, his daughters and sons continue the tradition of matrilineality whereby sons continue to be resident sons-in-law and going to their wife's residence to stay as *kobiya*.

To ascertain the present state of descent and marriage among the Hill Tiwa, fieldwork was conducted at Mugaguri, Tharakhunji, Singlangkhunji, Hadaw and Amsai village. Statistical data for these villages were also collected from the census reports of 2011.[20] In Table VIII, we have incorporated the field data, census data and the data collected from the electoral roll of the 2014 Lok Sabha election,[21] to understand the recent trends in marriage and descent system and the impact of literacy and Christianity in the last 15 years.

Brief profile of the villages:

Mugaguri:

Mugaguri is a Tiwa Catholic village founded by the people of Borongkhoi village after their conversion to Christianity during the early 1990s. It is situated in the Amri Development Block of West Karbi Anglong district of Assam. This village is not connected with metal roads and the people have to walk at least 3 kilometers to reach the nearest state highway. There is no primary school in the village. The children have to go cover 3 kilometers to attend their lower primary and middle school at Morten. The nearest health care centre in Umpanai is about 12 kilometers from the village. The main occupation of the people of this village is *jhum* cultivation. They also cultivate broom stick, betel leaf (*paan*), ginger and bamboo for commercial purposes. As per the census data of 2011, the total number of households in this village is 35 and the total population above the age of 6 is 212(Male: 117, Female: 95)

Singlangkhunji:

Singlangkhunji is situated at a distance of 29 kilometers from the nearest market and urban centre at Nelli, along the national highway 37. This village comes under the Amri Development Block of West Karbi Anglong district. This village is not connected with metal roads and even the village(*kutcha)* road is not well developed for vehicular traffic. The nearest health care centre is also located at Nelli. It has a government-aided lower primary school. The main occupation of this village is *jhum* cultivation. Beside, they also cultivate broomstick, bamboo, betel leaf, ginger, turmeric for commercial purposes. As per census data the total number of household is 66 and the total population above 6 years is 438(Male: 209, Female: 229)

Tharakhunji:

Tharakhunji is located at a distance of 25 kilometers from the nearest weekly market and medical health centre at Nelli. It comes under the Amri Development Block of West Karbi Anglong district. The village is not connected with metal roads and the people have to walk 5 kilometers to reach the nearest highway. It has a lower primary school with a good percentage of enrollments. There are a few persons in government service in the village but more than 90% population is dependent on *jhum* cultivation. They also cultivate broomstick and bamboo for commercial purposes. According to the census data of 2011 the total number of households is 81 and the total population above 6 years is 462 (Male: 227, Female: 235).

Hadaw:

Hadaw village is situated on a hillock in the Amri Development Block of West Karbi Anglong district. The nearest weekly market is situated at a distance of about 10 kilometers at Birsingki and the nearest health care centre is at Umpanai which is about 12 kilometers from the village. It has a government-aided lower primary school with a very low percentage of enrollments due to absentee teachers. The main occupation of the people of this village is *jhum* cultivation. They also grow broomstick, bamboo, *eri* cocoon, ginger, and betel leaf for commercial purposes. According to the census data of 2011 the total number of households in the village is 52 and the total population above 6 years is 311(Male: 151, Female: 160).

Amsai:

Amsai is one of the twelve root villages of the Tiwa. It is situated adjacent to the Umswai weekly market and is well connected with metal roads. This village is flanked by three Karbi villages namely Umswai Model, Maikramsa and Langorkhon and two Khasi villages of Mawlen and Romphom. The village has a government aided lower primary school and the nearest high school is at a distance of 1 kilometer. The nearest medical health centre is at a distance of 13 kilometers in Umpanai. The village has a few numbers of persons in government service but 70% is dependent on both wet rice and *jhum* cultivation. Besides they cultivate broomstick and bamboo for commercial purposes. As per the census data of 2011, the total number of households in the village is 114 and the total population above 6 years of age is 647 (Male: 349, Female: 298).

Pantalu:

Pantalu is a Catholic Tiwa village established by some people of Bormarjong village after their conversion to Christianity. The road connectivity with this village is very poor. It has a government-aided lower primary school. The nearest weekly market is at a distance of 7 kilometers at Umswai. The main occupation of the people of this village is wet rice cultivation and *jhum* cultivation. They also grow broomsticks and bamboo for commercial purposes. According to the census data of 2011, the total number of households in this village is 46 and the total population above 6 years is 257(Male: 138, Female: 119).

The following table shows the number of matrilocal residences (*Kobai*) and patrilocal residence (*pohari*) in the last 15 years:

Table: VIII

Village	Clans in the village	Total houses	*Number* of *Kobai* in last 15 years	Number of *Pohari* in last 15 years	% of *Kobai*	% of *Pohari*	% of literacy
Mugaguri	Khorai, Puma, Kholar, Amsong, Madar	35	15	20	43	47	12
Tharakhunji	Amshi, Mithi and Puma	81	40	41	49	51	64
Singlanghunji	Amsong, Puma, Sagra, Mithi, Khorai, Muni, Malang and Madar	66	39	27	59	41	19
Hadaw	Puma, Sagra, Maslai and Madar	52	39	13	75	25	13
Amsai	Sagra, Hukai, Maslai, Kholar, Malang and Phamjong	114	75	39	66	34	14
Pantalu	Kholar, Lumphui, Malang, Amsong and Puma	46	20	26	43	47	31

The above table shows that Hadaw has the highest number of family following the matriocal residence pattern (*kobai*) with 75% and Mugaguri and Pantalu at 43% each. Tharakhunji has the highest number of literates (64%) and has slightly more people following the patrilocal residence pattern (*pohari*) than the matrilocal residence pattern (*Kobai*). Amsai the largest village under study has 66% matrilocal residence (*Kobai*) but the literacy rate is only 14%. The above table further indicates that 55% of Hill Tiwa in the six villages favours the matrilocal residence and matrilineal descent over the patrilocal residence pattern. The two Christian villages, Mugaguri and Pantalu have more number of patrilocal residences than the matrilocal residence pattern.

The highest number of matrilocal residence at Hadaw may be attributed to limited interaction with other patrilineal tribes due to its remote location. Lack of proper road connectivity and transportation has limited their interaction with their counterparts from the plains and they still prefer to follow the traditional system. According to our informant,[22] who himself married in the *Kobai* system(matrilocal residence)stated that they still prefer the *Kobai* than the *pohari* system as it has been handed down by their ancestors. According to him the *pohari* system has been introduced around 30 years ago in his village. Before that, the boys used to go to his wife's house after marriage. However, due to the influence of neighbouring tribes like the Karbi and other Assamese communities including the Plain Tiwa has encouraged some of the Tiwa youth to adopt the *pohari* system (patrilocal residence).

According to our informant Pirlu Amshi, the village headman of Tharakhunji, in the last five years, the number of persons married in the *pohari* system has gradually increased in their village. He stated that during the early 1980s and early 1990s he saw some of his friends getting wife (*pohari*) into their houses. He told us that now-a-days it is hard to find a young Tiwa male who prefer to stay at his wife's house as a *kobiya*. Rather they prefer to stay in their respective houses and bring their wives as a *pohari* just like the neighbouring tribes (Karbi and Nepali)[23] that practice a similar marriage system. His statement suggests that there has been a change of attitude among the Hill Tiwa boys regarding the continuity of the matrilocal residence system due to the impact of the other patrilineal societies. However, it is also to be noted that there has been a gradual shift of attitude and perspective with the progress of time. During our fieldwork at Amsai village we found that the youth have respect for their matrilineal descent system but prefer to stay at their residence and bring *pohari* rather than going to the wife's house as a resident son-in-law (*kobiya*). According to a young informant[24] who is married to a Plain Tiwa girl from Morigaon, now-a-days very few boys prefer to go to their wife's house as they feel more comfortable and dignified at home than in his wife's house where he cannot exercise his will. Another reason, he stated for the preference for the *pohari* system among the Tiwa youth is the issue of inheritance. He stated that after becoming a resident son-in-law the boy loses his right to inherit his parental property but if he remains at his residence and brings a *pohari* then he gets his share of his mother's property, which is preferable. He further stated that due to growth of education, Tiwa youth prefer to work and spend their earnings on themselves and to look after their parents. It is to be noted that property may be in the name of either the mother or the father depending upon the type of residence decided at the time of marriage. We have a few examples where a boy has inherited his mother's property after he got married and brought his wife to his mother's house. However, with his marriage in the *pohari* system, the rule of inheritance has changed from mother to daughter to mother to son. Nevertheless, our field data from Amsai shows that during the last 15 years the number of matrilocal residences is recorded at 66% and patrilocal residence is at 34%. From the above discussion, we can see a rising trend towards patrilocality and the gradual development of patrilineal descent and inheritance which is an indication that the Hill Tiwa society is in a process of transition.

The changes in the marriage and descent among the Tiwa have impacted the traditional village administration and Tiwa religious belief system. Our fieldwork at Amsai and Bormarjong, two important root villages of the Tiwa suggest that the Tiwa traditional village administration which revolves mainly around the head priest (*Loro*) has been affected due to the gradual change in the descent system. It is worthwhile to mention that the *Loro*, is the most important person in a traditional Tiwa village. According to Tiwa tradition the incumbents for the post of *Loro*, should be an individual who married in the matrilocal system (*Kobai*) to a particular clan that has traditionally enjoyed the right to offer the *Loro* to the village. In Amsai, it is the *Kobai* of the Kholar clan who is eligible for the post of *Loro* of Amsai. Similarly, the Amsong clan has the legitimate right to provide the *Loro* for Bormarjong village. It means, the primary qualification[25] to become the *Loro* of Amsai and Marjong is that the individual should be married in the *Kobai* system.

Presently Mildon Pumah is the *Loro* of Amsai and he will continue to hold this position till death. In case of his demise, he has to be succeeded by a Tiwa individual who is married in the Kholar clan as a resident Son-in-law (*kobiya*).

As we have discussed above in absence of a *kobiya* the *Loro* system will be badly affected which means the Tiwa traditional beliefs will also come under serious threat. According to our informant[26] if no *kobiya* is found among the Kholar families to replace the present *Loro* of Amsai, than the *Loro* system will be profoundly affected. He apprehended that either they may need to alter the entire tradition of selection and installation of the *Loro* or they have to end this system and move to some sort of loose system for the continuance of their culture and tradition. It means renouncement of their age-old customs and beliefs. This suggests that, the shift of descent system has impacted the village administration as well as the Tiwa traditional belief system.

The Plain Tiwa has adopted the patrilinieal system both in marriage and descent. In the plains, a joint family is composed of a male head of the family, his wife, married and un-married sons, un-married daughters, daughter-in-laws, married and un-married brothers, their wives and children etc. The head of the joint family is always assisted by the other adult members of the family in matters like taking decisions in important issues, economic activities, management of family property, affairs of marriage etc. The members of the joint family show due respect to the head and all of them heed his advice. The residence after marriage is patrilocal and the descent affiliation is patrilineal. The property is inherited by the sons after the death of the father. Their clan (*khul*) is patrilineal and exogamous. The daughters do not get a share of the paternal property. But till marriage, their brothers have to take care of them and it becomes their duty to arrange the marriage of sisters in the absence of the father. If a joint family breaks into nuclear families after the death of a father, the widowed mother may live with her son's family.

According to our informant [27] until the 1960s the Plain Tiwa also practiced matrilocal marriage along with patrilocal marriage. In such cases, the children born out of that couple had to accept the lineage or descent and clan of their mother. However, with the growth of education and the influence of other Assamese communities, they have completely abandoned matrilocal marriages. N.K. Shyamchudhury and N.N. Das[28] who worked among the Plain Tiwa in the 1970s recorded that, the young boys of Tiwa villages who own more agricultural land, did not want to leave their village. The families which have in their possession more land do not want to lose their economic advantage by allowing the working hands (sons) to go away after marriage.

Continuity and Changes in the Traditional Belief System:

Among the Hill Tiwa traditional health care system such as infant care, sickness management etc. are still common. It may be due to the lack of proper access to modern medicine and health care in the hills that they are still adhering to their traditional healing system. Besides they still believe in offering sacrifices to the spirits to get rid of sickness. In traditional Hill Tiwa villages, we have observed that almost every household performs the annual sacrifice to propitiate ancestor spirits. They seek blessings and protection from their clan deities to keep them and their livestock safe and healthy. The Shamans (*Oja*), fortune teller (*Phamari*) and the village priest (*Loro*) play an important role in the Tiwa traditional belief system. These individuals with special qualities are believed to have the capacity to deal with various sickness and misfortune. Similarly the Hill Tiwa and some Plain Tiwa still practices the *jallai* system when a new baby is born in a family. In the *jallai* system a newborn baby is identified with his previous life identity. The Tiwa believes in the reincarnation of souls. Hence according to them, an individual after demise can be reborn in the families of his/her close relatives. Generally, when a father dies, it is expected that he will take rebirth at his son's house as his son. Similarly, any close relative can be reborn in different houses simultaneously. According to our field study every Tiwa in the hills and even in certain villages in the plains, an individual has two identities. One identity is his present name and another is his or her previous life's name. We have met several individuals whose identity is also known by the previous life's name.

However, the introduction of modern education, medicine and health care practices has gradually impacted the Tiwa traditional belief system. The establishment of a rural hospital at Umpanai under the Amri development block in the 1980s, have greatly contributed to spreading awareness on the use of the modern health care system among the Hill Tiwa. Educated people now-a-days prefer to visit doctors in case of sickness rather than going to the village priest (*Loro*) or the shaman (*Oja*) for treatment. They use modern medicine instead of divination and animal sacrifice to get relief from sickness. According to our informant,[29] when they were young, most of the Tiwa people used to visit the *Oja* or the *Loro* to seek remedy for sickness and problems in the family. They firmly believed in the role of ancestor spirits, spirits of natural objects like the rivers and hills. They used to offer sacrifice to propitiate these spirits for the safety and prosperity of their families. However, the growth of transport and communication and the availability of modern medical facilities, most of the Tiwa have started visiting hospitals and prefer to use modern medicine. Our observation during the fieldwork indicates that presently the Hill Tiwa have access to both traditional medicines as well as modern health care system. As there is only one rural hospital in an area of around 25 square kilometers, it is difficult for every villager to visit the hospital. Due to lack of proper road connectivity, the people are unwilling to travel 20/25 kilometers to see a doctor unless severe. Thus they still have to depend on the village *Oja* and the *Loro* to get rid of sickness.

Introduction of Neo-Vaishnavism:

An integral part of Hinduism, the Neo-Vaishnava[30] cult initiated by Sankardeva during the early part of 16th century in the Brahmaputra valley transformed into a religious movement in subsequent years after his death. The official creed of Sankardeva is *ekasarana nama dharma*, which means worship of one god that is Vishnu, especially in the incarnation of Krishna, and interdicts the votaries from the worship of any other deity. According to Maheshwar Neog,[31] the great Neo-Vaishnava movement of Assam of the sixteenth century brought about a new and comprehensive outlook on life, a distinctly healthy tone to social behaviour with an all-pervasive organizational setup, and accelerated the pace of literature and the fine arts like music and painting. S. L. Baruah[32] stated that Neo-Vaishnavism united the diverse tribal communities of the Brahmaputra valley and gave it a culture, to be identified later as the Assamese culture. In the Brahmaputra Valley, many ethnic groups belonging to the Indo-mongoloid group such as Bodo, Thengal, Sonowal, Deuri, Moran, Chutiya, Tiwa etc. came under the sphere of influence of this movement. The impact of this movement was such that large numbers of individuals belonging to these tribes converted to the creed.

How and when the Neo-Vaishnavism was introduced among the Tiwa of the Brahmaputra valley is not known. Apparently, the process of conversion entered among the Tiwa through chiefs of the minor principalities in Kolong and Kapili valley. According to the *Deodhai Asam Buranji*,[33] the Ahom King Jaydhwaj Singha during the mid-17th century established three minor principalities of Topakochiya, Baropujia and Mikirgoya as a tributary to the Ahoms. Subsequently, during the reign of Rudra Singha and Rajeshwar Singha nine more minor principalities were created. [34] These minor principalities were administered by a 'tribal chief'[35] called *Raja* and they were collectively known as *Puwali Raja*. These principalities were placed under the direct supervision of the Ahom officer stationed at Raha known as Rahial Baruah and the Jagial Gohain stationed at Jagi post. The *Aai Lakhi Charit*[36] mentioned that Aai Kanklata, the granddaughter-in-law of Sankardeva wanted to have pilgrimage at Barduwa, the birthplace of her grandfather-in-law which was under the Mikirgoya principality and pleaded for the Barphukan's (Ahom governor at Guwahati) help, who in return ordered the chief of Mikirgoya principality Chetuwa *Raja* to provide all possible help. Accordingly the chief himself escorted the team of Vaishnava saint Aai Kanaklata and Damudar Deva to Borduwa. During the journey the Mikirgoya chief accepted '*saran-bhajan*'[37] in 1665 apparently because the Vaishnava saints had refused to accept food cooked by him as he was not a follower of Vaishnavism. This incident impacted the other minor principalities. Following the footstep, chief of Baropujia, Khaigarh, Topakhuchi and Khora also accepted *eksarana nama dharma*.[39] Subsequently the Neo-Vaishnava saints established *satras*(centre of Neo- Vaishnava cult) in and around Tiwa villages to cater to the need of the newly converted members and expedite the process of proselytisation.

British ethnographer[40] recorded that,

> Typically a *satra* consists of a *Namghar* or prayer house, which is a large open shed supported on massive wooden pillars. The roof is generally made of thatch supported on massive wooden pillars, and at one end there is often a shrine in which the titular idol is carefully screened from the vulgar eyes. The floor is made of beaten earth and there are generally a few drums and cymbals lying about which are used in the daily ritual.

S.L. Baruah writes,

> The *satras* were the centers of Neo-Vaishnava cult which consists of *Satradhikar, Bhakats* and *Sisyas*. The *Satradhikar* or the head of the *satra* was popularly called *Gossain* or *Mahanta*, the *Bhakats* were the devotees who led intensely devotional life and remain celibates throughout their life, and the laity were called *Sisyas* who lived in scattered villages, leading the life of a householder.[41]

According to S.N. Sarma[42], one of the significant contributions of the *satra* was that, it brought the non-Aryan tribes like the Koch, the Moran, the Chutiya, the Ahom and the Kachari under the fold of Vaishnavism. Some of the major *satras* that worked among the Tiwa were Kalisila,[43] Aaibheti,[44] Itakhuli,[45] Kuji,[46] Suktal Borbori and Suktal Sorubori[47] *satras* in Nowgaon district.[48] The Gossains or the head of these *satras* took the initiative to convert members of the tribes like the Tiwa and Karbi who were in the vicinity of these *satras*. B.C. Allen recorded that the Gossains of the *satras* used to tour through the villages once a year and received/ induct) into the Hindu faith (Neo- Vaishnavism) from the members of the aboriginal tribes who were considered to be worthy of conversion.[49] It implies that those who pledge to give up from a tribal way of life like eating pork and drinking rice beer and those who were ready to accept the *eksarana nama dharma* or only adherence to lord Vishnu considered to be worthy of conversion to Neo-Vaishnava cult.

The process of conversation not only made the Tiwa a member of the *satra* but also facilitated a change in their ethnic identity. With conversion, they were given the status of *Soru Koch* or Junior Koch which was considered to be a higher position in the Assamese caste hierarchy. According to B.C. Allen,[50] a Koch is a respectable sudra-caste divided into two principal subdivisions of *Bor Koch* and *Soru Koch*. The first category of Koch was looked upon as a clean *sudra* caste and from whose hands Brahmanas will take water. However, the *Soru Koch* was not accorded the same distinction as the *Bor Koch* though they conform in most essentials to the somewhat lax standard of Hinduism exacted in Assam. Edward Gait[51] recorded that "the Koch was a name of Hindu caste rather than a tribe in Assam which received the converts to Hinduism from the ranks of the Kachari, Mikir, Lalung and other tribes."

The census report of 1962[52] has explained the process of conversion of Lalung (Tiwa), Mikir (Karbi and Kachari (Dimasa) into Hinduism (Neo-Vaishnavism). It stated that the Gosains, the head of *Satras* or some of its subordinates usually select certain families of aboriginal tribes who reside in the vicinity of Hindu villages and at distance from the main village of the aboriginal tribes (Tiwa, Mikir). These families are frequently lectured upon the purity of the Hindu religion and the easy way in which they can get salvation, and how they can acquire a position in the Hindu society if they give up their habit of eating pork and other forbidden food and strong liquor, and conform to the Hindu method of eating and drinking and worship. As these people are frequently feeling the inconvenience of their isolated position they are easily tempted to become Hindus, and thereby be associated and move with their Hindu neighbours, by whom they are hated and looked down upon as a degraded class so long as they remain unconverted. When these people after frequent lectures show some inclination towards giving up their religion and becoming Hindus, a certain propitious day is selected and they are questioned as to whether they would like to give up their former habits and customs and become perfect Hindus or that they would simply take *saran* (religious instruction) from the Hindu Gosain and remain free as too their habits of eating and drinking. When they express a desire of entire conversion to the Hindu religion they are made to fast for a day or two and then to undergo a *prayachit*(atonement) for which they have to spend some 5 to 20 rupees according to their circumstances. They then receive their *saran-bhajan*(religious instruction and mode of worship) from the Gosain, whom from that day they look upon as their spiritual guide. These people then change all former utensils of cooking and eating and also their dwelling houses and become quite hinduised. The Gosain then makes them over to a *khel*(group of people with shared identity) with whom the converted men are so associate. The converted people then give a feast to their new associates to whose habits and mode of worship they entirely conform. The converted men are closely watched by their new associates as to whether they take any of the forbidden food or strong liquor or not and if they are found to be entirely given up these things, they are freely admitted into the Hindu society and are called *Soru Koch*. For the first three generations from their conversion, they are looked down upon a little by their society and they are not allowed to take any leading part. From the third generation they become quite as good as any of the Koch caste.

According to the report, it appears that the families of the tribes who reside in the neighbourhood of the followers of the Neo-Vaishnava cult were mainly targeted for conversion as it was easy to motivate them because of their isolated position. The entire process of conversion was a gradual one, as there are at least three stages that a person has to go through before getting the status of a Koch or a Vaishnavite. Nevertheless, soon after conversion, the family adopts the Assamese language, dress and food habits prescribed by their religion and give up their former way of worship and tribal identity. Subsequently, the converts effectively severed ties with their community and way of life. They acquired a new identity with Assamese patronymic surnames such as Deka, Bora, Kakati, Thakuria etc. It led to the negative growth rate of the Tiwa population in the plains. The census recorded that the number of Tiwa population fell from 52423 in 1891 to 35513 in 1901, a decrease of 16910 persons.[53] During this decade the Tiwa population witnessed a decline of 32.2 percent. Whereas in the previous decades from 1872 to 1881 had a healthy growth of 36.6 percent.[54] The report further stated that the main reason behind the imbalance in the population growth was largely due to change of ethnic identity from Tiwa to Koch because of conversion to Neo-Vaishnavism.[55] This process continued unabated till the 1970s when some Tiwa nationalist organisations started protesting against the proselytisation and raised voice of concern of the Tiwa people.

Organisations like *Lalung Darbar, Sodo Asom Tiwa Sanmiloni* organised awareness campaigns among the Tiwa against conversion to Koch and appealed for preserving their ethnic identity. It was partially successful in containing the process of conversion. But it was the establishment of the All Tiwa Students' Union in 1989 which brought the conversion to an end. The organization was by and large successful in building a common Tiwa identity and infused a sense of Tiwa nationalism.

The long association with the neighbouring Assamese communities the religion of the Plain Tiwa has become a combination of both the traditional way of worship/sacrifice and elements of Brahmanical as well as Vaishnavism. Among them, both ancestor worship and worship of Hindu deities is a part of their religious practices. While professing their traditional religion, the Plain Tiwa not only incorporated Hindu elements into their religion but also accepted the dress, language and lifestyle of their neghbouring Assamese communities. According to Maneshwar Dewri,[56] from the 1960s-70s onwards the influence of Assamese rituals in marriage, birth and death ceremonies was visible among the Plain Tiwa. According to him, the trend of having a puberty ceremony for girls called *tuloni biya* which was earlier unknown to the Tiwa became an important part of Plain Tiwa society.

Introduction of Christianity:

The Khasi-Pnar Presbyterian missionaries were the first to introduce Christianity among the Tiwa in the early 1920s. They preached Christianity to the Tiwa through the medium of Khasi language, Khasi hymns, Khasi prayer books etc. which did not make much impact. Subsequently, the Presbyterian evangelist used the Karbi language to preach Christianity also without much success. According to Simon Mithi, those Tiwa were converted by the Khasi Presbyterian mission became Khasi and those who converted by Karbi Presbyterian missions had to accept the Karbi identity. He stated that, the Khasi Presbyterian Mission at Nongpoh was the first to make contact with the Tiwa of Morrow village, an offshoot of Amsai with twenty eight families. After their conversion they had to pray and practice the newly embraced faith in Khasi language as the pastors were Khasi and preaching was in the

Khasi language. Due to these difficulties, some of the families decided to move to the Khasi village at Mawlen and Umsingup, and some went to the Karbi village at Umswai Model. After their settlement in those villages, they either converted to Khasi or Karbi. However, those who refused to convert settled at Amsolong. During this period the Catholic German Salvadorian missionaries made contact with some Tiwa and Karbi of Umswai area. Their occasional visits attracted the attention of many Karbi and Tiwa of that area. Langtuk Hanse and his friends, who were impressed by a catholic priest while working in Garo hills, met Fr. Chrysostomus Lefef Mayr and expressed their eagerness to embrace Christianity. Eventually, they were baptized and converted to the Catholic faith on 25th January 1914.[57] It was a significant event as far as the history of the Catholic Church in Karbi Anglong district was concerned. It was not only the beginning of the Catholic faith among the Karbi, but also led to the foundation of the Catholic Church in the Karbi Anglong district. Soon these newly converted Karbi impressed some Tiwa families in the nearby villages. Finally a few Tiwa from Bormarjong village were converted to Catholic faith in 1916.[58] Soon they were joined by some other Tiwa families and established a new village by the name Roman Marjong after the religious affiliation of its inhabitant's i.e the Roman Catholic Church, meaning thus Catholic part of Marjong.[59] As majority of the inhabitants were Karbi hence they were incorporated into different Karbi clans and identified as Karbi. According to Karotemprel, since the first Catholics were Karbi, hence the newly converted Tiwa had to accept the Karbi language, dress and prayers and eventually their culture.[60] It is to be noted that the German Salvadorian missionaries had to abandon their missionary work due to the outbreak of the First World War. The British administration in North East India arrested the German missionaries and put them in the prison camp at Ahmednagar.[61]

After the departure of the German Salvadorian Mission, the Catholic Mission at Nongpoh took a keen interest in the evangelisation of the Tiwa. In 1948 some of the Tiwa were converted to Christianity under the aegis of Fr. Potto, an Italian Salesian priest. One of them was Simon Mithi of Amsolong. He was a Presbyterian who settled at Amsolong after their fellow villagers at Morrow either became Khasi or Karbi. Meanwhile, in 1951 some of the Tiwa families of Amsai also embraced Christianity and left their village to settle at Punduri Makha. The families who came to Punduri Makha in 1952 were Bin Maslai, Lobon Kholar, Sing Mithi, Samual Lumphui and Panthai Amsi. After hearing the news of the newly established Punduri Makha village, Simon Mithi also settled there. Thus, the first Tiwa Catholic community was established at Umswai. In 1952 the number of Tiwa Catholic was twenty-six individuals out of whom fifteen were male and the rest were female. They constructed a small chapel in their newly established village. As they were the first Tiwa Catholics and there was no Tiwa bible or prayer book, Jonis Phangcho, a Karbi catechist of Roman Marjong village, preached in Karbi language.

Initially, the Tiwa Catholic community of Umswai was looked after by the Nongpoh Parish located at a distance of around forty-five kilometers. In 1958 a French missionary Fr. Michael Valavoine[62] popularly known as Fr. Balawan came to the Nongpoh parish as an assistant parish priest. He soon took a keen interest in the evangelization of the Tiwa and the Karbi. He started frequent visits to the Tiwa and Karbi Catholic villages' sometimes on foot and sometimes with his Mahindra jeep. Fr. Balawan was aided by two Tiwa catechists, Babus Maurus Amsong and Simon Mithi[63] With their active support the evangelization process among the Tiwa gained momentum. During his active involvement among the Tiwa, he realised the need for education. Fr. Balawan realised that without educating the Tiwa it would be very difficult to spread the message of Christianity. This point was brought out by Fr. Sebastian Karotemprel in early 1980s. He recorded that, "illiteracy was a major problem for evangelization among the Tiwa. It made the communication of faith which is itself a difficult subject even more problematic."[64] Therefore Fr. Balawan mastered the Tiwa language and extensively worked on its grammar. Eventually he came up with several books. In 1967 he translated the *New Testament* into Tiwa language and subsequently the Lalung prayer book (*Mindai Khruma*), *Lalung life of Christ(Jisu Krise Thanga), Lalung Bible History, Sunday Gospel, Lalung Grammer, Lalung Dictionary-English etc.* were published which contributed to the spread of the Catholic faith among the Tiwa.

Fr. Balawan set up a mission centre at Umswai in 1966. Subsequently, in 1968 alongside the mission house a multipurpose hall was built to cater to the various needs of the Catholics of Umswai. He used to visit and stay at the centre for a few days in a month and return to Nongpoh Parish. On 24th April, 1977 the Umswai Mission was established at Chikdamakha with Fr. Albano D Mello SDB as the first parish priest.[65] Soon a school was set up along with a small hostel for the boys. Within the Parish compound, the Franciscan Missionary Brothers[66] started a small dispensary to cater to the medical needs of the Tiwa and Karbi. The missionaries would visit different Tiwa villages located in remote areas. They would request the illiterate Tiwa parents to send their children to the mission schools. The missionaries would also distribute essential medicines to the sick and request them to visit the Mission Centre for further treatment. Karotemprel[67] recorded that,

The Franciscan Brothers could make their way into the Tiwa village through the medical care and assistance that was offered by them. It served as a passport to many villages which otherwise would not have welcomed them. It was almost impossible to pursue the villagers who have been for centuries living in isolation and the confines of their own villages to bid farewell to traditional practices in times of illness.

Within a short time the Umswai Mission Centre became popular for its school and modern health care facilities. It became a tool to impress easy going Tiwa people to convert to Christianity. After their conversion, they had to leave their traditional village as it was against the Tiwa tradition and culture. Initially many Tiwa after converting to Christianity came to live around the Mission Centre in Chikdamakha. But later, they moved to different places which resulted in the emergence of several new Catholic villages in Umswai.

In 1977 the Franciscan Brothers shifted their mission centre to Langradang about ten kilometers north of Umswai. Soon they established a boarding school and a church which could accommodate two hundred people. However, due to frequent transfer of the Franciscan Brothers the Mission Centre was handed to the Capuchin fathers on the 31st December 1998. But the Capuchin fathers could not hold their ground over the mission due to physical hardships and strong opposition from the local community against evangelization. Eventually, the mission was closed down in 1999. During their stay at Langradang mission the Franciscan brothers converted three Tiwa villages namely Umbormon, Sinani Roman and Mugaguri.

In 2014 the Catholics under Umswai parish stood at three thousand and five hundred out of which 80% were Tiwa. According to our field study, the following are the Tiwa villages which are scattered under the Umswai and Amkachi parish in West Karbi Anglong and Umsolait parish in Ri-Bhoi district of Meghalaya: Pundurimakha, Chikdamakha, Amsobra, Tipali, Mokoidhorom, Orlongluri, Similikhunji, Thawlaw, Sondrophali, Khumkhunji, Sapali, Tarikhunji, Umbormon, Sinani Roman, Solaikhunji, Mawpyenjeng, Mugaguri, Mayong, Ti-iami, and Orlongshadali.

Christianity among the Tiwa brought considerable interaction among the Tiwa and other tribes like the Karbi and the Khasi-Pnar. As a result, there have been many inter-tribal marriages among Tiwa Christian families. Christianity brought the three tribes close to each other as they have to come together for religious works. The Tiwa Christians have less reservation in accepting daughters-in-law from other tribes into their families. It facilitated the rise of patrilineal descent among the Tiwa. We have recorded several Karbi women married to Tiwa men living with their husband's family as daughters-in-law at Pundurimakha, Chikdamakha, Pantalu, and Simlikhunji village. Moreover, we also found several Khasi-Pnar women at Chikdamakha village married to Tiwa and living in their husband's house as daughters-in-law. Their children have taken the father's clan and the property is shared among the boys. It is interesting to find that women belonging to the matrilineal Khasi-Pnar society have come to live with their husbands in patrilocal residence.

With the spread of Christianity constant interaction between the Tiwa, Karbi, and Khasi tribes resulted in the development of language proficiencies among the people of these tribes. During the fieldwork, we have observed the tri-lingual interaction among the Tiwa, Karbi, and Khasi at Umswai which was a unique experience. It explains their peaceful coexistence and also their respect for each other's language and culture. Furthermore, it was through the constant efforts of Fr. Balawan that the Tiwa language was enriched. His contribution to Tiwa language and literature is well appreciated among the Hill Tiwa. Besides those who converted to Christianity received special attention of the missionaries who helped them gain access to higher education and employment opportunities.

Nevertheless, there has been a strong opposition against the conversion to Christianity among the Hill Tiwa since the very beginning of evangelization. It was mandatory to excommunicate and expel those who were converted to Christianity from the root village. It has been observed that due to the well organised traditional village administration, the Christian conversion among the Tiwa is much lower than the other Hill tribes of North-East India. Despite the efforts of the missionaries most of the Hill Tiwa have adhered to their traditional religion. During the 1960s a few farsighted Tiwa people founded *Lalung Darbar* a Socio-political organization with a primary aim to secure a district comprising the Tiwa areas both in the hills and plains. With the establishment of the first political organization the Tiwa became more conscious of the preservation of their cultural identity and heritage. The leaders of the *Lalung Darbar* initiated a process to revitalize the traditional religion and culture as it was the backbone of the Tiwa identity. Their effort yielded good results and the process of evangelization was minimized. Subsequently another organization *Sodo Asom Tiwa Sanmiloni* was established in the 1970s which also contributed to the preservation of traditional religion and cultural practices. Both these organizations were partially successful in containing the process of conversion. The establishment of All Tiwa Students' Union brought about a considerable change in the attitude towards the issue of conversion and advocated for upholding Tiwa ethnic identity. Their nationalistic appeals and porgrammes were readily accepted by the Tiwa general mass and contributed to the containment of proselytisation. Interestingly there were several Christian converts among the leaders of these organizations who advocated for the upholding of Tiwa traditional belief system.

From the 1990s several Tiwa organisations such as *Tiwa Mathonai Tokhra, Tiwa Cultural Society, All Tiwa Women's Association,* and in recent years the *Hindu Tiwa Kanthichuri Chomot* has been consistently working for the revitalization of Tiwa socio-religious and cultural values. Our observations suggest that these organizations have successfully carried out their activities to secure the Tiwa culture and tradition from external influences. With the intellectual support and advocacy for traditional institutions and culture, the Tiwa people revived their religious festivals, dances, traditional games etc. Our recent fieldwork found that there are very few conversions among the Tiwa during the last five years. There were only a few isolated cases of conversion on account of family disputes and other causes. On the other hand, we have come to know that several Christian Tiwa has resumed practicing traditional religion.

Changes in the *Shamadi* System:

According to Tiwa tradition having a *Shamadi* (bachelor's dormitory) in every Tiwa village was mandatory. It was an integral part of Tiwa folklife and an institution in itself. However due to lack of proper access to building materials the villagers have been facing difficulties in repairing and rebuilding of *Shamadi*. During our fieldwork, we observed that the *Shamadi* of Khromkhunji, Lumphui, Makro, Amjong, and Khaplangkhunji are in deplorable condition. While asked about the problem the village elders mentioned that due to lack of building materials such as big trees for pillars and thatch for roofing, it had become a major problem in repairing the *Shamadi*. Presently there is a trend among the Hill Tiwa villages to construct the village Shamadi with cement concrete. At present villages like Khawarakrai, Amsai, Borrongkhoi, and Bormarjong have *Shamadi* constructed of cement concrete. The village elders of Amsai told us that they prefer to have the concrete *Shamadi* as it will last longer than the traditional *Shamadi* and hardly need to spend money on repairing work.

In many Tiwa villages, *Shamadi* has lost its significance as an institution. Nevertheless, a section of the Tiwa believes that the *Shamadi* should not be distorted by citing the difficulties of procuring building materials. They insist that the *Shamadi* should be preserved as a part of their traditional culture. According to them the significance of this institution will remain intact only when people make special efforts to preserve its original shape and design.

According to Pirlu Amsi, the shift from matrilineal to patrilineal descent and the modern education system has badly affected the *Shamadi* system of the Tiwa. He informs us that in the olden days when the kobai system was prevalent the unmarried male members were forbidden to sleep at their residence. Only the married male members like the resident son-in-law of the family and the head of the family are authorized to spend the night at their residences. In a traditional Tiwa house or nobaro, each room is specifically marked for different individuals of the family. For example, the grandmother and grandfathers always sleep on the right side of the *nukthi* or the main room and the left side is reserved for guests. In the absence of a guest, any girl of the family can sleep there. The *nomaji* is reserved for a married couple of the family. However, there is no specifically marked place for unmarried males of the family. Hence it was mandatory for a boy after he attends ten years of age to join the *Shamadi* where his place is specifically marked by its senior members. Earlier the boys used to leave their *Shamadi* life only after they go to live at their wife's parental house as a resident son-in-law or kobiya where he enjoys his rightful place. An unmarried boy can stay overnight at his residence when he falls sick or disabled. Otherwise, he has to be in the *Shamadi* along with his fellow mates. However, due to the shift from the *kobiya* to the *pohari* system, the male members preferred to stay at their residence and it has affected the social life of the individuals. In this system, a boy does not require to leave his place of birth due to marriage. Instead, he brings a girl from a different family to his own house which encourages other unmarried male members to remain within the house. In this type of marriage, the children take their father's surname rather than their mothers. Moreover, the introduction of the modern education system brought about a considerable change in the behaviour of the Tiwa individuals. Today Tiwa villages have access to lower primary and elementary schools. The government has also engaged the village elders to sensitise the public about the importance of education for their children. It is indeed a good sign as children are gradually getting educated at least at their village schools. However, due to school education and its related academic activities, young boys have hardly any free time to spend at the *Shamadi*. Besides they are unwilling to stay overnight at the village *Shamadi* because of the academic activities which can be done only at home. Moreover, the young boys have to leave their village after they pass out of high school for their higher studies. They either has to go to Nelli or Jagiroad located around thirty to forty-five kilometers away from the villages.

Earlier the *panthai khel* or the youth body used to manage the *Shamadi* with strict discipline handed down by tradition. Every boy in the village had to report to the Changdoloi and Changmaji and other senior members of the *Shamadi* about their presence in the evening. The junior section (*jokha khel*) has to do all kinds of work related to the *Shamadi* like procurement of firewood, storing of water, cleaning and securing the musical instruments. Our fieldwork has found that the youths of Tharakhunji, Borrongkhoi, and Bormarjong hardly spent quality time together in the *Shamadi*.

Changing Pattern of Traditional Economy:

The *jhum* cultivation is still a major source of income among the Hill Tiwa. However, the method of cultivation has gone through some basic changes. Earlier the Hill Tiwa used to cultivate paddy and other food crops along with cotton, but from the 1990s they have changed the pattern of cultivation in the field. One of the major changes in the *jhum* field was the introduction of broom and bamboo along with paddy and other food crops. Earlier the patch of land remains fallow for five to seven years, before it was considered suitable for cultivation. Now the cycle of *jhum* is changed. To earn more profit from the same plot of land for several years, they plant either bamboo or broom along with paddy during the first round of cultivation. Paddy needs only four to five months to harvest but the bamboo and broom take more than two years before it can be sold in the market. Hence the bamboo or broom does not create any problem when it is planted along with paddy and other food crops like pumpkin, sweet potato, yam etc. after the harvest of food crops they leave the plot of land for bamboo and broom to grow for two to three years. Very little care is required to grow broom and bamboo in the hills of Karbi Anglong because of favourable climatic and soil conditions. The broom cultivation was first introduced to the Hill Tiwa by some student leaders of the *All Tiwa Students Union* in the early 1990s as an experimental project which was very successful. The high demand for broom outside North-East India and abroad encouraged the Hill Tiwa and other communities in the hills to take up its commercial cultivation. Similarly, the bamboo cultivation picked up momentum after the establishment of the Hindustan Paper Corporation at Jagiroad which provided an ample bamboo market for the Hill Tiwa as well as other tribes like the Karbi and the Khasi. Along with wild bamboo the domesticated bamboo species grown on the hill slopes proved to be good source of income. At present almost every village household has broom and bamboo fields which were once used for growing food crops. They sell their bamboo as and when the grove becomes mature. They get an annual lump-sum income from bamboo and broomstick selling during February to April each year. The changing pattern of agriculture and incorporation of bamboo and broom cultivation provided better economic prospects among the Hill Tiwa.

The traditional Tiwa economy was based on reciprocal help and the barter system. Barter of commodities among the families in the villages was an important facet of the Tiwa economy. They exchanged paddy with physical labour, cloth, animals etc. and vice versa. The measurements of bartered commodities were decided on mutual consent of both parties. However, with the establishment of the weekly market at Umswai during the late 1960s and the establishment of the Hindustan Paper Corporation at Jagiroad in the 1980s, the market economy entered among the Hill Tiwa which affected the barter system. Nevertheless, during our fieldwork at Borrongkhoi, Singlangkhunji, Tharakhuni and Boramni village, we have found evidence of the continuance of the barter system. They still practice barter between families to fulfill their domestic requirements. The rate of exchange is fixed according to the value of the article based on its demand through a mutual understanding of the parties. At Tharakhunji village our informants told us that generally a fowl is exchanged for bamboo and paddy. Paddy is also exchanged for physical labour (wage) and cloths such as *kasong* and *joskai* etc. for pig, goat, fowl etc. However, they like to take money if an outsider from the plains wants to trade with them. Continuance of the barter system in these villages can be attributed to the absence of a market in the immediate neighbourhood and mutual trust and understanding between the people.

Figure 1. Modified Shamdi of Amsai Village *(credit. Leander Lumphui)*

Figure 2. Getting Ready for Sogramisawa *(Credit, Leander Lumphui)*

Figure 3. *Langra,* **traditional Gate,** *(credit, Tilok Thakuria)*

Notes and References:

1   B.K. Gohain, *Continuity and Change in the Hills of Assam*, Omsons Publication, Guwahati, 2006, p. 106.

2   Thomas Dietz, Tom R. Burns and Frederick H. Buttel, "Evolutionary Theory in Sociology: An Examination of Current Thinking", *Sociological Forum*, Vol. 5, No. 2, Springer, 1990, pp. 155-171.

3   http://www.sociologyguide.com/social-change/evolutionary-theories, online access on 12/08/2016

4   *Ibid.*

5   https://study.com/academy/lesson/structural-functional-theory-in-sociology-definition-examples, online access on 12/08/2016.

6   https://courses.lumenlearning.com/alamo-sociology/chapter/conflict-theory, online access on 12/08/2016.

7   *Ibid.*

8   G. M. Trevelyan, *English Social History*, Penguin, U.K., 1987.

9   M.N. Srinivas, *Social Change in Modern India* (Reprint), Orient Black Swan, New Delhi, 2015.

10   Carol R. Ember, Marvin Ember, *Cultural Anthropology*, Prentice Hall, New Jersey, 2002, p. 26

11   C.V. Furer Haimendorf, *Tribes of India*, Oxford University Press, New Delhi, 1985.

12   Eric Hobsbawm, *On History* (reprint), Abacus, London, 1999, p.17.

13   *Ibid.*

14   Late Bangthai Bordoloi of Rupaiburi village in the Ahatguri area of Morigaon district of Assam spent his entire service period as a lower pimary school teacher in the Hill Tiwa dominated area from 1965 to 2005. He stated that, he used to walk up to Nelli market along with the Hill Tiwa villagers who would come on Sunday morning and spend the night at temporary sheds within the market complex.The following day(Monday) they would exchange their goods with the local traders before noon and then leave for their respective villages. While returning to his school, he would continuously ascent the hills along with the co-travellers for more than 10 to 12 hours to reach his destination. He further stated that the present PWD road from Nelli to Ulukhunji was in a deplorable condition and there was no bus or any other vehicle that were to be seen until the late 1960s.

15   Nelli is located along the 37 national highways in the present Morigaon District of Assam.

16   B.K. Gohain, *The Hill Lalungs*, ABILAC, Guwahati, 1993, p. 39.

17   He is a resident of Amsai village.

18   Thomas R. Williams, *Cultural Anthropology*, Prentice Hall, New Jersey, 1990, p. 267

19   S.K. Bhuyan (ed.),*Deodhai Asam Buranj*(4th edn.), DHAS, Guwahati, 2001, p. 96-98

20 Census of India 2011, *Assam District Census Handbook: Karbi Anglong* (Part: B), Directorate of Census Operations, Assam.

21 The electoral rolls of different polling stations have been collected from the Chief Electoral Officer, Assam website, www.ceoassam.nic.in/electoralroll.html online access on 12/1/2016.

22 The informant is a resident of Hadaw village.

23 There are around two hundred Nepali origin people living in and around the Hill Tiwa village in Umswai valley since the 1970s. They are mainly dairy farmers and small traders who came to that area in search of livelihood.

24 The informant is a young entrepreneur of Amsai village.

25 However besides being the *Kobai* of the Kholar clan the individual has to prove his ability to handle the religious functions which is indispensable after being installed as the *Loro*.

26 He is the village headman of Tharakhunji village.

27 The informant is a resident of Meruagaon in Morigaon district.

28 N.K. Shyamchudury & N.N. Das, *The Lalung Society*, A.S.I., Calcutta, p. 96.

29 Ton Maslai, age 60 years, a resident of Pundurimakha.

30 The term Neo–Vaishnavism is applied to the Assam version of Vaishnavism preached by Sankardeva to differentiate this phase of Vaishnavism from its early phase that flourished in Bengal during Chaitanya Deva.

31 Maheshwar Neog, "The Vaishnava Renaissance in Assam", appeared in the *Aspects of the Heritage of Assam*, A Souvenir of Reception Committee, 22nd Session, Indian History Congress, Guwahati, 1959, p.31

32 S.L. Baruah, *A Comprehensive History of Assam*, Munshiram Monoharlal, New Delhi, 1985, p. 447.

33 S.K. Bhuyan (ed.), *op. cit.*, 2001, p. 99.

34 S.K. Bhuyan(ed.), *Harakanta Baruah Sadar aminor Asom Buranji* (4th edn.), DHAS, Guwahati, 2010, p.42

35 There were twelve minor principalities established by the Ahoms to administer the Tiwa and Karbi of the Kolong and Kapili valley. Among them Mikirgoya was headed by a Mikir or Karbi chief and rest were under the control of the Tiwa chiefs.

36 *Aai Lakhi Charit* is the biography of Vaishnava guru Aai Kanaklata who was also the granddaughter-in-law of Sankardeva, the founder of the Neo-Vaishnava cult in Assam. This book has been preserved at the Sukdal Barbori *Sattara* in Morigaon District.

37 *Saranbhajan* is the religious instruction and mode of worship given by the Vaishnava gurus to the converted *sisya* or laities.

38 Maneshwar Dewri, *Asomiya Jati aru Sanskriti Gathanat Tiwa Sakalor Abodan*, Assam Institute of Tribals and Schedule Caste, Guwahati, 2011, p. 82.

39 *Ibid.*

40 B.C. Allen, *Assam District Gazetteers: Nowgong*, Calcutta, 1905, p.91

41 S.L. Baruah, *op. cit.*, p.449.

42 S.N. Sarma, "The Satra Institutin", *Aspects of the Heritage of Assam*, A Souvenir of Reception Committee, 22nd Session of India History Congress, Guwahati, 1959, p.54

43 This *satra* was founded by Ram Chandra Mahanta in 1730 C.E.

44 The Aaibheti satra was established by Aai Lakshmi in 1790 C.E.

45 This *satra* was established by Biswanath Mahanta in 1800 C.E.

46 Established by Damodar Atta in 1660 CE.

47 Both the Suktal Borbori and Sorubari Satras were founded by Bhugali Aata in 1755 C.E.

48 B.C. Allen, *op.cit.*, p. 104

49 *Ibid.* p. 90

50 *Ibid.* p. 81

51 Edward Gait, *A History of Assam*(7th edn.), Lawyers Book Stall, Guwahati, 1983, p. 43.

52 E.H. Pakyntein, *Census of India 1962*, Vol. III, Assam, Part V-A, Government of India, Delhi, 1964, p. 57

53 J.H. Hutton, *Census of India*, 1931, Vol.I, Part II, Imperial Table, Govt. of India, Delhi, 1933, p. 549.

54 B.C. Allen, *Census of Assam* 1901, Vol II (reprint), Manas Publication, New Delhi, 1984, p.157.

55 B.C. Allen, *op. cit.* (1905), p. 84.

56 Maneshwar Dewri, *op. cit.* p. 83.

57 Souvenir of Roman Marjong Centenary Celebration,2014, pp.15-16

58 Pius Amsong, Monsing, Saldoi, Sabina, Konongma, Vincentious Doloi and some others accepted the Catholic faith along with thirty one Karbi people.

59 See Philippe Ramirez's paper Ethnic Conversions and Trans-ethnic Descent Groups in the Assam- Meghalaya Borderlands, *Asian Ethnology*, 01/2013, 72(2), pp. 279–297.

60 S. Karotemprel, *A Brief History of the Catholic Church among the Tiwa*, Sacred Heart Theological college, Shillong, 1981, p. 16

61 Souvenir of Roman Marjong Centenary Celebration, *op.cit.* p.15

62 Fr. Micheal Valavoine was a Frenchman who came to work in the Shillong Salesian Mission in 1948. He had contributed immensely for the development of Tiwa language and literature. His writings includes Tiwa-English dictionary, Tiwa grammar and he was first man to translate the New Testament in the Tiwa language.

63 This story was shared by Simon Mithi, 85 of Pundurimakha village who was closely associated with Fr. Balawan.

64 S. Karotemprel, *A Brief History of the Catholic Church Among the Tiwas*(*Lalungs*), Sacred Heart Theological College, Shillong, 1981, p. 23.

65 S. Karotemprel, *op. cit.* p. 20.

66   According to Fr. S. Karotemprel, the Franciscan Missionary Brothers came to North East India in 1971. Initially they settled down at Mawhati and Umsohlait in the present Ri-Bhoi district of Meghalaya where they set up a small agriculture school, dispensary and a boarding school. However differences of opinion among them and other stakeholders resulted in the dismantling of their mission. Later they were asked to work among the Tiwa at Umswai Mission Centre.

67   S. Karotemprel, *op. cit.*

CHAPTER VIII

Conclusion

The present work on the Tiwa is an ethnohistorical study. It is an attempt to understand the history of the Tiwa people and the changes that are taking place in contemporary Tiwa society based on extensive fieldwork supplemented by archival and secondary sources. The necessity of such a work has long been felt primarily because no full-length ethnohistoric study on this tribe has been attempted earlier.

The ethnohistorical study encompassing the origin, migration, settlement pattern, religious beliefs and practices, socio-political institutions as well as elements of continuity and change among the Tiwa indicates that the society is in a stage of transition. As one of the indigenous people of North East India, the Tiwa along with other tribes in the Brahmaputra valley and the neighbouring hills were recorded by the Vedic Aryans as "Kirata".[1] Similarly Greek merchants referred to them as '*Cirrhadae*', a race of savage men with flat noses in the 1st century C.E.[2] P.C Choudhury identified the '*Cirrhadae*' with the Kirata of North East India.[3] K.L. Baruah is also of the view that the Kirata mentioned in the Vedic texts are the ancestors of the various Indo-Mongoloid tribes of Assam such as the Lalung/Tiwa, Garo, Koch, Mech, Bodo and others. Thus the Tiwa could be said to have settled down in their present abode at a very early period.

The origin of both the terms 'Tiwa' and 'Lalung' is unclear. However, from various oral traditions on the origin of clan and stories of migration and linguistic interpretation, we can infer that the word 'Tiwa' is associated with water/river. An analysis of Tiwa oral traditions and religious practices suggests that the word "Tiwa" is derived from the word '*Tipharwali*' meaning a clan/people living along a large waterbody or river. This water body is believed to refer to the upper course of the Brahmaputra River which was known to the Tiwa as *Ti-leu/Leu-ti*. In Tiwa *leu* means long and *ti* means water/river meaning long river.

The term 'Lalung' by which the Tiwa were mentioned in the Ahom *buranjis* and some colonial accounts suggests that they were known to others as 'Lalung'. However, the tribe in question referred to themselves as Tiwa and considers the term 'Lalung' as derogatory. The the term "Lalung" may be given by others to the Tiwa people. There are several instances of exonyms or names given by others to the tribes of North East India. For example, the term Mikir for the Karbi, Garo for the Achik Mande and Dafla for the Nishi were the names given by others.

Based on an enduring folk song associated with *jhum* cultivation and oral tradition, it appears that the Tiwa have migrated from a place called Makha Koja meaning the Red Mountain. The Tiwa believe that their ancestors migrated from the east and Makha Koja is located in the Tibet region of the Himalayan mountain range. It also appears that they spent considerable time at different places like Langrathuli, Bortongkhara, Tumra Makha before reaching Sera Siri which is now identified with the present Umswai area of West Karbi Anglong district of Assam. The folk song also suggests that the Tiwa practiced *jhum* cultivation before they came to occupy the present homeland, using simple implements.

Oral traditions shared by knowledgeable Tiwa scholars suggest that the Tiwa of the Brahmaputra Valley had came down from the hills of West Karbi Anglong formerly known as *Jaytha Pahar* (Jaintia Hills) several centuries ago. Moreover, the accounts mentioned in *Datiyalia Buranji* as well as the oral traditions recorded by colonial officers has also suggested that the Plain Tiwa came from the Jaintia Hills in several batches and settled at different places in the present Nagaon, Morigaon and Kamrup district. The major factor that influenced the migration could be due to the outbreak of an epidemics and search for a better livelihood.

The ethnographic study of the settlement pattern of the Tiwa has brought to light certain difficulties in understanding the early settlement pattern of the Tiwa inhabited areas. As traditional Tiwa houses are made of perishable raw materials collected from the forest and most of the domestic items used by them are also perishable, potential archaeological traces are likely to be limited. In most cases, they construct a new dwelling house at the same spot where the old house was built. Before constructing a new house, the old house is dismantled, so that some of the strong wooden pillars of the old house can be reused in the new house. Wood and bamboo which could not be reused are used as firewood or burnt at the spot itself. The only probable traces could be post holes but once again these are easily covered by dense vegetation. Further, in many cases, flat stones are kept at the base of the pillars of the house which eliminates the chance of finding any postholes as well.

The Tiwa religion consists of veneration of spirits both of the village and ancestors. The Tiwa do not have any shrine or temple. Iconolatry is absent in their religion. According to them every spirit and deity has a specific area where they live and control humans and animals. A deity of a particular area does not go to the territory of others. Every Tiwa village has common deities that look after the well-being of men and domestic animals. They called these deities *mindai*. The principal deity of the village is called *mathiney giri* or the master of the area/village. However, based on the folk songs and prayers (*mindai songah/ lekhawa*) and other rituals, it can be said that the Tiwa has a concept of a supreme deity or creator god called *Sharipahai*. All Tiwa rituals are called the *Sharipahai ne nemnudi* or *Sharipahai's* rituals. The Tiwa believe the entire earth, *Sharipahai ne mathi* or *Sharipahai's* land. Besides *Sharipahai*, there are many village deities and ancestral spirits both benevolent and malevolent worshipped by the Tiwa. Some of these deities are Palakhongor, Bodolmaji, Moramuji, Silikhongor, Kanthaboroi, Nengorbala, Khatboroi, Yangli, Kabla etc.

Every clan has its ancestral spirits whose invocations are considered to be the most important part of the religious life of a Tiwa individual. The propitiation of ancestral spirits is done by offering animal sacrifices inside the Tiwa traditional house (*nobaro*)u nder the sacred post called the *thuna* on all important occasions such as birth, death and marriage. Because of its religious significance, the *nobaro* is not only a dwelling house of the Tiwa, but also a place of worship to the spirits of dead ancestors.

Among the Tiwa, the village priest (*Loro*) plays an important role in their socio-religious receremonies. He takes the lead in the sacrifice and offerings at religious functions in the village. Due to the religious significance attached to the *Loro*, he can be considered as the custodian of Tiwa rituals. Besides the *Loro*, other important functionaries include the shaman (*Oja*) and fortune teller (*Phamari*). All three have key roles to play in the Tiwa religious belief system.

A profound belief in different deities and spirits among the Tiwa suggests that they feared these spirits and their impersonal powers which always manifested themselves in various forms, omens and signs. They consider that the spirits and deities have the power to inflict harm if they are not given proper respect in the form of offerings and sacrifices. As a result of the power attributed to their deities, it is necessary to harbour friendly relations with them. The intimate relationship between the people and their deities is manifested in their seasonal rites and festivals which mark every stage of their agricultural cycle. The important festivals associated with the agricultural cycle are *Sogra Baro, Rokkara, Bor Chongkhong, Phidri Chongkhong, Khram Panthai Lamewa, Yangli, PisuRawa, Motih Lawa, Pakhukara, Mahadew Phujiwa, Langkhon Phuja, Thurlu Phuja,Sokrasa, Wanchuwa, Kabla Phuja* and *Khelchawa.* Oral tradition still current among the Tiwa indicates that they practiced human sacrifice or *pokhya tana* during the pre-colonial period.

An important contribution of the present work is the establishment of a linkage between human sacrifice the erection of megaliths during the *Phidri-Chongkhong* ceremony and a fertility cult among the Tiwa. This aspect has not been highlighted in previous studies. The tradition of erecting megaliths in the course of this ceremony is of great significance since the megalithic site coincides with the place where human sacrifice was performed in the past thereby suggesting its link with the cult of fertility. This point is further reinforced by the fact that *Phidri-Chongkhong* ceremony which is celebrated at the same location is associated with agriculture. The entire site is suggestive of a fertility complex.

The Tiwa strongly believes in the concept of the afterlife and reincarnation of soul. According to them after death, a person becomes a member of the spirit world and meets all ancestors who died earlier. Good souls are welcomed among the spirits but entry is restricted to wicked souls. Wicked souls have to take shelter in the jungle, hills and mountains. The reincarnated soul is called *Jalai.* Through a simple divination process, newborn babies are identified with the previous life of the soul. Among the Tiwa, it is believed that the spirit of the deceased takes rebirth among its close relatives such as daughters, sons, sisters or brothers. If a father dies, it is expected that he will be reborn in his daughters' and sons' family as their son. Our fieldwork indicates that all the Tiwa individuals especially the Hill Tiwa have two identities; one is the present name and the other obtained as the result of reincarnation.

The Tiwa also practices totemism. Some of Tiwa clans (Hukai, Mithi) consider certain animals as their totem and refrain from hunting or eating the meat of that animal. There are various taboos observed by the Tiwa. Some of the taboos that were recorded during fieldwork are the the entry of women inside the *Shamadi*, tilling of the soil, riding a bicycle etc. during the celebration of the *Sogra* festival, playing a musical instrument before the *Thurlu* ceremony, presence of women at the *Phidri-Chongkhong* ceremony etc.

The religious beliefs of the plain Tiwa can be classified in to two broad categories: a) those that follow a synthesis of both traditional as well as Brahmanical elements of belief and practice and b) those that follow Neo-Vaishnavism. An interesting aspect of the Plain Tiwa religious belief system is that veneration of ancestral spirits are combined with the practice of Brahmanical rituals in birth, death and marriage ceremonies. However, followers of Neo-Vaishnavism are guided by the virtues and principles of Neo-Vaishnavism propounded by Sankardeva and Madhavdeva which advocates *ekasarananama dharma* or the invocation of only one god that is Vishnu. The followers of Vaishnavism among the Tiwa do not practice traditional religion and it does not carry any significance. They consider the Tiwa traditional religious practices such as animal sacrifices and invocation of dead ancestors as irrelevant and even refrain from eating pork and drinking rice beer which are considered to be an important aspect of Tiwa cultural identity. The birth and death ceremonies among the Plain Tiwa have been influenced by Brahmanical traditions. The purification ceremony after the birth of a baby (*aukhush kheda*) and during funerary rituals like *tiloni*, *doha*, *shardho*, is suggestive of Brahamanical influences. Some of the religious ceremonies practiced by the Plain Tiwa are; *Deo Sewa, Suni Puja, Hogora*

Puja, Tusuma, Mal Puja, Borot, Bohag Bihu, Magh Bihu, Kati Bihu and Gosain Uluwa Utsav.

The intercourse of the Tiwa with the supernatural world of deities is characterised by a desire to secure their livelihood, especially agriculture. There is a systematic order of rationalisation in which the deities are propitiated. Ritual is the means of establishing a link with the deities but it is not an end by itself. The importance of the priest (*Loro* in the root village and *Dewri* in the offshoot of root villages) is that priest are specialised in the technicalities and knows the incantations. This enables them to monopolise the intermediation between them and the gods so that supernatural help can be sought only through them.

Both the Hill and Plain Tiwa recognize the rule of exogamy and marriages between members of a *Maharsha* or clan are forbidden. Matrilocal marriage is called *Kobai* and the resident son-in-law is called *kobiya.* Marriage ceremonies among the Tiwa are simple. Decisions taken at the time of marriage determines the type of descent pattern adopted and inheritance of property. Kinship terms and oral traditions still current among the Tiwa suggest that they were a matrilineal tribe and the progenitors of the twelve original clans were twelve sisters. In the *Kobai* system, children take the mother's clan and the property is inherited by daughters. The major share goes to the youngest daughter called *shodya* or *nomul.* Usually she lives in her house of birth and looks after her parents. In case a boy brings a daughter-in-law (*pohari*) into his house, he does not leave his house and gets a share of the parental property. In this system, children take the clan of the father. According to our ethnographic data, in the hills the matrilocal marriage and matrilineal descent is still the preferred system of marriage in villages which are located in remote areas. However, in the plains patrilocal residence and patrilineal descent have been adopted by the Tiwa. Our fieldwork, supplemented by statistical data collected from census reports and electoral rolls at five villages namely, Mugaguri, Tharakhunji, Singlangkhunji, Hadaw and Amsai village in the West Karbi Anglong suggests that the majority of Hill Tiwa still follow the matrilineal descent and matrilocal marriage system. However, there is an indication that the number of patrilocal marriages is on the rise in the last few years both in Christian and traditional Tiwa villages. An inclination towards patrilocal residence among the Hill Tiwa may be attributed to the change of attitude of the younger generations towards their cultural values due to the impact of modernity. It can also be partly attributed to the influence of Christianity as well as the impact of their counterparts in the plains who have already accepted the patrilocal residence system and patrilineal descent. With the change in the descent system from matrilineal to patrilineal, the rule of inheritance has also changed from daughter to son.

According to the study of the rules of marriage and descent system, the Tiwa can be grouped under the *ambilocal extended family kin group* wherein a married couple may choose to add their nuclear family kin group to the primary nuclear family kin groups of either the husband or wife. If a male goes to live with his wife at her paternal house than the girl inherits her mother's property and the children take the name of their mother. In case a boy brings a girl to his house after marriage, then he can claim a part of his parental property and the children born out of this kind of marriage take the name of the father's clan. Currently, it is found that both systems of marriage are prevalent among the Hill Tiwa. Their descent can therefore be termed as a bilateral descent pattern where descent is recognized culturally as taking place more or less equally in both the male and female line. However, the Plain Tiwa have already renounced the practice of the *Kobai* system from the mid-1970s due to the influence of their Assamese speaking neighbours and have adopted the patrilineal descent system.

Among the Hill Tiwa the position of the resident son-in-law (*Kobai*) is always considered to be the most important one because he gets due recognition as an individual in the traditional Tiwa society only after his marriage. An unmarried Tiwa individual has no place in the village administration as only married males are considered to be eligible for the various important positions in the village council of elders (*Pisai*). The significance of the *Kobai* can be gauged from the fact that, to become the head priest (*Loro*) who is also the head of the village council of elders (*Pisai*) the primary qualification is to be married into the dominant clan or the founding clan of a particular village only which can provide their *Kobai* as the *Loro*.

According to an oral tradition, the Tiwa had twelve root villages (*binung*) and each of the villages was administered by a twelve-member council of elders collectively known as the *Pisai* headed by the *Loro.* The members of the council of elders are selected from different clans. They exercise their responsibilities in connection with the socio-cultural affairs of the village. Being the leader of the *Pisai*, the *Loro* is called the *Pisaimul* meaning the head of the council of elders. To become a *Loro* a Tiwa individual has to be a *Kobai* or the resident son-in-law of the clan that has the legitimate right to provide the *Loro.* It implies that the selection of *Loro* is done based on the dominant position of the clan in a village rather than personal qualifications. The *Loro* discharges both religious as well as secular duties. The other important member of the village council of elders includes *Toloi, Phador, Shangot, Maji, Hadari, Barika Baro, Barika Pisa, Phayak Mul Kra, Phayak Mul Majowa, and two Phayak Mul Jokha.* According to tradition, each of the positions in the *Pisai* system is distributed equally among the clans of a village. Besides the *Pisai*, the *panthai khel,* the youth committee also plays an active role in the socio-cultural life of the Tiwa. The *panthai khel* is headed by *Changdoloi, Changmaji* and *Huruma.* In the *Shamadi* the Tiwa boys receive training and motivation essential for a traditional way of life at a crucial age. Dormitory life makes them understand and acquire knowledge about the community life. It enables them to take part in social activities, thereby allowing them to improve their personality and leadership quality. The *Shamadi* also provides security to the village. Moreover, the *Shamadi* is a common meeting place for the villagers where important decisions regarding socio-religious issues are taken. Due to its indispensable role in the social and cultural life, the *Shamadi* continues to occupy a prominent place in Tiwa society.

The Gobha *Raja* was the first central political authority of the Tiwa. According to oral tradition, the ancestor of Gobha was born at a place called Thinimoslong/Timowflong. Later it was shifted to Amsai and subsequently, the capital of the principality was moved to the present Gobha village. During the Ahom period, this principality played a significant role in diplomatic as well as military relationship between the Jaintia and the Ahom kingdom. The Ahom *Buranjis* and colonial reports suggest that initially Gobha was a vassal state under the Jaintia kingdom.

However, in many occasssions it had become a bone contention between the Ahoms and the Jaintia because of its strategic importance. During the initial years of British colonisation of North-East India the route from Sylhet via Nartiang to Gobha connecting the Brahmaputra valley was extensively used for transportation. R.B. Pemberton's report suggests that David Scott, the first agent of the Governor-General in the North East came to Assam in 1824 through this route. Subsequently this route was named as Scott's route.The Chief of Gobha Chattro Sing, resisted British occupation by killing three British officials in 1832. The incident has been described by colonial authorities as a pretext to annex the Jaintia and Gobha kingdom to the British Empire in 1834. A significant finding of the killing of the three British officials is that the Gobha Raja's soldiers took them to Amsai and sacrificed them at *Chongkhong Sal* in which the Jaintia King had played no role. The Jaintia King Rajendra Singh repeatedly claimed his innocence and denied any involvement in the issue. However, despite the repeated denial the British insisted that it was the Jaintia king who perpetrated the act and demanded the surrender of the Gobha chief to the British. With the failure of the Jaintia king to meet the demand of the British, on 15th March 1835 the Sylhet Light Infantry under the command of Captain Lister took formal possession of Jaintiapur, the capital of the Jaintia Kingdom and annexed it to the British Empire. A few weeks later Gobha was also annexed by the British in April 1835 by a detachment of the Assam Light Infantry. Though the British removed the political power of the Gobha *Raja* after its annexation, it continued to maintain socio-cultural influences among the Tiwa. The postion of the Gobha *Raja* is still occupies a significant place in the life of the Tiwa population both in the hills and the plains.

The distinctive eco-cultural features of the Tiwa economic organisation lie in its corporate activities and the inter-dependence between the families living within a village for the satisfaction of basic needs of food, clothing and housing. The Tiwa are mainly dependent on agriculture which includes both *jhum* and wet rice cultivation. Besides, the Tiwa also cultivate various kinds of vegetables both for consumption and for sale in the local markets. In recent years, bamboo and broomstick cultivation is gaining prominence among the Hill Tiwa which has largely contributed to their economic growth. The Tiwa has a tradition of cooperate activity called *hadari khel* and *kil* to share the agriculture work. The Tiwa also has a specialized form of a land measurement system called *jari* system. One *jari* is further divided into *Kawling, Khadisha, Tanglenger* and *Tangsha*.

From the field data supplemented by written sources, it has been found that both the Hill and the Plain Tiwa have undergone various changes. Several factors have contributed to the changes in different aspects of Tiwa society. Some of these factors are migration to the plains and contact with the Assamese speaking neighbours, the impact of Neo-Vaishnavism, the introduction of Christianity, and impact of modern education, western medicine and health care, development of transport and communication, and impact of the market economy.

The process of Sanskritization started gradually from the late 17th century after the subjugation of the Tiwa principalities of Gobha, Nelli and Khola by the Ahoms and establishment of the *Chokey* or military post at Roha in the present Nogaon district of Assam during the reign of Jaydhwaj Singha. Subsequently, this process gained momentum during the reign of Siva Singha. Our empirical data also shows that the conversion of Tiwa into Neo-Vaishnavism was largely the work of the *Satras* that were established by various Vaishnava *gurus* who gave *saron* or initiation to the newly converted tribes into Neo-Vaishnavism. Those Tiwa who were converted to Neo- Vaishnavism were initially given the status of *Soru Koch* or the Junior *Koch* which was considered to be a respectable position in the caste hierarchy of Assamese society. One very striking aspect of their culture is that the process of assimilation and acculturation is quite visible among this community.

Christianity was introduced among the Hill Tiwa by the Khasi Presbyterian mission as early as the first decade of the 20th century without any success. Subsequently, the Catholic Church came to work among the Tiwa through the help of Karbi families who were converted by the German Salvadorian Mission. However, there are evidences to indicate that those Tiwa individuals who embraced Christianity during that time had changed their ethnic identity to Karbi because they were excommunicated from Tiwa society. During the 1950s under the supervision of the Catholic Missionaries from Shillong the second phase of evangelization started with considerable success. The most significant contribution was that of Fr. Balawan, a French national who came to work as a Catholic priest in Shillong soon after the Second World War. He translated the Bible into the Tiwa language and also authored several Tiwa language and grammar books and compiled folk stories. Those who converted to Christianity had to leave their original village and settle at different places. It was because the traditional Tiwa villages were very strict in enforcing their customs through their village administration and whoever violates the rules has to be excommunicated from the village. As conversion to a different faith is against the custom of the village hence whoever accepts a different religion has to move out of the village. The Catholic villages which we have enumerated were the offshoots of various root villages established after their conversion. For example, the Pundurimakha village was created by the first five families who came out from their root village of Amsai, similarly, Chikdamakha was initially established by some Tiwa families from nearby Bormarjong village after their conversion to Christianity.

There has been a lot of change in the socio-economic aspects of the Tiwa society. Though the *jhum* cultivation still occupies an important place in the traditional economy, there has been a change in the pattern of cultivation. Now the Tiwa cultivate only once or twice in a selected plot of land and do not return to the same plot for a long period. It is because they grow either broom-stick or bamboo for commercial purposes. It gives them a good source of income as both bamboo and broom-stick have a growing market. The growth of markets in and around the Hill Tiwa area has considerably impacted their economic life. Earlier they use to barter their agricultural produce and bamboo made products with the plains people both in the weekly markets as well as in the villages. However, with the growth of weekly markets at Umswai and Birsengki during 1960s, the Tiwa has now discontinued the barter system. It has now been replaced with money economy. However our fieldwork at remote Tiwa villages like Singlangkhunji, Hadaw, Borrongkhoi found that they still practice barter within the village to procure essential commodities.

Notes and References:

[1] Sukla: Yajur Veda, Vajasaneyi Samahita, XXX, 16, and *Artharva Veda* X, 4, 14, quoted in S.K. Chatterji, *Kirata Jana-Kriti*, (4th Reprint), the Asiatic Society, Kolkata, 2014, p. 17.

[2] Wilfred H. Schoff, *The Periplus of Erythraean Sea*, Longmans, Green and Co., Calcutta, 1912, pp.47-50

[3] P.C. Choudhury, *The History of Civilization of the People of Assam to the Twelfth Century A.D.* (3rdedn.), Spectrum Publication, Guwahati, 1987, pp. 28-32

Glossary

Amsai	: A root village in the West Karbi Anglong district of Assam.
Barika	: The messenger of the village elder's council responsible for transmitting messages and collection of funds for religious ceremonies.
Binung	: A Tiwa root village.
Bokheya	: A human victim for sacrifice.
Buranji	: Assamese Chronicles.
Shangdoloi	: The head of the youth dormitory (*Shamadi*).
Shangmaji	: The deputy of the *Shangdoloi* and an important leader of the *Shamadi*.
Chokey	: A military station during Ahom rule.
Comphor	: An open space of a traditional Tiwa house (*Nobaro*).
Chongkhong	: A religious ceremony.
Datiyalia	: People of the fringe.
Harikhungri	: The senior most female of a family, generally the grandmother, mother or aunt.
Jallai	: Reincarnation of soul.
Jela	: The senior most male member of a family, generally the maternal uncle or elder brother of a woman.
Kabla	: A Tiwa deity worshiped by the Magro group.
Kachong	: Wrapper used by women.

Khara	:	A sword used in human sacrifice.
Kobiya	:	A resident-son-in law associated with matrilocality.
Khul	:	Tiwa clan.
Khunji-phara	:	A farm house near the *jhum* field.
Kobai	:	Marriage System within the matrilineal framework.
Koja	:	Red colour.
Krai	:	A village.
Maji	:	Personal assistant of the village head priest, the *Loro* and a member of village elder's council.
Laloo	:	A clan of the Jaintia tribe.
Libing	:	Human being.
Loro	:	The head of the village elder's council as well as the head priest of a Tiwa root village.
Mahar	:	Group of matriclans.
Makha	:	Hill or mountain.
Mathi- ne-Giri	:	The principal deity of specific area.
Moinari-Kanthi	:	A form of dance performed during the *Kabla Phuja* at Magro village.
Mindai	:	English equivalent to deity or god.
Namghar	:	An open prayer hall in Assam.
Nam-Kirtan	:	Invocation of Lord Krishna and Vishnu through devotional song and music by devotees.
Nara	:	A piece of four to five feet long waist belt made of cotton yarn.
Nem-nudi	:	Traditional rituals.
Nobaro	:	Tiwa traditional house.
Nomaji	:	Middle part of a traditional Tiwa house (*Nobaro*).

Nukhuri -Khunji	:	A legendry village located in West Karbi Anglong.
Nomul	:	Inheritress of the family, generally the youngest daughter.
Nukthi	:	A Part of the Tiwa House (*Nobaro*).
Orlong	:	Stone.
Palakhongor	:	A Tiwa village deity.
Pator	:	A member of the village council of elders.
Pham	:	A branch of root village.
Phar	:	River bank.
Phidri	:	Ancestral spirits.
Phayakmul	:	A member of village council of elders (*Pisai*).
Pisai	:	Council of elders of a traditional Tiwa village.
Pohari	:	Daughter-in-law.
Rate-chiniwa	:	A ceremony to introduce the resident-son-in-law to the village elders.
Sal	:	A place of worship/sacred place.
Sangot	:	An important member of the village elder's council.
Satra	:	The Centre of Neo-Vaishnavism in Assam established by Sankardeva in late 15th and early 16th century.
Sera-Siri	:	A legendry hill in east of Amsai village.
Shamadi	:	Bachelors dormitory.
Shodya	:	Youngest daughter of a family.
Sogra	:	A Tiwa annual religious ceremony held in the month of March/April.
Tagla	:	A kind of sleeveless traditional coat with floral designs.
Tewri	:	A Tiwa priest.
Tham Khunda	:	The sacred pillar of village youth dormitory.
Thanese	:	A loin cloth.

Thuna	: Sacred post of a Tiwa traditional house(*Nobaro*).
Thurlu	: A Tiwa festival.
Ti	: Water or river.
Ti-khumur	: Purifying water.
Toloi/Doloi	: An important official of the village elder's council and deputy of the village priest (*Loro*).
Wali	: A suffix to denote matriclan.
Wanchuwa	: A Tiwa agricultural festival celebrated once every four years.
Wasirawa	: A religious ceremony associated with agriculture.

Select Bibliography

Assamese Chronicles:

Bhuyan, S.K.(ed.), *Kamrupar Buranji* (3rdedn.), Department of Historical and Antiquarian Studies, Assam, Guwahati,1987.

__________(ed.), *Deodhai Asam Buranji* (4thedn.), Department of Historical and Antiquarian Studies, Assam, Guwahati, 2001.

__________(ed.), *Kachari Buranji* (3rdedn.), Department of Historical and Antiquarian Studies, Assam, Guwahati, 1984.

__________(ed.), *Satsari Asam Buranji*(3rd edn.), Lawyers Book Stall, 1999.

__________(ed.), *Jayantia Buranji* (3ndedn.), Department of Historical and Antiquarian Studies, Assam, Guwahati, 2012.

Colonial Accounts:

Allen, B. C., *Administrative Report on The Census of Assam*, 1901, Shillong, 1902

__________, *Assam District Gazetteers, Volume X: The Khasi and Jayantia Hills, the Garo and the Lushai Hills*, Pioneer Press, Allahabad, 1905

__________, *Assam District Gazetteers Nowgong*, part VI, Calcutta, 1905

___________, *Census of Assam* 1901, Vol II (reprint), Manas Publication, New Delhi, 1984

Butler, John, *Travels and Adventures in the Province of Assam: During a Residence of Fourteen Years* (reprint), Munshiram Manoharlal Publishers Pvt. Ltd. New Delhi, 2009.

Dalton, E. T., *Descriptive Ethnology of Bengal*, Superintendent of Government Printing, Calcutta, 1872.

Dutta, S.K (ed.), *Assam Buranji*(1648-1681) 2nd edn., DHAS, Guwahati, 1991,

Endle, S., *The Kacharis*, The McMillan Company, London, 1911.

Gait, E.A., *Census of India1891, Assam*, Shillong, 1892.

Grierson, G. A., *Linguistic Survey of India, Vol-III, part-I* (reprint), Low Price Publication, New Delhi, 2005.

Gurdon, P.R.T. *The Khasis* (reprint), Low Price Publication, Delhi, 2010.

Hamilton, Francis, *An account of Assam*, DHAS, Guwahati, 1940.

Hunter, W.W., *A Statistical Account of Assam*, Vol-I, Trubner & Co., London, 1879.

Hutton, J.H., *The Sema Nagas*, Macmillan, London, 1921.

Mackenzie, Alexander, *The North-East Frontier of India* (reprint), Mittal Publications, Delhi, 1979.

M'Cosh, John, *Topography of Assam*, G.H. Huttman, Bengal Orphan Military College, Calcutta, 1837.

Mills, A. J.M, *Report on the Province of Assam*, Thos. Jones, Calcutta Gazette Office, Calcutta, 1854.

___________ *Report on the Khasi and Jaintia Hills 1853*, NEHU, Shillong, 1985.

Pemberton, R. B., *The Eastern Frontiers of India* (reprint), Mittal Publication, Delhi, 1979.

Playfair, A., *The Garos*, David Nutt, London, 1909.

Shakespeare, J., *The Lushei Kuki Clans*, Macmillan, London, 1912.

Waddell, L.A., *The Tribes of Brahmaputra Valley: A Contribution of Their Physical Types and Affinities*(reprint) Concept Publishing Company (P) Ltd., New Delhi, 2011.

Vernacular Literatures:

All Assam Tiwa Yuva-Chatra Sanmilan(ed.), *Tiwa Sampradyar Parichay*, Asom Sahitya Sabha, Jorhat, 1975.

Dewri, M., *Tiwa Samaj*, Asom Sahitya Sabha, Jorhat, 1983.

__________, *Tiwa Janajati aru Bhashar Itihas*, Guwahati, Tribal Research Institute, Guwahati, 1988.

__________, *Asomiya Jati aru Sanskriti Gathanat Tiwa Sakalor Abodan*, Assam Institute of Tribals and Schedule Caste, Guwahati, 2010.

Gogoi, L., *Tiwa Sanskritir Ruprekha (PrathamKhanda),*Harihar Mandir, Nagaon, 1986.

__________, *Tiwa Sanskritir Ruprekha(DetiyoKhanda),*Udhab Senapati, Nagaon, 1987.

Pator, R. D., *Tiwa Samaj aru Sanskritir Acherenga*, Tribal Research Institute, Guwahati, 2007.

Rajkumar, Sarbanada, *Itihase Soaura Chashata Bachar (1226-1826),*Banlata, Dibrugarh, 2000.

Sadow Asom Tiwa Yuva-Chatra Sanmilan, *Tiwa Sampradayar Parichay*, Asom Sahitya Sabha, Jorhat, 1975.

English works:

Agnihotri, S. K., *The Lalungs*, S. Kumar & Associates, Delhi, 1996.

Axtell, James, Ethnohistory: An Historian's Viewpoint, *Ethnohistory* 26, 1979.

Barpujari, H. K. *The Comprehensive History of Assam, Vol-I* (2[nd]edn.), Publication Board, Assam, Guwahati, 2004.

Barua, K. L., *Oral Tradition and Folk Heritage of North-East India*, Spectrum Publication, Guwhati, 1999.

Baruah, B. K., *A Cultural History of Assam* (early Period), 2[nd]edn., Lawyers Book Stall, Guwahati, 1969.

Baruah, A. K., *The Lalungs (Tiwas)*, Self Publication, Guwahati, 1989.

Baruah, S. L., *A Comprehensive History of Assam* (Reprint), Munshiram Manoharlal Publishers Pvt. Ltd., New Delhi, 2009.

Bhuyan, S. K., *Anglo Assamese Relations* (2nd edn.),Lawyers Book Stall, Guwahati, 1974.

Boas, F., *The Mind of Primitive Man* (reprint), The McMillan Company, New York, 1944

Chang, K. C., "A Typology of Settlement and Community Pattern in Some Circum-Polar Societies," *Arctic Anthropology* 34, 1962.

Chatterji, S. K., *Kirata-Jana-Kriti: The Indo-Mongoloids; Their Contribution to the History and Culture of India* (3rd edn.), The Asiatic Society, Calcutta, 2011.

Cohn, B. S., *An Anthropologist Among the Historians and Other Essays*(6th edn.), Oxford University Press, New Delhi,2000.

Crook, William, *Popular Religion and Folklore of Northern India,* Vol. I, Oxford, 1926

Choudhury, P. C., *The History of Civilization of the People of Assam to the Twelfth Century A.D.* (revised 3rd edn.), Spectrum Publications, Delhi, 1987.

Das, B. M., *People of Assam: Origin and Composition,* Eastern Book House, New Delhi, 2003.

Das, Jogesh, *Folklore of Assam* (reprint), National Book Trust, India New Delhi, 2010

Datta, B., *Affinities between Folkloristic and Historiography: Some Theoretical Implications in the Context of Medieval and Modern History of North-East India* (6th edn.), National Folklore Support Centre, Chennai, 2002.

Devi, Lakshmi, *Ahom-Tribal Relations,* Self Published, Guwahati, 1968.

Dube, Saurabh (ed.), *Historical Anthropology*(2nd edn.), Oxford University Press, New Delhi, 2011.

Dundes, A., *Interpreting Folklore,* Indiana University Press, Bloomington and London, 1980.

__________, *Sacred Narrative- Reading in the Theory of Myth,* University of California, Berkley and London, 1984.

Durkheim Emile, *Elementary Form of Religious Life* (New Translation), The Free Press, New York, 1995.

Eliade, M., *Myth and Reality,* George Allen & Unwin, London, 1964.

Elliott, Julia (ed.), *Oxford Dictionary and Thesaurus* III, New York, 2008.

Elwin, V., *Myths of North-East Frontier*, Director of Information and Public Relation, NEFA, 1958.

Ember R Carol, Ember Marvin, *Cultural Anthropology*, Prentice Hall, New Jersey, 2002.

Frazer, J. G., *The Golden Bough*, The McMillan Company, New York, 1925.

Gait, E. A., *A History of Assam* (7[th]edn.), Lawyer's Book Stall, 1997(first Published 1905).

Geddes, B. & Malcolm, C., *Research Methods in the Field* (Royal size),Anmol Publications, New Delhi, 2006.

Gohain, B. K., *The Hill Lalungs*, Anundoram Borooah Institute of Language, Art & Culture, Guwahati, Assam, 1992.

__________,*Continuity & Change in the Hills of Assam: Karbi Anglong District, Assam*, Omsons Publication, New Delhi, 2006.

Goody, J.(ed.), *The Character of Kinship*, Cambridge University Press, New York, 1973.

Gordon, R., "Willey, Prehistoric Settlement Patterns in the Virú Valley, Peru", *Bureau of American Ethnology*, Bulletin 155, Washington, D.C., 1953

Gupta, Das, P. K., *Life and Culture of Matrilineal Tribe of Meghalaya*, Inter-India Publications, New Delhi, 1984.

Haimendorf, Furer C.V., *Tribes of India*, Oxford University Press, New Delhi, 1985.

Henige, D. P., *The Chronology of Oral Tradition: Quest for a Chimera*, Clarendon press, Oxford, 1974.

__________, *Oral Historiography*, Longman, New York, 1982.

Hobsbawm, Eric, *On History* (reprint), Abacus, London, 1999.

Hudson Charles, "Folk History and Ethnohistory", *Ethnohistory* 13, 1966

Hutchinson, H. N., *Marriage Rites, Customs and Ceremonies of the World*, Concept Publishing Company (P) Ltd., New Delhi, 2009.

Hutton, J.H. *Census of India*, 1931, Vol.I, Part II, Imperial Table, Govt. of India, Delhi, 1933

Josh, U.V., *Tiwa-English Dictionary*, Don Bosco Centre for Indigenous Culture, Shillong, 2014.

Kakati, B.K., *The Mother Goddess Kamakhya*, Lawyer's Books Stall, Guwahati, 1948.

Karotemprel, S., *A Brief History of the Catholic Church Among the Tiwas* (*Lalungs*), Vendrame Missiological Institute, Shillong, 1981.

Kholar, V. Len, *Tiwa Matpadi*, (1st edn.), Tiwa Sahitya Sabha, Jagiroad, 1995.

Kirk, G. S., *Myth: Its Meaning and Functions in Ancient and Other Cultures*, University of California Press, Berkeley, 1970.

Laishram R., "Narrative Discourse and Aryan Imprint in Manipur Historiography", *Journal of History and Culture*, Vol. I, Gauhati University, Guwahati, 2014.

Levi-Strauss Claude, *Structural Anthropology* I, Basic Books, New York, 1963.

Lubbock, John, *The origin of Civilisation and the Primitive Condition of Man*, D. Appleton and Company, New York, 1898.

Mandal, P., *An Approach in Cultural Mapping of North-East India*, The Asiatic Society, Kolkata, 2009.

Miller, D., Barbara, *Cultural Anthropology* (2nd edn), Allyn and Bacon, Boston, 2002.

Malinowski, Bronislaw, *Magic Science and Religion and Other Essays*, The Free Press, Illinois, 1948

Momin M. & Mawlong C. A. (ed.), *Society and Economy in North-East India* (Vol. I), Regency Publication, New Delhi, 2004

Momin. M., "Contextualizing Origin Myths of North East India", *Proceeding Volume of North East India History Association, 22nd Session, Tezpur, 2002.*

Morgan, L. H., *Ancient Society*, Charles H. Kerr & Company, Chicago, 1877.

Nath, R. M., *The Background of Assamese Culture* (Reprint), Dutta Baruah & Co. Guwahati, 1978.

Neog, Maheswar, *Religions of the North-East*, Publication Board Assam, Guwahati, 2008.

Pakyntein, E.H. *Census of India 1962*, Vol. III, Assam, Part V-A, Government of India, Delhi, 1964

Pasayat, C., *Oral Tradition, Society and History*, Mohit Publications Pvt. Ltd., Meerut, 2008.

Phukan, S.K., *Onomastics Assam*, Vol. I, Students Store, Guwahati, 2004.

Radcliff-Brown, A. R., *Structure and Function in Primitive Society: Essays and Addresses*, The Free Press, Illinois, 1952.

Rahul, Ram, *The Himalayan Borderlands*, Vikas Publication, New Delhi, 1970.

Rajguru, S., *Medieval Assamese Society* (1228-1826), Asami, Milanpur, Nagaon, 1988.

Ramirez, P. *People of the Margins: Across Ethnic Boundaries in North-East India*, Spectrum Publications, Guwahati, 2014.

Rao, Venkata, V., *A Century of Tribal Politics in North East India: 1874-1974*, S. Chand, New Delhi, 1976.

Sangkima, *Mizo: Society and Social Change*, Spectrum Publications, Guwahati, 1992.

Sarma, Satyendranath, *A Socio-Economic & Cultural History of Medieval Assam (1200 A.D.-1800 A. D.)*, Pratima Devi, Guwahati, 1989.

Sen, S., *Social and State Formation in the Khasi-Jaintia Hills*, B. R. Publication Corporation, Delhi, 1985.

Shyamchoudhury, N.K. & Das, M. M., *The Lalung Society: A Theme for Analytical Ethnography*, Anthropological Survey of India, Calcutta, 1973.

Singh, G. P., *Historical Research into Some Aspects of the Culture and Civilization of North East India*, Gyan Publishing House, New Delhi, 2009.

Sinha Surajit, *Tribal Polities and State Systems in Pre-Colonial Eastern and North Eastern India*, K.P. Bagchi & Company, Calcutta, 1987.

Srinivas, M.N., *Social Change in Modern India* (Reprint), Orient Black Swan, New Delhi, 2015.

Thakur, Sharma, G. C., *The Lalungs (Tiwas)*, Tribal Research Institute, Guwahati, 1985.

Thompson, Paul, *The Voice of the Past: Oral History* (2nd edn.), Oxford University Press, New York, 1988

Tylor, E. B., *Primitive Culture*, Vol. I, John Murray, Albemarle STI, 1871

Vansina, J., *Oral Tradition as History*, James Currey Publishers, London, 1985.

Weltfish, Gene, The Question of Ethnic Identity, an Ethnohistorical Approach, *Ethnohistoy* 6, 1959.

Wheeler-Voegelin, E., "An Ethnohistorians Viewpoint", *Ethnohistory* 1, 1965.

Williams, R., Thomas, *Cultural Anthropology*, Prentice Hall, New Jersey, 1990.

Wright, H.M., *Oral Tradition: A Study in Historical Methodology*, Routledge, London, 1965.

Zeigen, R. S., *The Family in Matrilineal Society: A Functional Comparative Analysis of Five Preliterate Cultures*, University of Utah, Utah, 1952.

Web Pages:

www.archives.gov

www.assamarchives.gov.in

www.censusindia.gov.in

www.courses.lumenlearning.com

www.easycalculation.com

www.merriam-webster.com

www.shodganga.inflibnet.ac.in

www.study.com

www.symbolic-meaning.com

www.thoughtco.com

Index